D1084092

Federal Reserve Monetary Policy 1917-1933

CONSULTING EDITOR: *William Letwin*
MASSACHUSETTS
INSTITUTE
OF TECHNOLOGY

Federal Reserve Monetary Policy 1917–1933

Elmus R. Wicker
INDIANA UNIVERSITY

RANDOM HOUSE
New York

First Printing

 Published in New York by Random House, Inc., and simultaneously in Toronto, Canada, by Random House of Canada Limited
Library of Congress Catalog Card Number: 67–10164
Manufactured in the United States of America by American Book–Stratford Press, Inc., New York, New York.

Designed by LEON BOLOGNESE

FOR CAROLYN

Introduction

WHEN I began a study of the history of Federal Reserve monetary policy several years ago, I assumed that its interpretation could be shaped primarily by familiar criteria such as the behavior of the money supply, interest rates, and price levels, and that well-known descriptions of monetary behavior represented by such labels as real-bills, gold standard, and managed money were adequate. But I finally realized that the traditional framework could not possibly do justice to the myriad strands of thought—professional and amateur, political and personal—entering into the complex process of monetary decision making. How could it? For a considerable period of Federal Reserve history the responsibility for decision making had been in the hands of men with little understanding of central banking theory and with little or no experience of central bank administration except that gained on the spot. This book, therefore, is an attempt to recapture something of the art of monetary policy formation during the first twenty years of Federal Reserve history with the view to revising our interpretation of the Board's early successes and failures.

It is my hope that it will also partially fill the need for a history of monetary policy which accords special emphasis to the role played by officials of the U.S. Treasury and the Federal Reserve System both in the formulation and administration of monetary policy. It is a regrettable fact that we know comparatively little about the thought of leading Treasury officials, individual Board members, Federal Reserve Bank governors or even that small but highly influential group of economic advisers. There is, of course, one notable exception—Benjamin Strong, governor of the Federal Reserve Bank of New York from 1914–1928. Lester Chandler's biography has done much to reduce the obscurity that surrounded the role Strong played in the evolution of monetary policy, though the extent of Strong's influence among Board members and other

System officials has been exaggerated.[1] Recently, materials have been uncovered which are now available for many more such studies and which open up a new and exciting frontier of monetary and financial history. Years ago, when Seymour Harris undertook to survey Federal Reserve monetary policy he had to rely primarily though not entirely upon the public record.[2]

We already have evidence of exactly how useful the more recent information can be as Chandler's biography of Governor Strong testifies. Chandler had access to the private papers of Benjamin Strong as well as to the records of memoranda and correspondence contained in the files of the Federal Reserve Bank of New York and the Board of Governors in Washington, D.C. Milton Friedman and Anna Schwartz, in their history of monetary policy, have used extensively the diaries of former Board member Charles S. Hamlin.[3] These diaries, now deposited in the Library of Congress, more a record of Hamlin's official career than a purely personal account of his private life, are our single most important source of information on the administration of monetary policy in the nineteen-twenties and early thirties apart from the records held within the Federal Reserve System. They contain fairly complete reports of what happened at Board meetings, and in those instances when he attended, of meetings of the Open Market Investment Committee and later the Open Market Policy Conference. When checked against the official files of the Board, the information in the Hamlin Diaries corresponds very closely to the Board's records. It would be difficult to exaggerate their importance in providing us with the only detailed account that we have of the way in which an individual Board member viewed his task, and how he performed it.

In addition to the Hamlin Diaries and the Strong Papers, the Papers of George Leslie Harrison, Strong's successor at the New York Federal Reserve Bank, are deposited in the Butler Library of Columbia University. Harrison served as governor of the bank from 1928 to 1941, and his memoranda, records of conversations, discussion notes and official correspondence provide a valuable guide to the administration of monetary policy during the era of stock market speculation and the subsequent Great Depression. The Papers of E. A. Goldenweiser, who was director of the Board's Division of Research and Statistics from 1927 to 1945, are now deposited in the Library of Congress. They contain important information especially for the period 1928–33, mainly in the form of confidential memoranda prepared for his own use. The memoranda of Goldenweiser enable us to see Federal Reserve action from the perspective of the professional who must find common ground with the decision makers in order to be effective. His incisive comments, summaries of Board meetings, and conversations with Federal Reserve officials add a new dimension to our understanding of how monetary policy was made. For an earlier period the Papers of Russell C. Leffingwell, Assistant Secretary of the Treasury during the Wilson administration, are indispensable if we are to understand the war and immediate postwar relationship which existed between the Federal Reserve System and the U.S. Treasury.[4]

I was granted permission by the Board of Governors to examine the records and correspondence contained in its official files, and it can be said that these records are probably the most complete, best organized, competently administered and historically meaningful collection of materials relating to the operation of a central banking system in existence. Our interpretation of some major episodes of monetary policy will need to be revised in the light of the information which these records reveal.[5]

The argument of this book can be stated very simply. The performance of Federal Reserve officials during the first twenty years was constrained by their attachment to certain specific economic goals, by their imperfect understanding of the tools of monetary management, namely, open market operations and the rediscount mechanism, and by their imprecise knowledge of how a central bank can exert an influence on the level of economic activity. Of lesser importance was the quality of leadership within the Federal Reserve System.

The framework is a chronological narrative, an appropriate technique when searching for and identifying episodes in Federal Reserve history which contribute most to our understanding of monetary performance. In each of the following chapters I describe and interpret a significant period in Federal Reserve monetary history. The narrative begins with the entrance of the United States into World War I in April, 1917. I have omitted the first two years of the System's history because the dominant problems confronting Reserve officials were not problems of monetary policy, but problems surrounding the organization and administration of the twelve Federal Reserve Banks. The book ends with the inauguration of Franklin D. Roosevelt and the declaration of the Bank Holiday.

Until June, 1920, monetary policy was dictated either by the needs of war finance or by postwar debt management problems, created by our wartime financial policies. In Chapters 1 and 2, I trace the origin of the policies pursued by the Federal Reserve and the Treasury and attribute their actions to a conflict of rival theories of how monetary policy works and, to a lesser extent, to a conflict of personalities. In interpreting how leading officials in the Treasury viewed the problem of monetary control and their relationship to the Federal Reserve System, I have relied mainly upon the new and important source of information contained in the official papers of former Assistant Secretary of the Treasury, Russell C. Leffingwell.

In Chapter 3, I explain why System officials maintained the same schedule of high discount rates throughout 1920–21, one of the sharpest deflationary periods in U.S. cyclical experience. Most critics have attributed this failure to reduce the rates to the overweening importance attached to the legal reserve ratio as a major determinant of monetary policy decisions. I argue that the crux of the explanation must be sought elsewhere. A money supply model consistent with the tenor of the Federal Reserve Act and the conduct of System officials shows that any positive action by the Federal Reserve either to lower rediscount rates or to reduce the huge volume of member bank indebtedness was improbable.

Monetary policy during that relatively brief period between 1922 and 1924, when Federal Reserve officials attempted to forge a criterion to guide the formulation of monetary policy independent of gold standard considerations is described in the next two chapters. According to R. F. Harrod and J. M. Keynes, the famous *Tenth Annual Report of the Federal Reserve Board* (1923) ushered in a new era of managed money. Although the Report did inaugurate a system of managed currency it did so only for the interim period before Great Britain and other European countries returned to the international gold standard. I refer to this brief episode as the managed money interlude.

Chapters 6, 7, and 8 analyze the so-called golden years of the Federal Reserve System under the leadership of the powerful and persuasive governor of the Federal Reserve Bank of New York, Benjamin Strong. During the period from 1924 to 1928, System officials supposedly learned how to use open market operations to cure the mild recessions of 1924 and 1927, how to maintain price stability, and how to free themselves from the discipline of gold movements by adopting a policy of gold sterilization and managed money. Was this, in fact, so? Did not international considerations decisively influence the formation of monetary policy in 1924 and

1927? Did the understanding of open market policy which evolved in the early nineteen twenties—the Strong-Burgess-Riefler tradition—constitute an adequate theoretical foundation for an aggressive open market policy? Was not the objective of open market policy limited to the much narrower task of eliminating the indebtedness of the member banks in New York and Chicago?

If monetary policy was so successful after 1922, how then can we explain the Federal Reserve's apparently poor performance after 1927? System officials were unsuccessful in their efforts to prevent either the stock market boom or the collapse in 1928 and 1929. Presumably to stem the outflow of gold, they raised the rediscount rate and tightened credit in the midst of the most serious depression in our history. They were reluctant to assume responsibility for preventing the widespread collapse of commercial banks beginning in the winter of 1930. The traditional explanation assumes that the administration of monetary policy somehow changed from good to bad between the two periods, mainly as a result of the death of Benjamin Strong. In the remaining chapters, historical evidence revealing neither a sharp break in the logic nor in the interpretation of Federal Reserve monetary policy is used to demonstrate that the behavior of System officials was consistent throughout the entire period.

I wish to thank those who read the manuscript and offered many valuable suggestions, especially Lester Chandler, Edward Simmons, and Alfred Hayes. To my colleague James Witte I am particularly grateful for his penetrating criticism and continual encouragement.

I also wish to thank the following for permission to use unpublished materials: the Board of Governors of the Federal Reserve System for permission to cite and quote from the Board's official records; Roland Baughman, head of Special Collections at the Columbia University Library for permission to quote from the George L. Harrison Papers; the New York Federal Reserve Bank for permission to use material in the Harrison Papers, part of the official record of the Bank; Mrs. E. A. Goldenweiser for permission to cite and quote from her husband's Papers deposited in the Library of Congress; John C. Broderick, Acting Chief of the Manuscript Division of the Library of Congress for permission to publish excerpts from the Charles S. Hamlin Diaries; Mrs. Edward Pulling for permission to publish the letters of her father, Russell C. Leffingwell; Francis H. McAdoo for permission to publish a letter from his father, William Gibbs McAdoo, to President Woodrow Wilson; and the Bank of England for permission to quote from a cablegram sent by Governor Norman to Governor Strong. Finally, I wish to thank the University of Chicago Press for permission to reproduce material which appeared in my article "Federal Reserve Monetary Policy, 1922–33: A Reinterpretation," in *The Journal of Political Economy,* Vol. LXXIII, No. 4, August 1965, copyright 1965 by the University of Chicago.

Financial assistance was generously provided by the Ford Foundation and the Graduate School of Indiana University.

My greatest single debt, however, is to Merritt Sherman, Secretary of the Board of Governors, who, together with Ralph Young, made it possible for me to examine large quantities of Board records. Without the assistance of the expert staff in the secretary's office, many valuable documents would not have been located. Economic historians owe a special debt of gratitude to those members of the staff of the Board who have worked diligently to make the files more readily accessible to scholars. The historian of American monetary policy need no longer be limited to the public statements and printed reports of System officials.

E.R.W.

Contents

Federal Reserve Monetary Policy 1917–1933

CHAPTER 1

The McAdoo Policy and World War I Finance

ON THREE separate occasions in the past fifty years, notably during World Wars I and II and the Korean War, the question of who is ultimately responsible for monetary policy in wartime has given rise to conflict between the Treasury and the Federal Reserve. By and large a history of American monetary policy in the war years has been a history of the unsuccessful struggle of the Federal Reserve to obtain the status of an equal partner within the councils of war finance. Since these Treasury-Federal Reserve conflicts have loomed so large in the evolution of wartime monetary policy, it is for more than historical interest that we understand the grounds upon which the Treasury based its views.

When the United States entered the war in April, 1917, the Federal Reserve System had been in existence for barely more than two years. Yet within that short time Reserve officials had made an impressive record of organizational achievement. Launching the twelve Federal Reserve Banks and establishing the administrative regulations governing their operations had been formidable tasks which required the greater part of the time and the energy of System officials. Inevitably there were some minor altercations between the Federal Reserve Board in Washington and some of the Reserve Bank governors and between some individual Board members and the Secretary of the Treasury, but none so serious or of such proportions as to threaten the System's existence. Initially both the Secretary of the Treasury and the Comptroller of the Currency were *ex officio* members of the Federal Reserve Board. Although Reserve officials were not inattentive to the inflationary effects of huge gold inflows from Europe, they lacked an effective tool for immobilizing them. Reserve requirements were fixed, and there were no government securities to dispose of in the investment portfolio.

The founders of the Federal Reserve System had worked diligently to design a central banking apparatus along the lines of the Civil Service and Interstate Commerce Commissions, which would be independent of both the President and the Congress. Although the President was given the authority in the Federal Reserve Act to appoint members to the Federal Reserve Board, active intervention by packing the Board with political appointees was restrained by staggering the terms of the original Board members. Neither he nor the Congress was expected to intervene directly in the administration of monetary policy.

War unavoidably upsets the regular peacetime mix of monetary and fiscal policy; the first major jurisdictional dispute between the Federal Reserve and the Treasury occurred after the United States entered World War I. The Treasury's understandable preoccupation with the problems of financing huge deficits in the budget each year and managing the rapidly expanding debt introduced a new element to complicate the formation of monetary policy. Treasury decisions concerning the tax-loan ratio, the terms upon which new securities are issued and the composition of the Federal debt not only challenged the alleged independence of the Federal Reserve, but severely weakened it.

Critics of Federal Reserve monetary policy employ a special language to describe its relations to the Treasury in wartime. They say the Federal Reserve was "conscripted" for war finance, that it abdicated its monetary responsibilities by becoming the "bond-selling window" of the Treasury, and that it was dominated by the Treasury.[1] Whatever the merits of dichotomizing the administration of fiscal policy in the Treasury and of monetary policy in the Federal Reserve during peacetime, the wisdom of such an arrangement in wartime is open to serious dispute. The principle of an independent Federal Reserve may simply become inapplicable, because the priority of goals is altered in war, as well as the margin of tolerance for their non-attainment. It is certainly not clear that its founders intended the Federal Reserve to be completely independent of Treasury policy in periods of national emergency. Since the major aim of financial policy in wartime is to contribute to the successful conduct of the war, ultimate responsibility for financial policy during wartime must rest upon the President and the Congress. The President and the Congress would therefore need to intervene and to participate more frequently in the formulation of monetary policy.

If we grant the necessity for responsibility jointly shared, we must examine the policies initiated by the Federal Reserve Board within a broader context of general financial policy. The Federal Reserve is not thereby relieved of its share of the burden, but the problem of assigning responsibility reveals itself to be far more complex than it might otherwise appear.

Grading Federal Reserve performance is made more complicated not only because of the difficulty of knowing where to draw the line between monetary and fiscal policy but also because of the dual role performed by the Secretary of the Treasury. As head of the Treasury he was responsible for the administration's financial policy. As *ex officio* chairman of the Federal Reserve Board, he presided at meetings whenever he attended. One purpose of this chapter is to describe the character of this wartime partnership and the manner in which it evolved. When Secretary McAdoo assumed leadership of wartime financial policy, he was disinclined to share the responsibility with officials of the Federal Reserve System. They were equally disinclined to relinquish monetary control to the Secretary of the Treasury. This chapter sets out their relationship in terms, first of all, of a conflict of personalities and, what is more important, of monetary theories. The role of the Federal Reserve is explained in those terms rather than in terms of the overworked traditional explanation. It may be that treasuries generally have a vested interest in easy money policies, are overly conservative in planning debt strategy, assign a low priority to price stability, and are slavish in their regard for public opinion. But this tendency cannot be assumed to explain each case without a prior investigation of the facts.

A Conflict of Personalities?

The conflict between the Treasury and the Federal Reserve did not originate during World War I; it had its roots in the personal animosity between some Board members and Secretary of the Treasury William Gibbs McAdoo. The Secretary as chairman of the Federal Reserve Board and member of the President's Cabinet was above the governor, the Board's chief executive officer, and the other Board members. Furthermore, because of his close personal relationship with President Wilson, he preempted the role of the Board's chief intermediary with the President and kept him personally informed of the business of the Board.[2] McAdoo exercised his influence more through the designation and reappointment of Board members than through intervention in daily affairs. Reappointment to the Board was especially important in the beginning because the terms of the original five Board members varied from two to ten years, and because the President redesignated the governor annually.

McAdoo's influence was bolstered by the fact that he had played a key role in guiding the Federal Reserve Act through Congress, and he had served on the three-man Federal Reserve Organization Committee. It is no accident, therefore, that the strongest influence by the Secretary of the Treasury on Federal Reserve monetary policy was exercised by two men intimately associated with the passage of the Federal Reserve Act—Secretary McAdoo, who headed the Treasury from 1914 to 1918, and Carter Glass, who was Secretary from 1918 to 1920.

The mere fact that the Secretary was a member of the Federal Reserve Board insured a certain minimum cooperation and coordination of financial policy. The Secretary's presence at Board meetings permitted Board members to express their views on policies for which he was responsible. Nevertheless, this relationship appears to have been spoiled from the outset by a dispute within the Board concerning its status *vis à vis* the Secretary of the Treasury. The situation was even strained by something as inconsequential as the Secretary's authorization to designate rooms in the Treasury for the Board's use. Some members of the Board were jealous of their independence from Treasury supervision—notably Paul M. Warburg, Adolph Miller, and Frederick Delano—and were quick to find provocation that their independence was being challenged. C. S. Hamlin, a Board member and a former Undersecretary of the Treasury in the second Cleveland administration, explained why the tension was high between the Board and the Secretary. He wrote in his Diary that "[the] real underlying trouble arose from failure to give definite status to [the] Reserve

Board—that they [the members] felt degraded and humiliated and that, while Secretary McAdoo treated them respectfully personally, yet they felt that officially he rather looked down on them."[3] Part of this complaint stemmed from a failure to define the social status of Board members in relation to other departments of government and especially to Secretary McAdoo. McAdoo told the Board that President Wilson did not believe that it should be placed in the order of precedence above the Interstate Commerce and Civil Service Commissions, and that Wilson would be willing to place them on a par with Assistant Secretaries. Hamlin thought that this would not appease the Board because "it seemed to them anomalous to have the Secretary preside at a meeting of [a] Board of which the members ranked only as high as Assistant Secretaries; that the very fact of disparity [in] rank of itself tended to magnify the importance of the Secretary as a member and to minimize the importance of the other members."[4] Hamlin wanted the Board to have the status just below a member of Congress and above the Assistant Secretaries. But to this suggestion McAdoo replied that "this would make the Board more obstructive than ever and it would swell their heads," a view unlikely to discourage jealousy and friction between himself and the Board.[5] McAdoo eventually informed President Wilson of the Board members' discontent over their status and requested that he decide their rank in the scale of social precedence. McAdoo relates that when he asked the President, Wilson reflected a moment, then looked up with a broad smile and replied: "Well, they might come right after the fire department!"[6]

Parker Willis, the Board's first Secretary, who later became its first unofficial historian, also thought that ranking Board members below Assistant Secretaries had seriously impaired the group's morale.[7] The Board in his judgment "never had the courage to act upon its own instincts" and it also "became more and more dependent upon Treasury dictation and less and less able to assert itself independent of the Treasury authorities."[8] Willis considered this the most serious mistake made during the organization of the Board.

Governor William P. G. Harding of the Federal Reserve Board accused McAdoo of not favoring the establishment of independent boards and commissions but preferring cabinet supervision of all Federal government agencies. According to Harding, McAdoo actually advocated a change in the law making the Board dependent upon a specific appropriation of Congress. Harding's suspicions are confirmed in the following letter that McAdoo wrote to President Wilson on November 5, 1915:

> Another unfortunate thing is the provision that the Federal Reserve banks shall pay the expenses of the Federal Reserve Board. The Federal Reserve Board is the sole judge of the amount of its expenditures, there being no control over them anywhere, and they levy an assessment upon the Federal Reserve banks for the amount thereof. This, I fear, influences members of the Board to feel that they are less of a Government institution than a part and parcel of the reserve banks themselves. Every other board and every department of the Government has to submit estimates of its expenditures to Congress, which reviews them and determines the amount of the appropriations, and these are paid out of the Federal Treasury. Consequently, every other board and every department of the Government feels that it is directly the servant of the Government, which pays all salaries and expenses. I feel confident that that provision of the Federal Reserve Act should be changed and that the expenses of the Federal Reserve Board should be approved by the Congress and paid out of the Federal Treasury.
>
> This is submitted merely for your information, and as the basis for any discussion we may have to have about this matter later on.[9]

So by the time America entered the war in April, 1917, instead of a smooth working machinery of coordination and a cooperative spirit between the Treasury and Federal Reserve, there was personal animosity, conflict, and rivalry destined to influence financial policy. The war and the financial problems it created merely aggravated the situation.

The Policy of War Finance

The key to World War I financial policy and its aftermath is Secretary McAdoo's decision to finance war borrowing at rates below those prevailing in the open market. His decision derived in part from a conviction about what was a desirable mix between tax receipts and borrowed funds as a means of paying for the war, and also, in part, from a belief in the political necessity of widely spreading the financial gains of war. He was convinced, either rightly or wrongly, that the volume of long-term borrowing necessary to finance the war was too great to be carried out on a purely commercial basis. He thought that the attraction of higher rates on government securities might draw funds away from other uses, creating a serious financial disturbance. His fear of a financial disturbance was the principal reason he gave for setting a maximum rate of 3½% on the First Liberty Loan. Concerning this, he has written:

> I decided tentatively on a three and one half per cent interest rate for the first loan because, for one thing, this rate was a little lower than the rates usually paid by savings banks. They were afraid that large withdrawals of their deposits would be made if the rate was higher, just at a time when the great shrinkage of their investments would make it difficult for them to stand the strain.[10]

McAdoo also recognized that the prices of newly issued government securities might fall below par and thereby discourage the public from further purchases. But initially, at any rate, he was prepared to accept that risk by placing all of his faith in the strength of the patriotic motive to absorb securities below commercial rates. Later he obtained Congressional approval to support the market for Liberty Bonds.

McAdoo's skepticism about setting commercial rates for government bonds was confirmed by the advice he received. Banking opinion on the whole tended to mislead him concerning the availability of funds. Of all his advisers, only Paul M. Warburg, a member of the Federal Reserve Board and a former member of the banking firm of Kuhn, Loeb and Company, correctly gauged the temper of the market. Warburg alone thought that the issue could be above $2 billion.

If the bonds were not to be sold on a strictly commercial basis, how, then, did McAdoo intend to unload them? He expected to accomplish through an appeal to patriotism what others had said could only be done with the lure of the profit motive. By calling for what in effect amounted to a financial mobilization for war, McAdoo, through a network of war loan committees, induced, cajoled, and pressured millions of people who had no previous experience of securities into buying variable price Liberty Bonds. People were expected to "work and save" and to resist temptation either to switch to other securities or to increase consumption by selling their Treasury securities. This way he was probably able to encourage voluntary saving, but by how much it would be impossible to say. Since only a little more than one-third of wartime expenditures were financed out of tax receipts, it was imperative, if inflation was to be minimized, to step up the amount of private saving, preferably by voluntary means. As an expert politician, he felt that by carrying his campaign to the public he would be successful. It was a bold assumption, and McAdoo had the courage and the political acumen to translate it into action. The Federal Reserve Banks played a vital role in all of McAdoo's patriotic bond campaigns by setting up War Loan Committees and by acting as fiscal agents for the Treasury. Apparently Treasury officials never seriously considered the problems which their methods of finance would raise in the immediate postwar period.

Congress gave its approval to McAdoo's strategy of war finance in the War Loan Act passed on April 24, 1917. The Act specified a maximum rate of 3½% on Liberty Bonds, thus giving Congressional endorsement to the policy of the President acting through his Secretary of the Treasury. The maximum-rate-of-interest clause of the First Liberty Loan Act was omitted in subsequent War Loan Acts.

The Board recognized immediately that it bore some responsibility for insuring the success of the Treasury's large-scale borrowing policies, even though they disapproved of the terms on which the securities were issued. If they had insisted on a policy of high rates, despite Congressional will, the Board could have jeopardized the war loan campaigns by depressing the prices of other outstanding securities. Be that as it may, the Board was simply not equipped politically to frustrate the mandate expressed by both Congress and the President without explaining its position to the American people. Clearly the Federal Reserve Act made no provision for this kind of political behavior.

To aid the Treasury in its borrowing and to maintain stability in the money market, the Federal Reserve decided to adjust the rediscount rate to the prevailing rate on government bonds. The measure was closely tied to borrowing methods the Treasury used to finance its expenditures. Much of the criticism of our wartime financial policy is directed at these specific methods of short- and long-term borrowing. Each will be taken up in turn.

Treasury Certificate Financing

To bridge the time gap in revenues between expenditures and the sale of Liberty Bonds the Treasury decided to issue short-term certificates maturing in less than one year. The certificates were to be issued at intervals to keep the Treasury supplied with a cash balance sufficient for a period of approximately three weeks. These were to be sold to commercial banks and others, to be redeemed out of the proceeds of Liberty Bond campaigns. To avoid disturbing the money market, banks were allowed to pay by simply crediting the Treasury's account held by them. Treasury deposits held by commercial banks were not subject to reserve requirements and, hence, there were no initial money market effects. Similar to current procedure, the Treasury did not write checks against these deposits at commercial banks but instead made periodical calls on the banks to transfer balances to the Federal Reserve Banks. When the Treasury did transfer its deposits to the Federal Reserve Banks, this reduced the reserves of the member banks and, if not counteracted, would tighten credit. The Treasury tried to minimize such effects by paying out these funds immediately and in the same district where the deposits were located. The ensuing net increase in demand deposits led to an increase in required reserves. Monetary logic called for some mechanism to supply the commercial banks' increased demands for required reserves without adding pressure to the money market. Two schemes were proposed for minimizing these effects: 1) the preferential discount mechanism, and 2) the Reserve Bank deposit scheme.

The Origin of the Preferential Discount Policy

Comparatively little is known about the origins of the Board's preferential discount rate policy since the public record contains no reference to it. The Board's private records, however, do indicate who initiated the policy, and how it came to be accepted. The First Liberty Loan came up for consideration at a joint meeting of the Board and Reserve Bank Governors held April 4–6, 1917. Secretary McAdoo had requested an "interchange of ideas" on the loan and had asked specifically for information on open market rates in the various Federal Reserve districts and their capacity to absorb securities. Out of the meeting came a report by a committee of Reserve Bank Governors which included the following recommendations: 1) use of installment purchases to dispose of government securities; 2) exemption of government deposits from reserve requirements; and 3) legislation authorizing Federal Reserve Banks to maintain balances in member banks, not to exceed the capital or combined capital and surplus of each member bank.[11] The purpose of the last recommendation was to minimize the money market effects of the drain on member bank reserves as Treasury deposits, from the proceeds of security sales, were shifted from commercial banks to the Federal Reserve. Perhaps the plan can be illustrated more clearly with the aid of T-accounts. Initially the sale of certificates leads to an increase in Treasury certificates and Treasury deposits at member banks (Figure 1). There is no change in required reserves, for Treasury deposits were exempt.

Figure 1

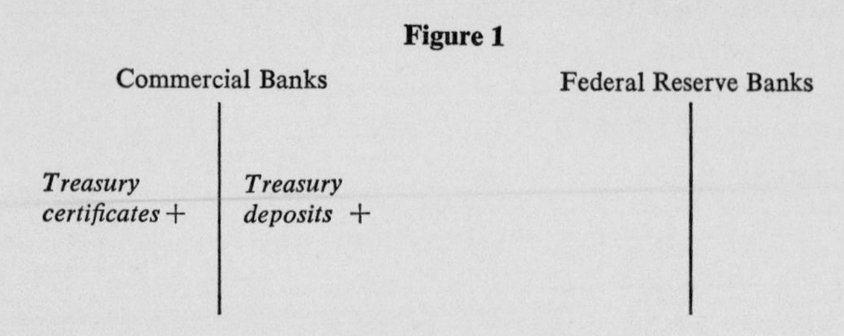

When the Treasury transfers these deposits to Federal Reserve Banks, Treasury deposits and reserves of member banks decline. Correspondingly, Treasury deposits at the Federal Reserve Bank increase and member bank deposits decrease (Figure 2).

Figure 2

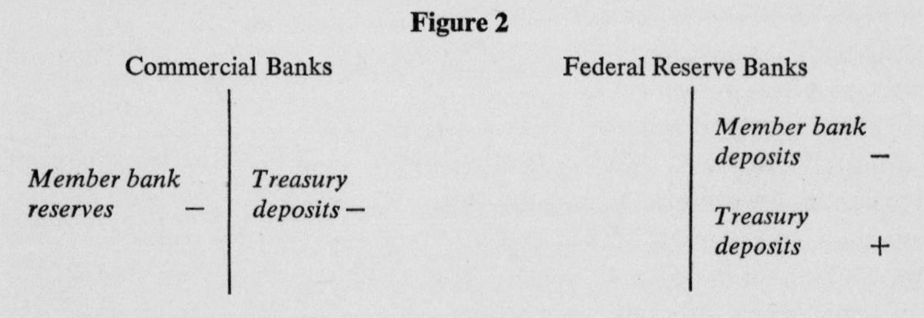

To offset the decline in member bank reserves, the special committee of governors recommended that Reserve Banks should be given authority to deposit balances at commercial banks (Figure 3).

Figure 3

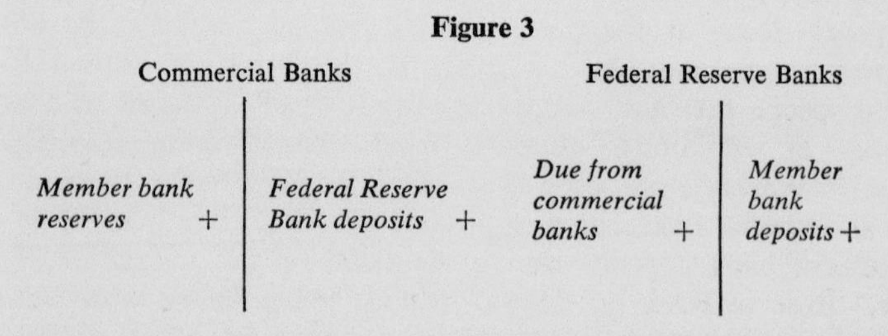

By allowing Federal Reserve Banks to hold deposits in commercial banks, the reduction in Treasury balances could be offset up to a limit imposed by capital or capital and surplus. This control over reserves would remain, therefore, with the Federal Reserve. The withdrawal of Federal Reserve deposits from commercial banks would mean additional restraint on bank credit expansion. The technique described above is superior to the one actually adopted, for the preferential discount plan, unlike the Reserve deposit scheme, placed the initiative with the commercial banks who borrowed to replenish reserves.

A week after the meeting of the Board and the Reserve Bank governors, the Comptroller of the Currency asked if the Board had considered the forthcoming Treasury loan, and Governor Harding replied that the matter had not been referred to the Board. When he addressed a joint meeting of the Federal Advisory Council and the Federal Reserve Board on April 17, he again stated, "The policy of the Secretary of the Treasury had been that of keeping his own counsel up to such time as the new bond Act should be passed."[12] At the same meeting Warburg warned that a 4% rate on government bonds would adversely affect savings banks by encouraging deposit shifts which could in turn depress the prices of corporate securities, a warning Secretary McAdoo apparently heeded when he set the rate on the First Liberty Loan.

The Liberty Loan Act passed Congress on April 24, 1917, and although McAdoo had consulted with Federal Reserve officials earlier in the month on the amount and terms of the loan, he had reached no decision concerning the role the Reserve System would play. Two days after Congress approved the Act McAdoo urged Reserve Bank officials to arrange some plan for redepositing the proceeds of government loans with the member banks. By that time, however, the Reserve authorities had no other recourse but to accept Congress's mandate and to set up ways to carry out the Treasury's borrowing plans. According to the Board's minutes, Harding said that McAdoo's plan for redepositing the proceeds of government loans at commercial banks was not feasible, and he suggested a rediscount plan "whereby the member banks would be given a special rate and would continue to hold the funds as the proceeds of rediscounts obtained from their Federal Reserve Banks."[13] Warburg proposed the use of member bank collateral notes at a special rate. The Comptroller of the Currency endorsed the Reserve bank deposit scheme suggested by the committee of Federal Reserve Bank governors. Adolph Miller joined with him and said that the plan in his judgment could be effective. An executive committee composed of Warburg as chairman, Miller, and the Comptroller, John Skelton Williams, was appointed to prepare a regulation. On May 17 the Board approved the preferential discount plan by adopting a preferential rate of 3% on fifteen-day collateral notes. It seems a little strange that the Board adopted this plan considering that of the three-man committee two members, at least initially, were opposed to it. In a memorandum dated October 17, 1917, and read at a Board meeting on October 19, Miller explained the reasons for the Board's adoption of the preferential discount rate plan:

> These rates were established by the Board at the time when the First Liberty Loan was in process of placement and when fear was expressed in banking circles that the flotation of the loan would be hindered unless distinct encouragement was given to bankers (who were expected to co-operate liberally in placing the bonds with their customers) by fixing rates for borrowings at Reserve Banks on Liberty Loan account, at 3½ per cent for the longer maturities and at 3 per cent for the fifteen-day maturities.[14]

To give the banks an incentive for taking the new certificates, the Board set the rate of discount on government paper below the certificates' rate, to absorb the cost of handling them. Since at the time of the Third Liberty Loan all banks were expected to contribute 1% of their resources to buying certificates, the preferential rate could be defended as necessary not to impair the earnings of many small banks. The general attitude was that individual banks ought not to be penalized by having to carry the certificates at a net cost to themselves. The special rate was probably a concession to the bankers to insure their active and willing participation. Undoubtedly the price paid for banker cooperation was underestimated both within the Board and at the Treasury. Adequate safeguards, they thought, existed in the form of moral suasion, that is voluntary discrimination by the banks themselves in making loans. The obnoxious by-product of this mechanism was the inducement of the commercial banks to borrow for profit at a time when the so-called tradition against borrowing had not yet become firmly established.

Long-term Bond Financing

The policy of issuing Liberty Bonds at infrequent intervals was, of course, related to the Treasury's policy of meeting its short-term cash balance needs. Proceeds of Liberty Bond campaigns were used to retire the more frequent certificate issues. The Treasury hoped that the public would purchase Liberty Bonds either out of current or future savings, and thus compensate for the low tax-loan ratio. But it was doubtful whether or not the necessary amounts could be sold strictly on a cash basis. There was a slim chance that installment purchases might even have a tendency to increase private saving. Buying bonds on credit, referred to at the time as the policy of "borrow and buy," put an extra burden on the banks, for they would be required to extend credit for a specified period to any would-be purchaser. To induce the public to borrow and buy, the lending rate at commercial banks could not be in excess of the rate on Liberty Bonds. To induce the banks to lend to prospective customers, the Federal Reserve thought they would have to supply reserves at a rate equal to or below the coupon rate on the bonds. Placing Liberty Bonds with commercial banks was ruled out in principle, for it implied an inflationary expansion of bank credit. Both the Treasury and the Reserve Board decided that the preferential discount mechanism would furnish the incentive to get these securities sold.

A frequent test used by the Board and the Treasury to gauge the success of a bond campaign was the amount of bonds still in the banking system. The continued aim was to keep this amount to an absolute minimum. Liquidation of the bond portfolios of the commercial banks was one index the Treasury used in the postwar period to judge the success of its anti-inflationary strategy.

Pressure from the Secretary of the Treasury to finance the war at low rates was reflected in the money market by declining bond prices on existing securities, generating concern about the success of future borrowing policy. McAdoo's emphasis on the patriotic motive was not sufficient to overcome the formidable strength of the economic motive. The disparity of rates between public and private security issues created a constant temptation to switch assets for the purpose of making a profit, enough to destabilize bond prices. The Treasury could not resist the tide of rising market rates of interest and in the next four successive Liberty Bond campaigns raised the rates from 3½% to 4½%.

After each Liberty Loan closed, there had been for a short time more sellers of bonds than buyers. When McAdoo requested approval for the Third Liberty Loan, he decided that some form of support for the market price of Liberty Bonds was obligatory. In testimony before the Ways and Means Committee on March 27, 1918, he said:

Very careful and earnest attention to the situation which has developed since the last Liberty loan has convinced me that the United

States must do what each of the warring countries in one form or another does, and prepare itself to support the market price for its bonds.[15]

In response to this, Congress included a Bond Purchase Clause in the Third Liberty Loan Act. McAdoo envisioned the Bond Purchase Fund as a pool out of which the prices of bonds could be protected during the intervals immediately following a new issue. He also reasoned that the existence of a sinking fund, coupled with the Treasury's willingness to use it, would inspire confidence in government bonds. The terms of the Bond Purchase Clause were quoted in all of the circulars publicizing the new issue. After the war the existence of this clause proved a source of embarrassment to the Treasury, for it was extremely reluctant to sanction any policy which would depress bond prices and raise market rates of interest. The Treasury viewed this as a serious breach of confidence.

Unlike Treasury policy during World War II, the object of the Fund was not to peg the price of Liberty bonds at par but to keep it "measurably around par." McAdoo rightly rejected pegging bond prices at par on the grounds that it would turn long-term government bonds into demand obligations.[16] He insisted that the price should fluctuate the same as other securities. All he wanted to eliminate was "violent and unnecessary fluctuations in price."

Congress authorized the Secretary to purchase annually in the open market not more than 5% of each outstanding issue. Purchases were made at market prices and not at par. The procedure was to sell certificates of indebtedness and use the proceeds to buy bonds on the New York Stock Exchange. The total purchases from April 4, 1918, to January 31, 1919, are shown in Table 1.

Table 1

Bond Purchase Fund Acquisitions at Par Value
April 4, 1918 to January 31, 1919
(*$000*)

Liberty Loan	To November 15, 1918	To January 31, 1919
1st	656	656
2nd	190,345	195,345
3rd	70,936	115,936
4th		35,000

SOURCE: *Report Operations of the War Finance Corporation*, 65th Congress, 3rd Session. House Document No. 1513, December 3, 1918 and *Bond Purchases*, Letter from The Secretary of the Treasury, December 1, 1919. House of Representatives, 66th Congress, 2nd Session. House Document No. 393, pp. 2–3.

The *Annual Reports* of the Secretary of the Treasury show that during the war most purchases were made to support the market while the Treasury was engaged in the Third and Fourth Liberty Bond drives. Subscriptions to the Third Liberty Loan closed on May 4, 1918. In the subsequent two-week period the Treasury acquired through the Bond Purchase Fund $631,000 of government bonds. The amount purchased daily during the operation of the Fund ranged from $15,000 to $25 million.

The Treasury regarded the existence of the fund as an important factor contributing to the success of the final wartime bond drives. Prices of government securities remained around par up until the final Victory Loan in 1919. What is important about the establishment of the Fund is not so much the degree of stability imparted to the bond market during the remainder of the war, but that the Treasury assumed responsibility through open market purchases for the relative stability of interest rates. The full consequences of the Treasury action did not become apparent until after the war when the Treasury and the Federal Reserve were locked in a bitter conflict. The mandate, it must not be forgotten, came directly from the Congress.

According to Parker Willis the Federal Reserve Board did not accept passively the McAdoo strategy of war finance. It was understandably reluctant to adjust the discount rate of the Reserve Banks to the coupon rate on the new bonds. Willis, always an ardent supporter of central bank independence, summed up the Board's attitude in the following manner:

> they were faced with the facts, namely that the Treasury Department was in a position to override the Board, and had it chosen to do so could with the assistance of the reserve banks themselves undoubtedly attain their object. . . . In these circumstances prudence and practicalities of the case dictated an acceptance of the Treasury policy and the Board almost inevitably felt itself driven to the making of a rate which should be substantially identical with the coupon rate on the bonds.[17]

Although he relates that the opposition of the Board to McAdoo's policies "culminated at meetings held during the midsummer of 1917, in which a firm but positive protest was lodged against the borrowing plans of the Treasury," there is no evidence in the Board's official files to corroborate this.[18] It may simply not appear in the written record. McAdoo was in no mood to brook such an attitude and announced that it might be necessary for the government to take over the funds of all the banks for the purpose of winning the war! Willis said that some consideration was even given to the possibility of resignations in protest, but the attitude of most of the members, he recalls, was that the more courageous policy would be "to remain at the post of duty even though the policies which might be forced by circumstances upon the organization could not be approved by it."[19] Willis' judgment is valid that the System was "neither strong enough nor independent enough of government authority at the opening of the war to adopt any such course of resistance to the public powers, even had the members of the System been inclined to pursue it . . ."[20] No useful purpose could have been served by such resignations. Not only would the System have been literally conscripted for war finance but also a competent and independent voice within the councils of war finance would have been lost.

Whether or not the borrow and buy strategy of the Liberty Loan campaigns was essential to their success is still open to dispute. Benjamin Strong thought that it was. On the other hand, Willis maintained that the First Liberty Loan would have been successful even without Federal Reserve support, and he was probably right. The ratio of cash payments to allotments of Liberty Bonds was 73%, and out of a total of $2 billion subscribed only one-half remained due. Moreover, many of the banks accommodated their customers at the coupon rate without any profit to themselves. The Board reported in the *Federal Reserve Bulletin* that the proportion taken by installment purchase was "unexpectedly small." They estimated that the banks took between 20% and 25% of the issue for their own account. In the second war loan 53% of the subscription was by credit. In the third, 80% was fully paid at the time of subscription.

The Treasury's View of Wartime Inflation

The Treasury had no official theory about the wartime rise in prices. However, the Papers of Russell C. Leffingwell offer the views of the Assistant Secretary of the Treasury who was responsible primarily for financial affairs. Leffingwell was a brilliant and articulate spokesman for Treasury policy. He was fully as intelligent, persuasive, and strong-willed as his arch-rival in the Federal Reserve System, Benjamin Strong. Although Leffingwell and Secretary McAdoo did not always agree, McAdoo praised his work highly and gave him credit for sharpening his own views of Treasury policy.

In a statement read to the American Economic Association in 1921, Leffingwell defined the goals of Treasury policy during World War I as having been to finance the war so that it could be won without "avoidable inflation."[21] To Leffingwell "avoidable inflation" meant first and foremost the maintenance of the gold convertibility of the dollar. This was not an unorthodox interpretation, for R. F. Harrod has recently reminded us that prior to 1914 inflation was taken to consist of either a reduction in the official gold valuation of the monetary unit, or the existence of a discount on currency in relation to its valuation in gold.[22] Almost from the outset of the war there was fairly unanimous agreement among American economists and financial specialists that our policy of war finance, unlike that of several European countries, should be the maintenance *at home* of the gold convertibility of the dollar, thus ruling out the possibility of an inconvertible paper currency. The European experiment which resulted in the issue of paper money convinced U.S. policymakers that its effects in the United States would be reckless spending by the government, loss of public confidence in the currency, and extreme inflation. This belief was reinforced by the widely held view that inflation was the necessary concomitant of the issue of an inconvertible paper currency. A "sound" currency and domestic gold convertibility were indistinguishable and formed the basis of public opinion regarding currency matters. In a memorandum prepared for Walter Hines, Director General of the railroads, in August, 1919, Leffingwell denied that the rapid increase of wartime government expenditures was inflationary:

> That expansion was accomplished without depreciation of our currency. There never was at any time a premium on gold in the United States . . . The Federal Reserve System has a gold reserve of about 50% [August, 1919] . . . which is greatly in excess of the practical and legal limitations upon a sound currency. The currency and credit structure of the United States is sound and true and the *charge of inflation is contrary to fact* and is a direct aid to the profiteers, furnishing their principal argument for exorbitant prices.[23]

In this instance, Leffingwell completely divorced inflation from the rise in prices, but later he was to give a different analysis of the wartime price increase.

In a seventeen-page letter to Paul Warburg written after Warburg had retired from the Federal Reserve Board, he attempted to refute the charges levied against the policy of certificate borrowing by Jacob Hollander, professor of political economy at Johns Hopkins, the author of a classic of war finance.[24] The main point of

Hollander's criticism was that the Treasury's war borrowing techniques were inflationary; that is, they led to an expansion of the money supply and on the grounds of crude quantity theory tended to raise prices. The Assistant Secretary of the Treasury denied both charges that certificate borrowing increased the money supply and that increases in the money supply were responsible for the wartime inflation. Since the Board endorsed Hollander's two propositions, a fundamental disagreement emerged between the Treasury and the Federal Reserve over the monetary effects of the former's war borrowing policies. The clash of personalities was aggravated by a deep-rooted conflict of rival monetary theories. It was this latter conflict that explains the persistence with which the Treasury's views took precedence over those of the Federal Reserve Board.

Leffingwell denied that the quantity theory of money could explain general price behavior although he admitted that it might explain some special price movements in the past. He objected especially to Hollander's position that the quantity theory was behind wartime price advances. The wartime price increase he attributed to an "excess demand over supply of commodities" caused by the enormous rise in government expenditures. The supply of money, he maintained, simply accommodated itself to the increased expenditures:

> when an excess of demand over supply exists in very extreme form for a considerable period of time an increase in the quantity of money must follow as the effect of that excess unless the currency and credit structure breaks down and catastrophe results.[25]

The other alternative he ignored, that is, the failure of the monetary authority to increase the money supply, might have reduced expenditures and hence inflationary pressures. He went even further to state that the increase in the quantity of money in every instance *followed* the increase in prices and did not precede it! He reasoned that since prices on government contracts were made months, and even years, ahead of time and Treasury cash balances were sufficient for only a few weeks, then the rise in prices could not be attributed to an increase in the supply of money. Leffingwell thought that Hollander had the causation reversed—money to prices, instead of prices to money, as it should be. As he put it, "Hollander, then, starts with the erroneous assumption that prices during the war were attributable to inflation, when, as a matter of fact, the inflation was consequent upon prices."[26]

Hollander correctly argued that the mechanism of the preferential discount rate, designed to cope with certificate borrowing, increased the quantity of money. But Leffingwell labeled this "sheer nonsense." The confusion, he thought, was the result of calling bank deposits money:

> All of these people who believe in the quantity theory of money in its extreme form choose to call bank deposits money, but bank deposits are not money. Bank deposits cannot be paid out without money. Money which can be paid out over the counter cannot be gotten just by writing an entry into a book. Hollander has become so convinced that bank deposits are money that he has now got himself into a state of mind where he thinks that the entry of an item into the books of the bank puts the banks into a position to increase the supply of money without more ado. . . there was in the mere process of payment by credit something which involved inflation *ipso facto*. This, I take it, is sheer nonsense and would only result from the confusion of thought which follows from the misuse of terms, as in the case of calling a bank deposit money.[27]

Leffingwell based his position on the following argument. Government deposits at commercial banks fail to satisfy the quantity theorists' criterion of money inasmuch as they are never checked against; payment by credit for Treasury certificates does not provide a depository bank with loanable funds.

Leffingwell obviously failed to understand the money supply effects of the Treasury's practices of certificate borrowing. Moreover, he denied the validity of the quantity theory explanation of wartime price inflation. No wonder then that the Treasury was not prepared to accept the leadership of the Federal Reserve and follow its counsel in forming monetary policy. In his analysis of wartime price inflation, with its emphasis on expenditure flows and not the money stock, Leffingwell was on solid ground, more solid than that of his critics, but the subject remains highly controversial. His view that price inflation was not solely the consequence of bad banking policy is a tribute to his economic intuition, but his failure to grasp the money-creating effects of certificate borrowing must be roundly condemned and is hardly justifiable in an official whose responsibility it was to administer the financial policies of the Treasury.

The Reserve Board's Theory of Wartime Inflation

In sharp contrast to the Leffingwell approach to an explanation of price inflation is the position of the Federal Reserve Board. The foundation of the Board's inflation theory was the quantity theory of money, while recognizing the existence as well as the importance of the "cost-push" explanation. Unlike the Treasury, the Board confined its use of the term inflation to a rise in prices. Reserve officials identified correctly the phenomenon which we designate as pure price inflation: the supply of money increasing more rapidly than the volume of "current and available goods." They realized that the response of prices to an increase in the supply of money was not necessarily immediate nor was it related exactly to the amount of the increase.

Because of the tendency to overemphasize the Board's allegiance to the so-called "real-bills doctrine," its acceptance of the quantity theory of money has not been given the attention and publicity it deserves. Adolph Miller, the only professional economist on the Federal Reserve Board, attempted a reconciliation of the two doctrines which furnished the intellectual framework for the Board's official position. Two relatively long but extremely illuminating passages from the *Federal Reserve Bulletin* for June, 1918, summarize the Board's approach:

> Creation of additional bank credit, for the purpose of buying bonds or paying taxes by obtaining bank accommodations rather than by saving, results only in a technical increase of purchasing power, since it is not based upon a commensurate increase in the production of goods—in other words, is not offset by genuine savings. The consequence of making such additions to bank credits is necessarily an increased tendency toward the bidding up of prices, and results in the menace called "inflation."[28]
>
> . . .
>
> Whenever the volume of current purchasing power, in terms of money, whether in the form of actual currency or in the form of credit, grows or is increased faster than the volume of current and available goods, the resulting situation may be ascribed to the excess of currency and credit, or both, above normal requirements or, more briefly, to the distention of currency and credit. This alteration of the proportion between existing goods and purchasing power eventually results in increase of prices, not necessarily in the exact degree in which the volume of purchasing power has been increased but in the degree in which it is actively used to effect the purchase and transfer of goods. *When loans are made by banks upon the security of bonds or other claims to the product of future industry or its share in fixed capital, the tendency is to advance prices.* Funds obtained by the Government, in the form of such credits, result therefore in the bidding up of the prices of commodities, especially of those for which the Government has the most need.[29]

The Board reasoned that creating money to finance either government expenditures or fixed capital leads to no immediate increase in "current and available goods" and hence is *prima facie* inflationary. But in the case of spending on fixed capital there is a distinct lag between initial expenditure and the resulting stream of consumption goods. To be consistent the Board should also have argued that prices will rise during the period of construction and fall again when the production process is completed. The real culprit was identified as credit creation by the banks on the basis of government securities. Or to put it in a slightly different way, it is not the volume of money which is crucial in the determination of prices but the way in which the money tap is turned on.

Shortly before America's entry into World War II, our World War I financial policies were reviewed by a panel of economists.[30] They concluded that the principles of war finance were imperfectly understood by officials of the Treasury and the Federal Reserve Board inasmuch as they failed to identify the real problem of war finance as the curtailment of private spending. They censured the financial authorities for focusing too much attention on the problem of raising funds. Perhaps the Treasury at times did appear to be guilty of such a misunderstanding. However, the charge cannot be made against the Federal Reserve Board. The Board continually emphasized the necessity for saving and conserving resources and was fully aware of the dangers of creating excessive credit to finance government expenditures. Inflation was thought a threat as long as the public refused to purchase government securities out of current saving.

Given the scope and character of Treasury policy, probably too much reliance was placed upon voluntarism, exhortation, and encouragement of private thrift and not enough upon higher taxes and direct controls. The importance of restricting private expenditures was understood by Treasury officials, but they preferred a policy of voluntary restraint, rather than compulsory restriction through a more vigorous policy of taxation. If they were indeed guilty of any offense, it was the crime of being overoptimistic in their expectations about the effectiveness of voluntarism. Whether they could have done more, given the political climate, remains pure conjecture.

At least one Board member, Adolph Miller, in a paper, "War Finance and Inflation," clearly anticipated Keynes' analysis of inflation contained in *How to Pay for the War*.[31] Miller perceived correctly that the fundamental problem of war finance was that of defraying war expenditures out of the current income of the community. To consume less, Miller argued, "must be our national formula of finance. We must produce more of the things which the nation of war requires and, in order to set free the nation's productive forces to accomplish this result, we must consume less of the things which the nation in wartime does not require."[32] It could hardly be put better today. Miller produced some relatively crude national income arithmetic very similar to Keynes. He estimated the gross annual product of the country's industrial and business activities in 1917 at $50 billion which corresponds reasonably well with Kuznets' estimate of GNP of $57.5 billion. Miller's estimate of saving for 1917 was approximately $15 billion from which he inferred that $12 billion could safely be raised by government borrowing. He thought that the Treasury's fiscal policy was inadequate. Furthermore, he declared that the policy of voluntarism had failed. Miller did not shy away from unpopular remedies, for he concluded by saying:

> Whether it may mean taxation carried to the farthest limits, compulsory saving, industrial conscription, priority of industry or priority of credits, the response will be made by the people if the call is authoritatively made upon them.[33]

These austere and ascetic sentiments were shared neither by the Secretary of the Treasury nor by members of Congress. But it is one thing to have the benefit of wise counsel, another thing to act upon it. At least the Board had not failed in its duty to analyze and to defend a more stringent fiscal policy to cope with the restraints imposed on a purely monetary policy. The Board continued to plead for a higher tax-loan ratio, moral suasion to raise the savings ratio, and direct controls over the allocation of industrial materials to supplement credit rationing.[34]

CHAPTER 2 Postwar Financial Policy: The Inflation Phase, 1918–1920

Treasury-Federal Reserve Discord

"Financially, the War is by no means over."
FEDERAL RESERVE BULLETIN, June, 1919.

THE END of hostilities in Europe in November, 1918, did not bring an end to our wartime financial policies. Government expenditures continued at a rate of $2 billion a month during the final months of 1918 and January, 1919. From February until the end of May spending was halved, dropping to a little over $1 billion a month. The continuation of these large war-budgeted expenditures led Secretary McAdoo to send a letter in November, 1918, to all bank and trust companies outlining the Treasury's borrowing plans and announcing the resumption of the issue of Treasury certificates to be funded in a final bond campaign sometime in the spring. He called upon each national and state bank to subscribe biweekly 2½% of its gross resources or a total of 5% monthly. The commercial banks were almost literally conscripted to finance the Treasury deficit. In the five-month period running from December 5, 1918, to May 1, 1919, the Treasury issued over $6 billion of certificates.

From a purely financial standpoint, the situation had changed very little from wartime. The same problems faced the Treasury after the armistice as before, only in a more acute form. The patriotic motive was less intense, and the banking system faced increasing pressure to finance the demands of business. The formula of "work and save" diminished in effectiveness as the wartime economy gradually reconverted to a peacetime basis. Moreover, there was growing pressure to dismantle the apparatus of wartime controls.

The aim of Treasury policy was to fund all of the floating debt by July, 1920, except that part issued in anticipation of income and profit taxes; to accomplish this objective, Treasury officials decided to issue a final postwar loan. They hoped that the floating debt could be funded without disturbing the market for Liberty Bonds. Relatively stable bond prices remained therefore an important objective of fiscal policy as long as debt operations continued on a large scale. The behavior of existing bond prices also influenced the Treasury's plans concerning the appropriate maturity of the new issue. From the standpoint of the Treasury, then, the war was not over in a financial sense. And it would not be until the Treasury withdrew as a dominating influence from the money and the securities markets.

The banking system was the principal intermediary through which the success of Treasury policy was guaranteed. The question is whether or not the ending of the "hot" war brought about any change in the wartime relationship between the Federal Reserve and the Treasury. Had the primary responsibility for monetary policy reverted to the Federal Reserve? Those who charge the Federal Reserve with incompetent management during this period answer in the affirmative, but the situation was far more complicated.

First, there are personality considerations. During this period leadership of the Treasury changed hands twice: from Secretary McAdoo to Carter Glass on December 16, 1918, and from Carter Glass to David F. Houston on February 2, 1920. Secretary McAdoo announced his resignation on November 22, 1918, and in his place President Wilson appointed Carter Glass, a member of the House of Representatives and the "father" of the Federal Reserve Act. Glass understood as well as anyone the role that Congress expected the Federal Reserve to play in relationship to the Treasury. As a congressman from Virginia he guarded jealously the integrity of the System and defended it against attack.

One might have expected a Secretary of the Treasury as sympathetic as he to the Federal Reserve to have released it from "bondage" to the Treasury. Instead he vowed to continue without change the policies of his predecessor. It was not out of a greater loyalty to the Treasury than to the Federal Reserve that he championed the Treasury cause. Rather it was a fundamental difference of opinion about how monetary policy works. He eschewed the use of the discount rate to curb inflation; he preferred discriminatory credit controls and the separation of essential from non-essential credits. Yet he voted, albeit reluctantly, for an increase in rates in January, 1920, a decision which he very much regretted in later years.

One other consequence of McAdoo's departure from the Treasury was that Russell C. Leffingwell's influence became stronger. Glass relied heavily upon his analysis and judgment in forming and executing fiscal policy. Leffingwell's memoranda for Secretary Glass on major policy questions are significant documents in American financial history. The Treasury-Federal Reserve relationship cannot be understood adequately without a knowledge of the monetary and fiscal theories of Leffingwell and the influence which he exerted on the Board during the critical debate on discount policy in the last months of 1919.

The Treasury continued its policy of low interest rates because it regarded the existence of a large floating debt within the banking system as *prima facie* inflationary in the sense that the volume of credit extended by the commercial banks was thereby excessive.[1] That is, Treasury officials interpreted the quantity of government bonds held by the banks, both commercial and Federal Reserve, as a symptom of inflation. For this reason they had refrained from direct sales of securities to the Federal Reserve Banks during World War I. The sale of certificates to the commercial banks was only supposed to be a temporary expedient. Presumably they would be retired from the proceeds of bond sales to the non-bank public. Fortunately, the Treasury's debt strategy was on the whole successful. When the armistice was signed, there was no short-term indebtedness not covered by deferred installments of the Fourth Liberty Loan. However, $2 billion of Liberty Bonds were still held by the banking system. The Treasury viewed this residue of the war loan campaigns as unavoidable "inflation" to be "liquidated" as quickly as possible, thus squeezing the amount of "inflation" out of the banking system.

The maturity structure of the Federal debt, as shown in Table 1, reflected the Treasury's strategy. Evidently Secretary McAdoo had deliberately left open the intermediate maturity range to accommodate the postwar financial situation, for the gap there provided a "safety valve" with which to relieve the pressure on the long-term market.

Table 1

Maturity Structure as a Percentage of Federal Interest-Bearing Debt 1917–1920

Year	Less than 1 year	1–5 years	5 years and over	Total interest-bearing debt (*$ million*)
1917	11.1	2.4	86.5	2,713
1918	14.9	2.9	82.6	11,986
1919	14.3	17.5	68.2	25,234
1920	11.5	21.1	67.4	24,061

SOURCE: E. R. Van Sant, *The Floating Debt of the Federal Government 1919–1936* (Baltimore: Johns Hopkins, 1937), p. 21.

Unfortunately immediately after the war Congress dismantled the apparatus of money and capital market controls designed to effect the Treasury's low rate policy. Their continuation might have proved helpful in buttressing the Treasury's policy of stable rates. Hamlin expressed some surprise in his Diary when McAdoo agreed to the abolition of the Capital Issues Committee, originally established to control the amount of new security issues. According to Hamlin, McAdoo said "he would even prefer to pay a higher rate on future bond issues than to hold up the country's development until next April—the probable time for a new bond issue."[2] Because of Leffingwell's strenuous objections, he agreed finally to make a statement that all issues would be approved *except* those involving present economic waste. But McAdoo might have consented eventually to an increase in the discount rate if he had remained in the Treasury. He was less doctrinaire than either Russell Leffingwell or Carter Glass and was certainly capable of providing the necessary national leadership if convinced of the necessity for a change in rates.

The Board agreed in principle with the Treasury's views of the importance of placing war obligations outside of the banking system. How it proposed to deal with the situation is set out in the *Sixth Annual Report* (1919):

The remedy for this condition is the absorption by investors of the undigested securities. This process could not be accelerated, as in normal times, by sharp declines in value, as the large volume to be digested precluded that possibility. Absorption can be brought about only by time and saving; and it often happens that a rising price causes better absorption than a falling quotation. A consideration of these facts makes it clear that abnormalities were imposed on the banking system by the war and that a restoration of normal conditions must be brought about through the gradual elimination of war paper from the banks. It was necessary to cooperate with the Treasury in every way to facilitate first the sale of Government securities and then their absorption by investors.[3]

But the question arose very soon after the war as to the desirability of continued Federal Reserve support for Treasury debt management operations. Could the final Victory Loan be successful without Federal Reserve cooperation and support? The Federal Reserve Board reviewed carefully two aspects of Treasury-Federal Reserve policy: 1) the continuation of the preferential discount rate; and 2) the borrow and buy strategy of selling government bonds. Hamlin discloses that every member of the Federal Reserve Board felt that borrowing for future bond issues should be discouraged. And in his account of the Board meeting held on January 17, 1919, he indicated that Adolph Miller favored the elimination of the preferential rate on 15-day notes collateralled by government securities.[4] In all but three of the twelve Federal Reserve Banks the existing rate was 4%. Miller wanted it raised immediately to 4¼%, the bond rate of interest. Hamlin agreed with Miller, but he said that he preferred to wait and to hear any reasons which might be advanced against it. Governor Harding then conveyed to the Board a message from Secretary Glass:

> Mr. Glass told him to say that he could not be present at the meeting but that he earnestly hoped that the Board would *not* advance these rates as such action would gravely prejudice the Government's interests; that it would necessitate immediate raising of rates on U.S. Treasury certificates and the rate on the next bond issue, that he was having the greatest difficulty in placing Treasury certificates now at the 4% rate on 15 day notes and Commercial paper secured by Government obligations.[5]

Both Harding and Albert Strauss, Vice Governor of the Federal Reserve Board, said that they agreed with the Secretary. Hamlin also intimated that he would support the Treasury's views until at least after the Victory Loan. At a meeting of the Board three days later Governor Harding relayed a second message from Secretary Glass reiterating that any increase in rates would seriously embarrass the Treasury in the forthcoming Victory Loan and "that the ease in local rates in New York was equivalent to an increase in the Federal Reserve rates."[6] Whereupon the decision was made with Adolph Miller concurring to make no change in prevailing rates.

The picture which emerges from Hamlin's account is definitely not that of a Board "dominated" by the Secretary of the Treasury. Apparently Glass did not consider it important enough to attend either meeting. There is good reason for believing that the Board accepted deliberately the leadership of the Treasury in questions concerning the probable success or failure of the Victory Note issue. There was considerable sympathy within the Board for the problems facing the Treasury. Understandably, the Board was reluctant to accept any responsibility for the outcome of the Treasury's debt management policy. But there is no evidence that the Board was particularly better, or even as well, informed as the Treasury on conditions in the capital markets to be in a position to challenge seriously the views of Treasury officials. To have done so would have invited the invocation of the Overman Act, an eventuality noted by Benjamin Strong, John R. Commons, Governor Harding and many others.[7] The Overman Act, passed in 1918, authorized the President during the war and for six months thereafter to redistribute functions of the various federal agencies including the Federal Reserve in the interest of more efficient government.

These discussions by the Board in January settled effectively the question of the Federal Reserve-Treasury relationship at least until after the conclusion of the Victory Loan campaign. Although the Reserve Bank governors met aagin in March and reviewed the question of an advance in rates, they did not favor an increase. Miller said that the System would be in an indefensible position if discount rates were raised while the reserve percentage was high. He held out hope that rates could be raised when and if the gold embargo were lifted. Strong summarized the gist of the meeting of governors as follows:

> It is the opinion of the meeting that present differential rates in favor of notes, secured by Government obligations, should be continued until after the fifth loan is placed, and for such reasonable period thereafter as will permit a considerable liquidation of such borrowings without imposing undue penalties upon the banks which are required to rediscount with Federal Reserve Banks.[8]

Subscriptions for the Fifth Loan opened April 21, 1919, and closed May 10. To avoid undue disturbance to the market for

Liberty Bonds, which the Treasury felt was practically saturated, they issued $4½ billion of four-year notes in two series at 3¾ % and 4¾ %. The Treasury had decided to fill the "McAdoo gap" in the intermediate maturity range of government securities (Table 1).

An important feature of the Fourth Liberty Loan was the commitment made by almost all national banks to lend to their bond purchasing customers at 4¼ % for ninety days with renewals *at the same rate* for one year. The various Liberty Loan organizations had made this request with the approval of the Federal Reserve Board and the Federal Reserve Banks. A similar arrangement existed for purchasers of Victory Notes; these Notes could be purchased on an installment basis over a period of six months running from May 10 to November 11. The Board sent a confidential telegram to all the Federal Reserve Banks dated April 16, 1919, the contents of which have never before been revealed. The text in part reads as follows:

> Board is informed that many banks are still carrying considerable amount of Fourth Liberty Loan bonds under commitments to carry them for a year, and this engagement will terminate in October or November next. Board suggests that unless there should be some unexpected change in situation, reserve banks discourage member banks from making agreements in connection with Victory Loan for a longer period than six months, thereby leaving situation with respect to loans secured by Government bonds entirely clear after November. Board invites comments on policies proposed in this telegram.[9]

On the same day Governor Strong replied to Harding. He telegraphed:

> Referring your telegram to Jay regarding rates of discount. Suggestion contained is exactly that adopted by this bank and by Liberty Loan Organizations as to loans by member banks to subscribers. Liberty loan committee discussed advisability of urging banks to agree specifically not to lend beyond 6 months period but we felt such agreement would not appear well on record and would be unwisely restrictive in certain special cases like large life insurance companies so general understanding exists that period will be limited to six months unless special circumstances demand exceptional terms.[10]

Later Governor Harding explained the reasons for the action taken by the Board in April:

> We realized at the time that we could not do very much toward equalizing rates until November of this year, for the reason that when the Fourth Liberty Loan was being placed, a number of banks made agreements with subscribers that they would be carried for twelve

months at the coupon rate. This concession was made in order to get the banks behind the Loan.[11]

This explicit moral commitment to the bankers combined with skepticism about the efficacy of higher rates explains the Board's decision to delay an advance in rates until November. So it was not mere fortuitousness that the conflict between the Treasury and the Federal Reserve Board didn't flare up until late October and the beginning of November, 1919.

On June 7, 1919, the President lifted the restrictions on the export of gold. A large outflow followed immediately—$100 million during the first thirty days and $322 million for the year as a whole. The Board thought the export of gold would tend to "exert a sobering influence and cool the ardor for overtrading and speculation."[12] Adolph Miller had expressed some doubts earlier about whether or not the Board could raise rates as long as the central bank reserve percentages were high. He hoped that the gold outflow would be sufficient to reduce the reserve ratios and thus enable the System to raise rates. Leffingwell also considered this move to be an effective step to combat inflation. It failed however to have the intended effect.

In July some System officials again expressed their discontent with Treasury policy. The Boston Federal Reserve Agent, Frederic H. Curtis, recommended a general increase in rates, but the Board disapproved on the grounds that it might bring about the sale of bonds at a time when bond prices were improving. Later that month the Richmond Federal Reserve Agent, Caldwell Hardy, recommended higher rates. He maintained that the Treasury's arbitrary policy of distributing certificates had resulted in some banks in his district being forced to take certificates beyond their banking power, an obvious reference to the technique used by Assistant Secretary Leffingwell to guarantee absorption of Treasury certificates by commercial banks. Hamlin described Governor Harding's angry reaction as follows:

> Governor Harding was very ugly—said tired of being dominated by Leffingwell—that he should write a personal note to Federal Reserve agent Hardy expressing agreement with his views—that Treasury must adjust itself to Federal Reserve position and not vice versa. Strauss combatted this view vigorously.[13]

Hamlin questioned the sincerity of Governor Harding's response. He attributed his strong attack on Treasury policy to a desire to be reappointed governor. By some curious logic Hamlin reasoned that by opposing the Treasury position, Harding would have to be reappointed governor in order to keep him in line! But only a few weeks earlier Hamlin had accused Harding of destroying the Federal Reserve Board because of his willingness to cooperate with Treasury officials:

> Governor Harding has practically destroyed the Federal Reserve Board. He acts as if he were the whole Board. In fact, today, the Board consists of Harding, Strauss, Leffingwell and Governor Strong! I am satisfied the Treasury wants us to pull its chestnuts out of the fire, and by playing on Governor Harding's vanity it secures anything it wants. Evidently Governor Harding wants to be redesignated as Governor.[14]

There is no other evidence of opposition by System officials to Treasury policy during the summer of 1919. The Treasury planned to resume the issue of certificates on August 1 with additional issues scheduled for August 15 and September 2. Thereafter they contemplated no further issues before December 1.

Between March and July, 1919, the wholesale price index had advanced 8%. The Treasury had not ignored the sharp increase in prices. Leffingwell in his memorandum to the Director General of the railroads in August, 1919, referred to in the preceding chapter, stated bluntly that "the charge of inflation is contrary to fact."[15] But he used the term "inflation" in this instance to refer to the fact that there was no premium on gold, *i.e.*, no depreciation of the currency in terms of gold. He attributed the high cost of living (the rise in prices) to two causes: 1) the large increase in governmental expenditures for war purposes; and 2) profiteering. The remedies for the situation he enumerated as follows:

> 1) Strictest economy in Governmental expenditures.
>
> 2) Meet the Governmental expenditures out of taxes rather than loans.
>
> 3) Remove the artificial support of prices which has been furnished by the Government consistently since armistice, notably by the Food and Wheat Administration and by the War Department.
>
> 4) Early and frequent official statements to the effect that prices are too high and must come down. As soon as domestic stocks, which were very low when the armistice was signed, have been replenished and the temporary needs of Europe (which have been greatly exaggerated) are met, there will be necessarily a tremendous falling off in exports which, if the present overstimulated production were continued, would result in collapse.
>
> 5) Vigorous prosecution of offenses under the Sherman Law, Federal Trade Commision Act, Lever Law, etc. etc.

6) A campaign of education should be conducted among the people to encourage thrift and economy.[16]

Leffingwell ruled out monetary control as a device for restraining rising prices except by techniques of moral suasion because he thought the Treasury commitment to support bond prices for one year after the war took precedence over the Federal Reserve's desire to reestablish credit control. He said:

The Treasury was in honor bound to use the bond purchase fund established by Congress for that purpose to support the market for Liberty Bonds. Thus whatever pressure upon the money market resulted from the effects of the Federal Reserve authorities to control credit was automatically relieved by the Treasury. It is noteworthy that efforts to control credit never gave any sign of becoming effective until April, 1920, the Treasury's moral obligation having been satisfied, it discontinued purchases from the bond purchase fund.[17]

There was especially strong sentiment in the Congress for protecting the holders of Liberty Bonds with the consequent fear that if bond prices were allowed to fall pandemonium would be created in the government securities market. The strength of this sentiment and Governor Strong's evaluation of it can be gleaned from his testimony before the Joint Commission of Agricultural Inquiry:

Governor Strong: There was a strong outcry in Congress for the protection of the interests of holders of the previous loans, Liberty loans, which had suffered a decline in the market; and without discussing the wisdom or unwisdom of any such policy, I think there was possibly a sentiment which might be regarded as crystallizing, that might have forced a refunding of the entire war debt, which would have been a very difficult, and almost impossible task, and possibly one of great danger to the country.

Representative Ten Eyck: Well would not the public practically have demanded that, if the rate of interest had been increased?

Governor Strong: Well, I think that is a question of judgment. My own belief is that there would have been a very strong outcry. There was a very strong outcry. But I have a feeling—possibly because I do not live in the atmosphere of Washington—that it could have been resisted. I hesitate even to express it so strongly as that.[18]

Hamlin as late as November 13 remarked that he thought that higher rates "would certainly wreck Treasury policies and perhaps force a refunding of all outstanding bonds," and he did not believe higher rates at that stage would check speculation.[19] Strauss also did not believe rate increases could control the situation. The strong sentiments against rate increases were the result of honest differences of opinion within the Board as to the probable consequences of further advances in the discount rate.

Table 2 shows semimonthly purchases for the Bond Purchase Fund from June 1 through December 31, 1919. Between August and October monthly purchases of Liberty Bonds averaged $60 million, concentrated heavily on issues of both the Second and the Fourth Liberty Loans. The purchase of almost $200 million in November reflects both the sincerity of the Treasury's motives as well as the increasing uncertainty about the future course of bond prices occasioned by the rumors about the Treasury-Federal Reserve conflict over interest rates.

Table 2

Semimonthly Purchase of Liberty Bonds for 5% Bond Purchase Fund
June–December, 1919
(*$ million*)

Months		Liberty War Loan Issues				
		1st	2nd	3rd	4th	Total for month
June	1*					
	2				14.1	14.1
July	1				14.1	
	2					14.1
August	1					
	2				65.6	65.6
September	1		14.1		14.0	
	2		23.5		18.8	70.4
October	1				47.0	
	2				12.3	59.3
November	1	19.4	84.5			
	2			66.7	18.7	189.3
December	1		9.3	52.9	18.6	80.8
	2					
Total		19.4	131.4	119.6	223.2	493.6

SOURCE: *Purchases of Liberty Bonds and Victory Notes For the Five Per Cent Bond Purchase Fund,* House of Representatives, Document No. 905, 66th Congress, 3d Session, 1920, pp. 3–5.

* Inscript 1 and 2 refer to semimonthly periods—not June 1 and June 2.

In September, Leffingwell came before the Board and again attempted to explain the Treasury view. He began by emphasizing that:

So far as my personal view is concerned, I am not primarily interested in borrowing money cheaply for the the [sic] Government. That is not the thing that impresses me as our objective. In that respect, my view has not been the same as some others. The thing that interests me is the thing that interests you, and that is, liquidation of expanded credits. That is what we are really striving for when we discuss discount rates, I take it.[20]

He particularly stressed the need to place permanently the twenty-odd per cent of government bonds either held or loaned upon by the commercial banks. An increase in interest rates would have, he reasoned, two adverse effects: 1) It would tend to shorten the maturity structure of the debt by increasing short-term loans at higher interest rates and thereby "make it more difficult to finance through investors on the terms we are now enjoying"; furthermore, the new issues might be lodged within the banking system, thus, bearing in mind Leffingwell's theory of inflation, forcing "inflation" instead of "liquidation." 2) It would have a tendency to depress bond prices, the consequences of which he described in alarmist tones:

I do not hesitate to say that if the bonds go below 90 it would be necessary for the Government to refund its entire debt. I do not hesitate to say that the twenty million Americans who bought these bonds will not stand for a ten point loss on them. I think Congress would force the Treasury to refund the whole war debt. . . .[21]

Governor Harding asked him several times if the success of the Treasury strategy turned on the maintenance of a differential in favor of certificates. He replied: "So far as the Government financing is concerned, it is not a differential that I ask for. I ask that you do not increase your rates on paper secured by Government obligations."[22] Leffingwell anticipated a serious downturn in business activity which he thought would follow an inevitable contraction in export demand:

It is my firm belief that the international trade situation will force a contraction within not more than a year, possibly six months, probably nine months, and certainly a year; that the subsidized war stimulated exports must stop; that the enormously increased production which resulted . . . must stop, and when this stops you are going to have a slackening of industry, closed plants, reduced prices and easy money, and the Treasury does not propose to finance the balance of the war debt on more onerous terms.[23]

The Treasury argument opposing rate increases was three-pronged: 1) An increase in rates would be "inflationary" inasmuch as the commercial banks increased their holdings of government securities. 2) It would depress bond prices and encourage agitation to refund the entire war debt. 3) It would add to the burden of the debt in the forthcoming recession.

The Debate on Rate Changes

At the governors' conference on October 28, 1919, Governor Harding of the Federal Reserve Board presented a plan to increase all discount rates to 4¼%, a plan which Hamlin understood was agreed upon by Secretary Glass, Leffingwell, Strong, and Harding. Governor Strong said that he was prepared to recommend an increase to 4¼% on Treasury certificates to the directors of the New York Federal Reserve Bank, but that in his opinion the rate on 15-day paper secured by Treasury certificates should be raised immediately to 4½% and ultimately to 4¾%. Hamlin reported that "All of the Governors expressed themselves of [the] same opinion; that we could not bring about liquidation unless the Treasury as well as all other customers had to pay higher rates."[24]

When invited to appear before the Board to explain the views of the Treasury, Leffingwell declared that a rate increase to 4½% would "smash" the Treasury plans. Strong protested vigorously saying that he would accept a 4¼% rate only if the Treasury insisted. However, Leffingwell did say that an increase in discount rates at that time would have a valuable moral effect if adjusted so as not to embarrass the Treasury's borrowing plans or to injure holders of Liberty Bonds and Victory Notes. Although he did not intimate what specific changes in rate schedules he had in mind unquestionably he was opposed to any involving Treasury certificates. His main point was that an advance in rates would not solve the problem of increasing speculation and rising prices; it would only penalize the legitimate borrower and not deter the speculator. The problem, he concluded, should be attacked by a "firm discrimination in making loans." He said that he was "weary of the copybook texts" and that making credit more expensive would not be effective.

On the other hand, Governor Strong was equally firmly convinced of the futility of credit rationing. Both men were locked in a bitter struggle to win the Board's approval for their views. The basis of the conflict was primarily one of disagreement over how monetary policy works and how monetary control should be exerted. Leffingwell did not think that a rise in rates would check speculation whereas Governor Strong was convinced that there was no other effective alternative.

Secretary Glass was apparently very excited by Governor

Strong's position for he called Hamlin by telephone and told him: "Governor Strong was trying to dominate [the] Treasury and [the] Federal Reserve—that if we opposed the 4¼% rate he would come out publicly and protest . . . that credit should be rationed . . . He intimated even that he should press for removal of Governor Strong."[25] At this time Glass was steadfast in his determination not to use the discount rate to curb inflation or Wall Street speculation, a view which he held more resolutely during the 1928–29 stock market episode. He believed the appropriate policy to pursue was to ration credit by distinguishing between essential and nonessential loans. To one so firmly committed to credit rationing the use of the discount mechanism in a way which might penalize legitimate business was almost anathema. He felt that a rise in rates would not be in keeping with the legislative intent of the Federal Reserve Act.

It does indeed seem anomalous that heading the Treasury was a man whose whole banking outlook was permeated through and through by real-bills considerations and whose policies reflected the application of that doctrine. Secretary Glass' attempt to apply qualitative credit control in the autumn of 1919 led the Federal Reserve Board into a head-on clash with the Treasury. In his review of this episode R. G. Hawtrey discerned the real issue when he said that the Board "seems to have been infected with that skepticism as to the efficacy of the rediscount rate which has been so prevalent since the war."[26] What he should have added was that same skepticism lay at the back of Treasury policy as well; the Treasury was merely more skeptical than the Federal Reserve Board.

On October 30 Governor Strong called from New York and announced that the directors of the New York bank would not approve a 4¾% rate on Liberty Bonds because they were afraid that it would depress the price of Liberty Bonds to 90 and might cause a panic. In this important instance Governor Strong was not able to convince the directors of his own bank of the efficacy of a 0.5% increase in rates. On November 1, however, the Board approved an increased schedule of rates at the New York bank putting up the rate on Treasury certificates from 4% to 4¼%. And at a meeting of the Board in the afternoon Secretary Glass said "that it was monstrous for [the] Federal Reserve Banks to put up commercial rates to thwart Wall Street speculation etc."[27] But what is even more surprising is Hamlin's statement: "We all agreed—except Miller—that [the] proper way was to ration credit."[28] The Board was still not convinced that changes in the discount rate alone would be effective. They evidently preferred a policy of credit rationing to that of rate changes but decided for the time being to experiment and to observe the effects.

On November 12 the Board heard a report from Governor Harding and Albert Strauss on a conference with the directors of the New York bank. They both recommended a policy of "watch and wait" before taking any drastic action to which the Board readily agreed.

Governor Strong presumably was not in any physical condition to press his views further. Hamlin's picture of Strong during his controversy with Leffingwell is not that of a man able to inspire confidence:

> I can not help feeling some lack of confidence in Strong—his health is bad and he is inclined to be panicky as shown in recent rate discussions where he fought Leffingwell's 4¼ % rate, finally adopted it but said 4½ absolutely necessary—then went back to New York and said any increase would hurt Liberty bonds—then came back demanding higher rates and finally compromised.[29]

Strong continued to insist that the only effective way to combat inflation was to use the discount rate mechanism, but he made it clear that he "would see this particular crisis through, but after this he would resign rather than continue any such policy."[30]

Hamlin, Strauss, and Secretary Glass were firmly of the opinion that a change of rates would create havoc with the Treasury's financial plans and would demoralize the bond market. Governor Strong and Adolph Miller could offer no solid evidence to the contrary. Miller was by no means clear in his own mind about the desirability of an immediate increase in rates, for he stated at the governors' conference in November that:

> In the next two months, according to the statement of Mr. Leffingwell, there is going to be a very considerable change in the position of the Treasury. I question very much, even if I felt as optimistic about the effect of rates as Governor Morss does, whether the results you would obtain at this time, through anything like a moderate increase in rates, would be comparable with the injury that you would do to the Treasury through such a policy.[31]

And again:

> I do not believe any one in this room has any more faith in the necessity eventually, when we obtain control of the general situation

on a National scale, and in the efficacy of rates than I have, yet I believe it would be demoralizing, costly and ill-advised at this date to go ahead and attempt to operate control of the credit situation in general, when it would obviously be at so heavy an expense and embarrassment to the Treasury.[32]

He was still of the same opinion a week later and so advised the Board. Glass again reiterated his view that rates should not be increased until after the Treasury was out of the market. He said that what was needed was credit rationing. Hamlin described the angry exchange between Governor Strong and Secretary Glass as follows: "Whereupon Governor Strong with some vehemence said it could not be done—that [the] only way was [a] radical increase in rates. Glass replied with some heat that it could be done and must be done, that it was successfully done by [the] Money Committee during [the] war . . ."[33]

If any effective effort was ever made to refute Leffingwell's views by an appeal to the conditions of the capital market or to demonstrate that the Treasury's views were exaggerated about the possible effects of rate changes on the bond market there is no trace of it in official records. The issue was clearly drawn. Governor Strong's opinion differed from that of Leffingwell over the advisability of a rate increase, and there was good reason for going along with the Assistant Secretary unless it could be shown explicitly that he was wrong with respect to the relevant facts of the securities market.[34]

On November 21 Hamlin reported that all of the Board members felt that Leffingwell was wrong in putting out Treasury certificates on December 1 at 4¼%. The Board's attitude so alarmed Leffingwell that he made a dramatic appeal to the members on November 26 which represents the climax to the month-long struggle with Strong and the Federal Reserve Board. The statement is significant in that it lends credence to his remarks before the American Economic Association several years later where he stated that the Treasury would have felt honor bound to support the bond market irrespective of what rate the Federal Reserve established. Leffingwell made the following lengthy statement:

I do not think any of us, even the member banks, would like to see shaken out of the hands of bona fide holders the Government bonds purchased by them and this would be the consequence of a raise of rates at this time, particularly when we must agree that government bonds will be at par inside of two years. Nothing could stop the bonds reaching that mark until the floating debt is out of the way. It is for these reasons that the Treasury has be [sic] reluctant to submit to the demands of the Governor of the Federal Reserve Bank of New York. The Treasury looks upon the action of the New York bank in eliminating the 4¼% rate on paper secured by 4¼% certificates as a direct attempt to punish the Treasury of the U.S. for not submitting to dictation on the part of the Governor of the F. R. Bank of New York, even though it be at the cost of a shortage of funds of the Treasury to meet its outstanding obligations. The only other conclusion that the Treasury can draw is that when the Governor of the F. R. Bank of New York presented these proposed increases in rates to his board of directors he felt that they would not be approved by the F. R. Board. It would be absolutely impossible for the Treasury to sell 4¼% certificates were the 4¼% discount rates eliminated. Its elimination would mean a further decline in the market value of Liberty bonds and Victory notes. There is no question but that during the last 2½ months their market prices have been driven down 2½ points by reason of the agitation of the question of rates by the Governor of the F. R. Bank of New York with the support of his board of directors. The Treasury looks upon this situation with the utmost concern. As you know, on yesterday the Treasury had to purchase some $12,000,000 Liberty bonds to support the market. The Treasury has no doubt that these sales on the market were made by insiders who know of the agitation of the rate question. There can be no doubt as to that, for the bonds were offered in lots of $2,000,000 and more.[35]

The disturbance in the bond market is reflected in the amount of securities acquired for the Bond Purchase Fund. During the period November 26–28, purchases for the Bond Purchase Fund totaled over $75 million, $57 million of which were acquired on November 28 (Table 2). Leffingwell's statement had its intended effect. The Board capitulated. Miller, who believed in principle in increased rates, said he would vote to protect the Treasury. Did this episode represent a case of Treasury "domination"? There are those of course who will answer this question both ways. Nevertheless if voluntary agreement with an action is included in the arts of domination then the word loses much of its original emotive force.

Leffingwell followed his oral appeal to the Board with a memorandum to Governor Harding dated November 29 in which he again stressed the grave consequences of a change in rate policy.[36] He attempted to show that the substantial reduction of over $1 billion in the amount of bonds, notes, and certificates of indebtedness held by reporting member banks between June 6 and November 14 was conclusive evidence that the expansion of credit was not based on government war securities. He emphasized the "healthy absorption" of these securities by the investing public. Consequently, he saw no need to advance rates on government securities. One of Leffingwell's criteria for an overexpansion of credit was the amount of bonds held within the banking system. He did not consider the money supply effects because he denied that demand deposits were money! Furthermore, he denied that money was a causal factor in the price rise. Considering the kind of monetary theory espoused by Leffingwell, one can readily understand why he defended the Treasury's low rate policy. In the light of some remarks he made subsequently, Leffingwell probably exaggerated and overdramatized the alleged effects of a discount rate change. But the "reign of terror" in the bond market during mid-November gave him no grounds for optimism.

By December 9 the Treasury's position had improved considerably. Leffingwell said he would not offer any objections to the Federal Reserve Banks increasing discount rates on war paper to the same level as commercial paper. However, he wanted the rate on Treasury certificates maintained at 4½% on the 4½% certificates. The Board decided that maintaining 4½% on Treasury certificates was necessary to insure the success of future issues and involved no great danger because the profit spread—the difference between the rate at which they could borrow on these securities and their yield—to commercial banks was eliminated and offered an "inducement to distribute certificates among taxpayers and other private investors." On December 9 he drafted a memorandum to Secretary Glass in which he stated:

> I see signs of a recrudescence of speculative activity and of expansion of credit which cause me some apprehension . . . I do not think that at the present time the Treasury's position is such that it can justify imposing its views upon the Federal Reserve Board or the Federal Reserve Banks and thus relieve the Board and the Banks of the feeling of responsibility for the situation. I do not think that a moderate further increase in rates at the present time would have a disastrous effect upon the Treasury's position although, of course, it would require some modification of the Treasury's plan. The Treasury is now sufficiently fortified in its cash position to contemplate with some composure further effort to deal with the situation.[37]

The next day he wrote a letter to Governor Harding expressing the same views and hoped that what he said in his letter of November 29 would not deter the Federal Reserve Board from taking action.[38]

Governor Harding announced at a Board meeting on December

30 that the New York directors were unanimous in favor of increasing to 4¾% all rates at which the Federal Reserve Banks would lend to member banks on the collateral of Treasury certificates. What happened is recounted by Hamlin, as follows:

> We then decided to call in Leffingwell. He said he thought the directors were wrong but that if he were a member of the Board he would vote to sustain them, and he felt it would not injure the sale of the new certificates. We accordingly voted to do so, Williams for some unaccountable reason voting no.[39]

The conflict with the Treasury was resolved, and the Board entered the new year thinking it had regained control of the situation. But this was an illusion. The Treasury continued to purchase large amounts of government bonds for the Bond Purchase Fund. In this instance, unlike the famous 1951 agreement, there had been no "accord." The Treasury had completed part of its task and withdrew any objections it had to future rate policy of the Federal Reserve. The Treasury did not, however, discontinue support of the bond market. The Board was fully apprised of what was going on. Governor Harding wrote a letter to Senator Lee S. Overman dated January 29, 1920, informing him that the Treasury had not profited by purchases made for the Bond Purchase Fund:

> As you know, the Government is already doing everything in its power to protect the market for Liberty Bonds and the interests of Liberty Bond holders by means of the five per cent bond purchase fund provided for under existing law. These purchases have been made for the sole purpose of stabilizing the market and have resulted in preventing a more marked decline. The Treasury has not profited by purchases made from Liberty Bond holders who have forced their bonds on the market, for it has been obliged to borrow at higher rates of interest much of the money out of which purchases have been made.[40]

Purchases for the Bond Purchase Fund from January to June 1920 are set out in Table 3.

At a Board meeting on January 21, 1920, Governor Harding disclosed that Leffingwell wanted the Board to put the rate at which Federal Reserve Banks would lend to member banks on the collateral of commercial paper up to 6%, and Liberty Bonds to 5½%, leaving the certificate rate at 4¾%. The unexpected shift in his position arose ostensibly from the precarious gold reserve ratio of the Federal Reserve Banks which, in his judgment, placed the country dangerously near leaving the gold standard. Though the

Table 3

Semimonthly Purchases of Liberty Bonds for 5% Bond Purchase Fund
January–June, 1920
(*$ million*)

Months		Liberty War Loan Issues 1ST	2ND	3RD	4TH	5TH on Victory	Total for month
January	1*		2.8				
	2	1.9	1.8				6.5
February	1	0.9	12.0				
	2						12.9
March	1						
	2	0.9	1.4				2.3
April	1	6.4	8.7				
	2	0.4	50.0				65.5
May	1	0.2					
	2	0.05					.25
June	1						
	2	0.05	13.4				13.45
TOTAL		10.8	90.1				100.9

SOURCE: *Purchases of Liberty Bonds and Victory Notes For the Five Per Cent Bond Purchase Fund*, House of Representatives, Document No. 905, 66th Congress, 3d Session, 1920, pp. 3–5.

* Inscript 1 and 2 refer to semimonthly periods—not June 1 and June 2.

details of this meeting are quoted fully from Hamlin's Diary by Friedman and Schwartz, they nevertheless write: "Surprisingly, in view of the Treasury's earlier role, the sharp rate increase to 6% was adopted at the Treasury's suggestion, according to Hamlin's Diary."[41] But it was not surprising at all. The advance in rates accorded well with Leffingwell's monetary views that the central bank's gold reserve ratio is an adequate test of the soundness of the currency.

From the Friedman and Schwartz account of the vote on the increase in rates to 6%, one can easily garner the impression that the Treasury "dominated" the Board. Although Hamlin expressed some surprise at Adolph Miller's affirmative vote because he had previously told him he would vote otherwise, Miller's approval of an increase in rates is consistent with his general policy record. Miller had always favored a policy of raising rates to counter inflation. On the other hand, however, Secretary Glass' affirmative vote was a surprise because he had persistently opposed an increase in rates. Hamlin's discomfort at Glass' vote is thus obvious. Hamlin was unhappy about the sudden increase of rates to 6% and even considered resigning, but after some deliberation decided that this would not make the "*slightest* impression on the President, for I know that he has no idea of the importance of the Board and of its work and would see in my resignation only another office to be filled along political lines." [42]

What is indeed remarkable about the abrupt increase to 6% at the January 21 meeting of the Board was the fact that it was done at the initiative of Leffingwell and not the Federal Reserve Board. The Treasury was more concerned about the unfavorable gold reserve position of the Federal Reserve Banks than the Reserve Board and feared that the gold standard might be in jeopardy. The Treasury apparently assumed responsibility for the maintenance of the gold standard and was prepared to press hard for the adoption of a policy which they felt would insure its maintenance. This explains Secretary Glass' *volte-face* on the discount rate increase to fight inflation and speculation.

The declining gold reserve ratios of the twelve Federal Reserve Banks was the proximate cause of the rise in discount rates in January, 1920. But that does not mean that Federal Reserve officials were not equally desirous to control the rampant inflation. The two explanations are not inconsistent. The decline in the reserve ratios was the result of the expansion of bank credit, not a change in total gold holdings of the Federal Reserve. Miller explained the reasons for the System's behavior as follows:

> The action taken by the federal reserve banks in 1920 was taken not primarily to protect their reserves but to control the rate of expansion of credit. The solicitude of the board arose not because of loss of gold—for the total gold holdings of the reserve system showed little variation . . . but because of the unhealthy credit situation which threatened to culminate in disaster unless subjected to control.[43]

So that while action by the Treasury was inspired by gold reserve considerations it would be a mistake to infer that the Board acted solely because the reserve ratio had fallen.[44]

CHAPTER 3

Postwar Financial Policy: The Deflation Phase, 1920–1921

THE COLLAPSE of the boom in the spring of 1920 coincided with the more vigorous Federal Reserve rate policy. In May the wholesale price index turned down for the first time in over a year, and some Reserve Banks advanced discount rates to 7% for paper maturing in ninety days, 1% above the existing rate. Preferential rates continued on paper secured by government obligations. Borrowing rates on Treasury certificates on December 31, 1920, were 5½% at the Reserve Banks of Boston, New York, St. Louis, and Minneapolis and 6% elsewhere; on Liberty Bonds and Victory Notes the rate was 6% in New York and ranged from 5½% to 6% in other districts. This schedule of rates remained in effect until April, 1921, when Boston reduced the rate on commercial, industrial, and livestock paper from 7% to 6%. New York followed in May by a reduction to 6½%. Preferential rates on government securities were gradually discontinued but this entailed an upward revision of existing rates which did not commence until January, 1921. By the end of that year, however, a single rate prevailed for all classes of paper.

Altogether, then, it took about two years to dismantle the wartime apparatus of preferential discount rates, begun to aid the financial policies of the Treasury. Why? Both the Board and the Treasury embraced a theory of inflation identifying the source of trouble as large amounts of government securities present in the commercial banking system. A principal goal of policy, therefore, was to shift these obligations permanently from the banking system to private investors. The transfer involved the sale of government securities by the banking system and a reduction in loans secured by government obligations. Repayment of loans at commercial banks and purchases of government securities by the public from the banks was supposed to lead to a reduction in the amount of bank credit and demand deposits. Increasing rates on Treasury issues to levels competitive with others in the open market by eliminating the system of preferential discount rates was part of the mechanism to achieve the desired results. As long as the process did not disrupt the money and capital markets, all Federal Reserve officials viewed liquidation of bank credit as necessary for a return to "normal." The *Federal Reserve Bulletin* described the process as "necessarily more or less gradual and can be completed only when very considerable redemptions of bonds have been made and the remainder thoroughly absorbed by the public."[1] No other period in Federal Reserve history furnishes a better test of the effect of a faulty analysis of the process of inflation on the subsequent course of monetary policy. There is no reason to think that this particular experience will ever be repeated. The unexplained fact about this episode is why the Federal Reserve System maintained the same high rate schedule throughout one of the sharpest deflation periods in U.S. cyclical experience. By June, 1921, wholesale prices had fallen 56% of the level attained in May, 1920, and the money supply had declined 9%. Unemployment at its peak exceeded 10% of the civilian labor force.[2] In retrospect, judging by present standards, no other period in Federal Reserve history furnishes a better example of mistaken monetary policy.

Lester Chandler, Milton Friedman, and Anna Schwartz have attributed the failure to reduce rates sooner or to prevent a decline in the money supply to the central bank's gold reserve ratio.[3] There is some convincing evidence for this interpretation in statements by Governor Harding of the Federal Reserve Board and Governor Strong of the Federal Reserve Bank of New York. Governor Strong thought that no rate reductions were justified in the latter part of 1920. In reply to a question put by the chairman of the Joint Commission of Agricultural Inquiry in 1922, he answered:

> The demand for credit would not justify it. The peak of our loan account in New York, as shown by daily figures, did not come down until November, 1920. During that period we were right down at the

bottom of our reserve. In fact, the Federal Reserve Bank of New York was borrowing from $40,000,000 to $60,000,000.[4]

But he explained further that it was "the expansion of the loan account in which we were interested, and toward which we direct our rate." In this instance Strong referred to the level of member bank indebtedness rather than to the gold reserve ratio. Though he added that experience dictated high rates when the reserve ratio was at a minimum, he did not mean necessarily that the reserve ratio was the overriding consideration. The reserve ratio gave the Federal Reserve the excuse which the public not only could understand but also would approve. Governor Harding stated in his book, *The Formative Period of the Federal Reserve System,* that the Board may have been overcautious in not reducing rates, but that it was concerned with the effects of permitting reserves to fall below the prescribed minimum. He had in mind the fear that the public might try to redeem the more than $3 billion of Federal Reserve notes in gold, the effect of which could easily have been suspension of payment by the banks followed by a discount on notes in terms of gold. With these considerations in mind, he concluded:

the Board did not feel justified in suggesting to directors of Federal Reserve Banks that discount rates should be lowered without regard to current market rates; nor did it feel that it would be prudent, in defending its policy, to refer to the possible effect of a renewed credit expansion upon the ability of the banks and the Treasury to maintain Federal Reserve notes on a parity with gold.[5]

The Board's chief concern, if Harding is correct, was to maintain the domestic convertibility of notes into gold.

The reserve ratio was certainly important in determining System policy during this phase of its history, but the major part of the explanation must be sought elsewhere. R. G. Hawtrey has surmised correctly that the real reason for the failure of the Federal Reserve to have acted at all was "that the working of the 'vicious circle' of deflation was not understood. It was not realised that a deterrent rediscount rate, once it has taken effect, can safely be reduced, and that the falling prices and shrinking purchasing power will then do their work without extraneous aid."[6] He thought that both Montagu Norman and Benjamin Strong were "blind to the disastrous results of maintaining high discount rates when activity had already given way to depression."[7] Why the effects of maintaining high discount rates were not understood by

Federal Reserve officials is related to their implicit model of the money supply mechanism. David Houston, Secretary of the Treasury at the end of the Wilson administration, summed up the viewpoint of both the Treasury and Federal Reserve officials, as follows:

> There was not a great deal which could be done, except of a temporary character, to aid the people in distress. Time alone, and the readjustment of the industry of this nation and the world, could bring the necessary relief.[8]

Interference with the "normal" processes of recovery might tend to encourage rising prices and speculation in commodities and securities.

Three main questions arise in connection with Federal Reserve monetary policy during this period: 1) Why weren't discount rates reduced? 2) Why wasn't member bank indebtedness reduced more quickly? and 3) Why were the money supply and prices allowed to contract? The fact that the Board allowed the money supply to decline is not, or ought not to be, surprising.[9] The monetary model Reserve officials employed required a reduction in the volume of bank credit, the money supply, and the price level. It can be argued, of course, that they should have known better. But that issue can only be resolved by an extensive investigation into what they ought to have known, not what they in fact believed. The money supply model built into the Federal Reserve Act as interpreted by the Board precluded any action by Reserve Banks to either lower rediscount rates or reduce member bank indebtedness. In the view of System officials the money supply in 1920 was redundant (excessive) and should decline to restore the "proper" relationship between prices, credit, and volume of production. The term most frequently used to describe this process was "liquidation," the necessity for which was not disputed by either the Board or by any other Federal Reserve official including Benjamin Strong of the New York bank.[10] The money supply was excessive because a large part of it had been created to facilitate government borrowing through the purchase of securities by the banks and for which there was no corresponding increase in the production of consumers' goods. To eliminate the excess money created in this manner, the Federal Reserve thought it necessary to dislodge that portion of the debt still in the banking system by encouraging the public to purchase these securities out of genuine saving. The effect would be to reduce the volume of bank credit in the form of government securities, to contract demand deposits, and eventually to lower the level of prices.

The Money Supply Adjustment Mechanism

The 1913 Act was an attempt in part to provide elasticity to the currency supply in times of emergency and in part to eliminate the seasonal variation in interest rates by making the money supply more flexible. Paul Warburg, one of the initial members of the Federal Reserve Board, proposed to measure the benefits to the System by the extent to which these seasonal variations had been removed.[11] In the years immediately preceding the Federal Reserve Act, seasonal changes in the demand for money led to sharp variations in both credit availability and market rates of interest. There was no mechanism for smoothly adjusting the supply of money to seasonal demands. Similarly, abrupt changes in the demand for money resulting from a loss of public confidence in the banking system frequently precipitated a panic involving a complete breakdown of the financial system. Gold flows supplied the cyclical and secular increases in the demand for money. The Federal Reserve Act created the rediscount mechanism for the specific purpose of adjusting the supply of money to meet both seasonal and panic-originated changes in demand. No provision was made for adjusting the money supply to a demand arising out of cyclical and secular expansion. It is not unreasonable to assume then that, here, the rules of the gold standard applied.[12]

During the depression following World War I, the Federal Reserve's responsibility did not extend as far as the management of money to meet either cyclical or secular requirements. The Congress had failed to outfit the Federal Reserve with the apparatus to make *permanent* additions to the reserves of the member banks, and, hence, permanent additions to the money stock. Reserve requirements were fixed, and open market operations were not yet contemplated to serve this function. Central bank accommodation was temporary in nature which in fact meant that it was confined largely to seasonal variations in demand. The Board tended to view bank reserves as essentially a revolving fund adjusting almost automatically to seasonal demands.

The most complete statement of the Board's position at the time on the relationship of credit, prices, and the behavior of the money supply appears in the *Federal Reserve Bulletin* for November, 1918:

Bank credit when granted by commercial institutions upon the strength of, or for the purpose of liquidating, commercial transactions of early maturities, serves as a means of facilitating the flow of commodities from producer to consumer and the return of purchasing power from the consumer to the producer through the various channels of circulation. This process enables goods to act as a means of purchase and payment for other goods, and when the maturity of the average loan granted (or "credit" allowed) is no longer than that of the productive processes in which the community is engaged, the effect of it is only that of facilitating and promoting production and distribution . . . Credit expansion becomes inflation when the increase of prices it produces brings no commensurate or offsetting increase of production.[13]

The essential point seems to be that bank credit, if properly restricted to a loan maturity *equal* to the period of production and in accordance with seasonal needs, behaves as a revolving fund. Credit extended by commercial banks to supply the seasonal needs of business will therefore require little or no addition to the reserves of the commercial banks:

Ordinary extensions of credit made for the purpose of facilitating the exchange and circulation of goods require little or no addition to the reserve funds of the banks, because the credits thus granted in the main offset and cancel one another, leaving an unimportant margin to be redeemed in cash.[14]

The central bank can, therefore, remain indifferent to the problem of the level and rate of growth of member bank reserves, and, indirectly, to the level and rate of growth of the money stock!

The situation during World War I was quite different from that depicted above. Substantial amounts of bank credit were extended to the government to finance the war without an equivalent increase in purchasable output. An increase in reserves was necessary to sustain the new level of deposits which was accompanied by an increase in prices. This process the Board labeled credit inflation. The source of the difficulty was described as follows:

There is no means of permanently canceling or digesting such outstanding credits except one—their use by those into whose hands they come for the purchase of the securities against which the credits were extended, notably Government bonds in our present situation.[15]

The money supply and the volume of bank credit were redundant. The remedy seemed obvious: to reduce the quantity of bonds in the banking system by sales to the public, thereby canceling demand deposits and enabling member banks to repay their indebtedness to the Federal Reserve System.

The type of model described is easily recognized as belonging to the notorious real-bills family. But there is an important difference between the Board's interpretation and that usually ascribed to real-bills enthusiasts. In some formulations a form of bank credit is isolated which is always recognized as a legitimate basis for credit expansion by the commercial banks and by the central bank as well; that is, credit which meets the short-term working capital needs of business and trade. No distinction is made in this case between the seasonal, cyclical, or secular demands for working capital. But the distinction is important to central banking practice: *seasonal working capital needs supplied by bank credit require no mechanism for increasing reserves whereas cyclical and secular needs do.*

An increase in working capital induced by an expansion of output, defined as goods in process, will ordinarily increase the quantity of money demanded by business firms. The adjustment can take either of two forms: an increase in velocity or an increase in the supply of money, if the working capital needs are supplied through the banking system. The use of bank credit, however, implies a permanent increase in reserves to sustain the new level of deposits which is inconsistent with the money supply mechanism built into the Federal Reserve Act. According to the Board's interpretation, reserves can be regarded as a "revolving" fund only when the banking system is maintaining the aggregate of working capital intact. An increase in working capital financed by the banks for either cyclical or secular purposes entails a willingness on the part of the central bank to employ the rediscount mechanism as a source of permanent reserves, a position which cannot be reconciled with the Board's view as set out above.

The term "accommodation" appearing in the Federal Reserve Act should be interpreted as referring only to demand disturbances of a purely seasonal or "panic-like" character. Accommodation for cyclical or secular purposes requires either a reinterpretation of the role of the rediscount mechanism or the use of other monetary control devices which can hardly be justified by the actions and statements of System officials. What the difference comes down to ultimately is whether or not the rediscount mechanism as originally conceived precluded its use as a source of permanent or only temporary additions to banking reserves.

Too strong an attempt has been made to identify Federal Reserve thinking and practice closely with the nineteenth-century banking principle. Chandler, Friedman, and Mints apparently see more of a resemblance than I do during this earlier Federal Reserve period. What in effect the 1913 Act had accomplished was to create a money supply mechanism based solely on the seasonal and emergency demands for money.[16]

The weakness of a money supply model which considers only the seasonal and emergency demands for money is too obvious to bear repeating. Nevertheless, the neglect of the transactions and the liquidity motives is revealing. There can be little doubt that the Board as well as other Federal Reserve officials understood the nature of the transactions demand for money which suggests very strongly that founders of the System never intended the behavior of the money supply to be its primary responsibility. The efficient functioning of one part of the credit mechanism was its aim—the adequacy of seasonal credit flows to business firms. It was the intermediary function, not the money supply function, which the founders of the System had uppermost in mind in the formulation of a credit policy. A monetary policy in the broadest sense had not yet been formulated.

Application of the Money Supply Model

At the onset of the depression in the spring of 1920 member bank indebtedness to the Federal Reserve amounted to $2.5 billion. A substantial easing of credit required not only a reduction of discount rates, but also a swift decline in member bank borrowing which, perhaps, could best be brought about by large purchases of government securities. But large-scale purchases were ruled out because Federal Reserve officials had not yet learned how to use open market operations as an instrument of monetary policy. A reduction of rates by itself was not sufficient. Even with unchanged discount rates the amount of member bank borrowing continued to expand through December, 1920. Without the authority to reduce reserve requirements and a commitment to a theory of bank liquidity which excluded government securities from the portfolios of commercial banks, the Federal Reserve saw no alternative to a policy of "liquidation." The cure consisted of a campaign of thrift to induce the public to purchase government securities from the banking system out of current saving and thereby to reduce the excess supply of money. This policy was described in somewhat different language at the time as lodgment of the national debt in the hands of permanent holders. The diagnosis and prescription entailed a reduction in the supply of money. It ought not to be surprising then to find Federal Reserve officials presiding over a decline in the money supply. The abandonment of a theory of bank liquidity which excluded government securities from the portfolios of the banking system, both Federal Reserve and commercial banks, was a prerequisite for a countercyclical monetary policy.

Serious discussion to reduce rates did not begin until late December, 1920, the initiative originating with the Comptroller of the Currency, John Skelton Williams. In a letter to the Board, Williams recommended more liberal credit policies to restore confidence and to improve business conditions. Specifically, he favored a reduction of the rate of interest on loans secured by Liberty Bonds from 6–7% to 4½%, and the suspension of progressive interest rates applied to borrowings by member banks. Earlier in the year the Federal Reserve Act had been amended to permit Federal Reserve Banks to adopt at their discretion a graduated scale of rates based on the amount of borrowing by individual member banks. The Comptroller thought business conditions demanded definite and energetic action even if it meant a departure from accepted rules and tradition.

The Federal Reserve Board denied that the decline in prices had been due to either a restriction of credit or to a contraction of the currency by the Federal Reserve Banks. They explained that the most rapid decline in prices took place before November 5, 1920, while rediscounts and Federal Reserve Notes were both expanding. They argued that the consequences of a decline in the discount rate to 4½% on paper secured by Liberty Bonds:

> would be to induce a temporary and artificial ease in the money market, which could not be sustained, because the lending power of the Federal Reserve Banks has its limitations, and which might result in a temporary revival of the speculative spirit which was so strongly in evidence fourteen months ago and which had such an unhappy effect upon the commerce and business of the country.[17]

The Board reminded the Comptroller that there were $24 billion of government securities eligible to serve as collateral for borrowing at both commercial and Federal Reserve Banks. Under these circumstances they did not think it wise to encourage further expansion by a reduction in rates. Apparently they felt that member bank borrowing would be highly sensitive to a 1% to 1½%

reduction in rates and that further expansion of rediscounts would be sharply curtailed by the ceiling set by the gold reserve ratio. Between January and July, 1921, the Federal Reserve Banks of Dallas, Richmond, and Minneapolis were forced continually to rediscount with other Federal Reserve Banks to maintain their legal reserve position.

In February, Williams launched a scurrilous attack on the Federal Reserve Bank of New York and its administration of the discount window, an attack which led ultimately to the first Congressional investigation of Federal Reserve monetary policies. A Joint Commission of Agricultural Inquiry was appointed and issued its now famous report in 1922. At a Board meeting on February 11 the Comptroller introduced a motion to reduce discount rates to 6%. However, according to Hamlin, officials of the New York bank said that the reduction would encourage "wild speculation," and it was voted down.[18]

At the end of March the new Secretary of the Treasury, Andrew Mellon, expressed the view to Governor Harding that the time was ripe for a reduction of rates from 7% to 6%, and that the differential rates in favor of government securities should be eliminated. Harding replied that the reduction, he feared, might revive speculative activity in the stock market. Mellon's retort was that a little speculation in stocks would not be harmful.[19] On April 4 Mellon again repeated his opinion that rates should be reduced. The reduction, he thought, would in all probability have a "good psychological effect." The appointive members of the Board hesitated: Governor Harding feared renewed speculation; Miller preferred to wait; and Hamlin said that he would approve if the request came from Boston, feeling that the initiative should come from individual Federal Reserve Banks. The Board postponed the decision until after the meeting of the conference of governors scheduled for a week later. In the meantime Boston requested permission to reduce its rate to 6%, but the Board denied the request until at least after the conclusion of the conference.

Hamlin related that Governor Strong was violently opposed to a reduction in rates by the Boston bank on the grounds that if Boston lowered rates "public opinion would force the New York Reserve Bank to do the same and this would cause a violent speculative boom in stocks . . . that we should wait until wages were lower and the curve of wages, deposits, wholesale and retail prices were more nearly together at a much lower basis,"[20] in other words until a new equilibrium was restored at lower prices, lower wages, and a reduced money supply. At the conference which began on April 12, all of the governors opposed the reduction of rates except the governors of the Boston and the Atlanta Federal Reserve Banks. Governor Strong outlined his reaction to a reduction in discount rates at the conference, as follows:

> certain banks are not out of debt to the Federal Reserve Bank, and the influence of their surplus funds upon the market is gradually working toward establishing a rate that is equal to our rate, or lower than our rate, and up until that time comes about, until our rate is at least equal to the market rate for the money, we do not think that our rate should be reduced. The great bulk of the business now being done in New York is still, I would say, seven and one-half per cent or seven and three-quarters per cent, which is the rate at which commercial loans are being made. I feel that the time has measurably approached when we must consider a review of rates in New York, but that it would be too soon to make a change now. I think these conditions which are developing and which are sound and which we anticipated and hoped would arrive, have not yet progressed far enough to justify a reduction in rates.
>
> Now, the one reason why I say that is the influence which it would have upon distinctly speculative conditions . . . Stock exchange rates have been about the same for a long period, but the fact remains that the technical position is such that the sentimental influence of the change in our rate would be very strong to develop speculation, and I fear that the sentimental influence of any change by any Federal Reserve Bank just now would have that tendency, and it might extend to commodities. It might very well extend to commodities, and with general regard to the situation in New York, I think the sound policy is to leave the rate unchanged for a time.[21]

Throughout the remainder of April, Strong and the New York directors continued to oppose any alteration in rates. Miller changed his mind as to the advisability of the decrease in rates. At a Board meeting on April 18 he moved that the New York rate be fixed at 6½%. No change was made, however, until early May when Atlanta and Chicago reduced their rates with the approval of the Board.

CHAPTER 4 The Managed Money Interlude: 1921–1923

AN OPINION that is widely held though seriously misleading is that prior to 1922 Reserve officials had not the time to develop normal peacetime objectives. They were powerless to affect policy before 1917 because of large gold inflows, later because of the high priority assigned to the aims of war finance. Hence, according to this body of opinion, the System had no opportunity to map a peacetime monetary strategy. But, in fact, the failure to have mapped an explicit peacetime strategy does not imply the absence of one. The monetary theory governing Federal Reserve behavior before 1922 was just as applicable thereafter. Nevertheless, by 1922 the Federal Reserve had revised its theory of the relationship of credit, prices, and the money supply under the impact of three major events: 1) the tremendous wartime growth of the Federal debt; 2) the unusually sharp inflation of 1919–20; and 3) the severe but short depression during 1920–21. Each left its mark on Federal Reserve thinking and practice and led eventually to the revision of policy objectives. The increase in the Federal debt led to the abandonment of the theory of bank liquidity excluding government securities from the portfolios of commercial banks; and the behavior of prices convinced some Reserve Bank officials of the political necessity of avoiding the violent swings of prices of 1919 and 1920.

Gradually the public came to expect more in 1922 from credit policy than it had in 1913. Experience gained during the war and its aftermath proved inadequate to the new tasks ahead. This perceptible difference in Federal Reserve thinking was due as much to the fundamental change in the public's expectations after the inflation-deflation experience as to any improved knowledge by System officials of how monetary policy works.

The most important change in official thinking was the inevitable outcome of the enormous increase in the Federal debt. Forcing reconsideration of a bank liquidity theory which excluded government securities from commercial and Federal Reserve Bank portfolios hastened the use of open market policy. Open market operations could not become an instrument of monetary control until the Federal Reserve abandoned this fallacious doctrine of bank liquidity.

Two Views of the Banking Function

Traditionally the banking system is accorded two roles in the economic process: 1) as an intermediary in the saving-investment process; and 2) as the manufacturer of a substantial portion of the means of payment, i.e., the money supply. The efficiency with which these two tasks are performed determines the contribution that the monetary system can make to increasing economic activity and maintaining domestic stability. During the formative years of the Federal Reserve System more emphasis was placed upon the intermediary function than upon the money supply function.

The theory of central banking which evolved in the United States between 1914 and 1921 was distinctively an American product differing in important particulars from that which had evolved in Great Britain and on the Continent. In Europe the principal and most urgent problem of central banking was the adequacy of the money supply. In America, the more urgent problem was the viability and liquidity of the banking system. Repeatedly the U.S. banking system had collapsed in the face of a liquidity crisis. Since liquidity is a balance sheet problem, the emphasis of the Federal Reserve on the volume of bank credit and the composition of bank assets is not surprising. Thus the lending, and not the money supply, function received prior consideration.

Using the term "credit policy," not "monetary policy," to describe the Federal Reserve is significant. Within the context of intermediation, central bank "accommodation" of business takes on a definite and precise meaning—product flows should not be inhibited by temporary frictions arising in the credit markets. Smoothing out credit flows to accord with the "natural" flows of output became therefore a major objective of credit policy. The founders of the Federal Reserve System thought that they had set out a valid criterion by which to judge the adequacy of bank credit in the sense of loans and investments. They wished to restrict the supply of bank credit by limiting it to primarily seasonal commercial loans and by eliminating government securities and loans for purely speculative purposes. An excess of bank credit could be identified by these three criteria: 1) the behavior of the price level; 2) the presence of government securities within the banking system; and 3) the existence of speculation as evidenced by the accumulation of inventories and the movement of stock prices.

The idea of "passive accommodation" to meet the short-term borrowing needs of "legitimate" business is consistent with the view of commercial banks as intermediaries. Possible conflict between a bank credit criterion and a money supply criterion was the persistent theme of criticism leveled against the Board by Seymour Harris and Laughlin Currie in the early nineteen-thirties.[1] To maintain that Federal Reserve officials thought that both criteria were satisfied simultaneously is to fall victim to the real-bills myth.

The reduction of discount rates in 1921 at the Federal Reserve Banks did not begin before their reserve ratios passed the 50% mark and until the volume of member bank indebtedness had fallen to $2 billion in April, 1921. Both prices and industrial production emerged from the trough in June, 1921. Production recovered rapidly during the second half of the year while wholesale prices held approximately constant. By the end of December the volume of indebtedness amounted to $1 billion and the reserve ratio stood at over 70%. These results were achieved by a $750-million increase in the monetary gold stock and a reduction in currency in circulation by $360 million. Total member bank reserve balances remained unchanged.

The precipitous decline in bills discounted (55%) during 1921 raised anew the problem of adequacy of Reserve Bank earnings and the volume of earning assets, which for the twelve Reserve Banks fell from a high of $3 billion in December, 1920 to $1.5 billion in December, 1921. At the beginning of 1922 individual Reserve Banks initiated the purchase of government securities to offset the decline in bills discounted. Between January and June the banks acquired over $350 million of government securities. These purchases were uncoordinated and did not reflect a change in monetary policy. Their significance lay more in the final abandonment of the theory of bank liquidity set out in the *Federal Reserve Bulletin* in 1918. Because Federal Reserve officials failed to understand the effects of these purchases, the volume of earning assets continued to decline until June, 1922 when the total was not much over $1 billion. An increase in the gold stock of $133 million and a decline of $289 million in currency in circulation, coupled with the purchase of government securities, contributed to the further substantial reduction in member bank indebtedness by $743 million.

Adolph Miller wrote in *The American Economic Review* for June, 1921, that proposals to abandon the central bank reserve ratio in favor of a price level criterion as an indicator of discount policy were merely academic in tone.[2] The charge was only partly true, for Professor Oliver M. W. Sprague of Harvard had argued in the preceding issue that discretion exercised responsibly by the Federal Reserve Board would be a more satisfactory basis for monetary policy than the reserve ratio, especially in a period when the volume of credit was determined more by domestic economic conditions than by movements of gold.[3] (This was before Europe had returned to the gold standard.) Miller replied: "There is not, however, the slightest reason for supposing that such a procedure on the part of the Federal Reserve banks would be viewed with approval."[4] He defined the problem as one of not "finding a substitute for the reserve ratio as a guide to credit policy, but rather that of finding how to make our reserve ratio a more sensitive and immediate indicator of changing conditions in the credit situation than it now is."[5]

The strength of public opinion and the extent of its attachment to the central bank reserve ratio should not be underestimated. In the *Tenth Annual Report* the Board gave as its reason for supplanting the reserve ratio as a guide to credit policy the absence of an effective international gold standard. The Federal Reserve maintained that under current circumstances, with gold embargoes, exchange restrictions, and controls in foreign countries, gold movements were not self-corrective.[6] As long as the international gold standard remained inoperative, the gold reserve ratio could not serve as an appropriate guide for a single country. But there was no indication or statement to the effect that the gold reserve ratio should be *permanently* abandoned. To the contrary, it was the confident expectation of Board members that the reserve ratio would assume its former position of authority when abnormal gold movements ceased, and the international gold standard was fully restored.

Large inflows of gold created special problems for the Federal Reserve during the first seven months of 1922. Wholesale prices increased, and some Federal Reserve officials expressed concern about continuing a policy which might lead to further and more drastic inflation. Given the circumstances they began to reconsider seriously the appropriateness of the reserve ratio as a guide to credit policy. The results of these deliberations during 1922 and 1923 emerged for public inspection in the now justly famous *Tenth Annual Report* dated February 15, 1924.

The events leading up to the *Report* as well as the *Report* itself have generally been misconstrued in this country but particularly in England. There are two sources of this apparent confusion: 1) the extent to which the System abandoned the old gold standard orthodoxy; and 2) the extent of the Board's commitment to the so-called real-bills doctrine. The first can be called the managed currency myth and the second, the real-bills myth.

The Managed Currency Myth

The "managed currency myth" refers to the view that beginning sometime in 1922 the Federal Reserve System inaugurated a policy of managed money and adopted a permanent set of goals to replace the old rules of gold standard orthodoxy. The error of this view stems from a failure to distinguish between Federal Reserve policy prior to the full resumption of the gold standard abroad after 1925 and the policy pursued thereafter. Statements by Federal Reserve officials must be read and interpreted in the proper context of the period to which they refer. Governor Strong repeatedly expressed distaste for managed money and nostalgia for the so-called rules of the gold standard game. There were no substantial differences between Benjamin Strong and his old friend and archadvocate of the gold standard orthodoxy Montagu Norman. Even the Board preferred to interpret England's return to gold in April, 1925 as a first move in the restoration of the traditional international monetary framework:

> From the viewpoint of the banking situation in the United States the restoration of the gold standard abroad has the additional significance that gold movements will become more normal and will respond more

promptly to the forces which before the war related the movement of gold to changes in trade and credit conditions at home and abroad . . . With the re-establishment of an effective international gold standard the movements of gold between countries will again exercise the corrective influences that experience has shown to be safeguards against unsound credit developments.[7]

Governor Strong reaffirmed the efficacy of the old gold standard machinery in his testimony printed in the *Stabilization Hearings* (1928):

I still feel that everything important which is sought to be accomplished by this direction of the Congress [price stability], could be well accomplished, possibly with avoiding some misuderstanding [sic], through a scientific application of the well-known principles of the gold standard.[8]

He described exactly how the gold standard acted as a check to either inflation or deflation:

The creation of a great volume of credit, in excess of what the business of the country requires, immediately has certain reactions. Interest rates go down. You have an exodus of capital from the country and, if such a policy is so deliberate as to be generally recognized, there would be a flight of capital, and if it was a gradual policy of inflation, insidious and not readily perceived by the public, it would undoubtedly have in time some effect upon prices.

But in every case the consequence is the same: gold would leave the country. Gresham's law would operate at once, and it would be an apparently short time, particularly if the public were aware of the situation, before the reserves of the country would become so impaired that we would be facing a suspension of specie payment. I do not know of anything that would bring the country to its senses any quicker.

The reverse of this is equally true in a period of deflation of the credit and currency of the country, if it could be brought about.[9]

Strong expressed genuine skepticism about the efficacy of a managed money policy, that is, one requiring a large dose of human judgment and discretion, without the support of the gold standard discipline.

There would be no need to labor this point if Keynes and Harrod as well as others had not been misled by the statements in the *Tenth Annual Report*.[10] Since Strong has been credited with being the guiding genius of System policy in the twenties, it is all the more important to understand thoroughly what he thought the distinction was between a system of gold payment and one without. He maintained that:

> the gold standard is a much more automatic check upon excesses in credit and currency than is a system where gold payment, if you please, is suspended and it is left to the human judgment of men to determine how much currency shall be issued which they do not need to redeem in gold—do you see the distinction? And when you speak of a gold standard, you are speaking of something where the limitation upon judgment is very exact and precise and the penalty for bad judgment is immediate.
>
> Where you are speaking of efforts simply to stabilize commerce, industry, agriculture, employment, and so on, without regard to the penalties of violation of the gold standard, you are talking about human judgment and the management of prices which I do not believe in at all.[11]

He completed his testimony by re-emphasizing that an automatic system of gold payment including domestic convertibility of notes would "minimize the possibilities of bad judgment or abuse of power by a better method than any that has yet been devised."[12]

To Governor Strong the world-wide adoption of the gold standard was the best defense against both inflation and deflation. When Lester Chandler writes, "Before the end of 1922, he [Strong] had come to believe that promotion of price level stability should be a major policy objective, though he firmly opposed proposed legislation ordering the Federal Reserve to stabilize the price level,"[13] we must consider this statement in its proper context—that is, when the United States was alone in its adherence to the gold standard and when it was no longer politically expedient to reproduce intentionally violent swings in prices. It should not be taken to imply price stability, for example, in some literal sense of keeping an index number constant.

The Real-Bills Myth

The temporary rejection of the central bank gold reserve ratio as a guide to Federal Reserve discount policy had far-reaching implications which have not been fully appreciated. As shown earlier, the money supply mechanism built into the Federal Reserve Act was not designed to provide for cyclical and secular variations in the demand for money. Gold movements were expected to supply permanent additions to banking reserves without interference from the Federal Reserve. Optimal adjustments of the money supply, other than purely seasonal ones, were outside the discretion of the Federal Reserve. One might have thought that rejecting the reserve ratio as a guide to discount policy also entailed rejecting gold movements as a valid criterion for making additions to bank credit, reserves, and the money supply. Nevertheless, the money supply tradition associated with gold standard orthodoxy was so deeply ingrained that Federal Reserve policy was never fully consistent. At times the Board, rather than swim against the tide, drifted along with it, accommodating itself passively to inflows of gold. The rejection of the reserve ratio guide did, however, imply a major overhaul of the money supply mechanism. Formally detached from a gold criterion, Federal Reserve officials sought an alternative to replace it.

No progress whatsoever could be made towards this policy until the fallacious doctrine that government securities within the banking system are a source of credit and price inflation had been cast aside. Cyclical and secular expansion of the money supply requires some means for supplying reserves to the commercial banks, and the rediscount mechanism is not really suitable. The ideal instrument is open market operations. It is no accident, therefore, that the inauguration of open market operations happened to coincide with the rejection of the reserve ratio as a guide to Federal Reserve credit policy.

Although loans secured by government obligations for 800 reporting member banks declined by $400 million during 1921, the government security portfolio increased by $200 million. Between September 7, 1921, and December 27, 1922, government security holdings at 800 commercial banks doubled and their share in total loans and investments increased from 8.3% to 15.8%. In January, 1922, individual Federal Reserve banks began to purchase large amounts of government securities signaling the departure of the System from the theory of bank credit, prices, and the money supply set out in the *Federal Reserve Bulletin* in 1918. There was no official statement announcing the change in policy. It was almost inadvertent inasmuch as the alleged reason for the purchases was the decline in the volume of earning assets and the squeeze placed on Federal Reserve Bank earnings.

The *Tenth Annual Report* (1923), was an attempt to patch up the statement in the 1918 *Bulletin* with its emphasis on: 1) bank credit and reserves as essentially a revolving fund; and 2) a theory of bank liquidity which attributes "inflation" to the presence of government securities in the banking system. In the *Report* the Federal Reserve Board extended its responsibility for monetary and credit policy to include not only the "quality" of credit but also its "quantity" as well. To test for an excess supply of credit, a double criteria was proposed: a qualitative and a quantitative test.

1) The *qualitative test* is described as follows:

The Federal reserve system is a system of productive credit. It is not a system of credit for either investment or speculative purposes. Credit in the service of agriculture, industry and trade may be described comprehensively as credit for productive use. The exclusion of the use of Federal reserve credit for speculative and investment purposes and its limitation to agricultural, industrial, or commercial purposes thus clearly indicates the nature of the tests which are appropriate as guides in the extension of Federal reserve credit.[14]

So far as the first test is concerned, no change in Federal Reserve thinking is apparent. The real-bills emphasis is quite explicit though stated at greater length and more precisely in the 1918 statement.

2) *The quantitative test,* however, constitutes a significant departure from tradition and is concerned with "limiting the volume of credit within the field of its appropriate uses to such amount as may be economically justified—that is, justified by a *commensurate increase in the Nation's aggregate productivity.*"[15] The quantitative test, and not the qualitative, provided the Board with an effective substitute for the gold reserve ratio as a guide to credit policy and one which was actually employed for a time during the twenties. Given the availability of production indices, it was a fairly simple test to administer. Changes in the volume of bank credit were not thought to be excessive if they were accompanied by a corresponding increase in the volume of production. Presumably output maximization was given priority over price stability as the appropriate goal of policy, at least until output became highly inelastic with respect to changes in the volume of credit.

Lloyd Mints described the two tests but dismissed the second on the mistaken grounds that the Board thought that the first test would be sufficient.[16] The following sentence in the *Tenth Annual Report* has generated much of the confusion: "It is the belief of the Board that there will be little danger that the credit created and contributed by the Federal reserve banks will be in excessive volume if restricted to productive uses."[17] Mints suggests that the Board's statement meant that it thought the qualitative test was both necessary and sufficient. In the context in which this statement appears, his exclusion of the quantitative test is not easy to understand. The significance of both tests is adequately emphasized elsewhere in the *Report:*

> The Board is fully aware of the fact that the problem of credit extension involves the question of amount or volume as well as the question of kind or character; otherwise stated, involves a *quantitative* as well as a *qualitative* determination. But it is the view of the Board that it is not necessary to go outside of the Federal reserve act to find suitable methods of estimating the adjustment of the volume of credit provided by the Federal reserve banks to the volume of credit needs. The Federal reserve act itself suggests the nature of the tests, guides, or indicators—whatever they may be called—to be used in gauging the need for and the adequacy of Federal reserve credit.[18]

By recognizing the relevance of both tests, we can effectively exonerate the Board of the spurious charge that they were guilty of the so-called real-bills fallacy—that by simply looking after the quality of credit the money supply would look after itself—that attention to quality alone would be a sufficient safeguard against inflation. The Board showed that it was well aware that price inflation would follow if credit expansion continued beyond "full employment" even if there was no deterioration in the quality of credit. Moreover, the Federal Reserve Board's behavior reveals the use of a dual criteria and shows cognizance of the output and price response to a change in credit policy.

CHAPTER 5

The Application of the Quantitative Test: 1922–1923

THE QUANTITATIVE test for the adequacy of bank credit began to take shape slowly during the first six months of 1922 when the Federal Reserve Board found itself facing a rapid rise of prices. The wholesale price index increased 12% between January and July while unemployment remained abnormally high, probably exceeding 7% of the civilian labor force. Commodity output continued to increase rapidly as measured by the Board's Index of Business Conditions. The policy of the Federal Reserve during the price increase was one of relative ease, but this does not imply necessarily a deliberate, self-conscious action on the part of Reserve Bank officials. Some rise in prices was thought necessary to correct the extreme dislocation of production and trade in 1920 and 1921. The acquisition of $365 million of government securities did not, however, represent planned action to ease credit conditions further. The Federal Reserve merely accommodated itself to conditions as they found them and attempted to keep the level of Reserve bank credit from falling below a point where earnings might be impaired. The interest rate on prime commercial paper declined from 5% in January, 1922, to a low of 4.13% in July. Similarly, the yield on U.S. government bonds fell from 4.45% in

January to 4.12% in August. The rediscount rate at the Federal Reserve Banks of Boston, New York, and Philadelphia continued unchanged at 4½% until after the middle of June when both Boston and New York reduced to 4%.

In March when the Atlanta Federal Reserve Bank reduced its rate to 4½%, the Assistant Secretary of the Treasury, S. Parker Gilbert, Jr., addressed a memorandum to Secretary of the Treasury Andrew Mellon expressing some concern about the effects of discount rate reductions.[1] He suggested that it would be a mistake for the Federal Reserve Banks to reduce discount rates from 4½% before completion of the March 15 financing and until the future of the Soldier's Bonus Bill was more clearly ascertained. He feared that a reduction in rates would encourage adoption of the bill by Congress. At the beginning of April he again urged Mellon to postpone action on further rate decreases until after the governors' conference on May 2. The reason he gave is revealing. Gilbert maintained that if the 4½% rate could be established on a "proper basis," that is, above commercial rates, it would tend to limit access to the discount window to seasonal and emergency needs rather than to accommodating the usual course of business.[2] Apparently he thought the motivation for member bank borrowing for a profit from the Federal Reserve was still strong. It may well have been, since the volume of member bank borrowing in March still remained over $600 million.

According to C. S. Hamlin, Adolph Miller introduced a motion at a Board meeting on May 23, 1922, stating that the New York bank could with advantage lower its discount rate.[3] He defended his motion on the grounds that the reserve ratio was high, and a reduction in market rates would have a stimulating psychological effect. The Board approved Miller's motion by a vote of 4 to 1, Governor Harding not voting. Hamlin voted "no" following his practice of withholding his support until after the New York bank requested approval for a change in rates. The Board minutes for June 2, 1922, show, however, that the New York bank did not favor an immediate reduction. It did not think that "local conditions" warranted a decrease. Pierre Jay, the Federal Reserve agent in New York, in a letter to Miller, expressed some doubt about lowering rates because he thought it might induce speculation. He did not think it was necessary to give an additional stimulus to business activity, for lower rates might spark an inflationary movement that would be difficult to deal with later.[4]

Miller prepared a memorandum in response to Jay's reservations about the possible effects of a rate decrease. The memorandum was dated June 22, 1922, the same day the New York bank announced a reduction in rate to 4%.[5] Since Miller, with Walter Stewart, the Board's director of the Division of Research and Statistics, was largely responsible for drafting the famous *Tenth Annual Report,* his memorandum is interesting, for it shows that all members of the Board did not hold the view that the qualitative test of credit adequacy was sufficient. He denied that any speculative reaction would accompany a change in attitude on the part of the Federal Reserve. As evidence that Miller was no doctrinaire proponent of qualitative credit control, he reminded Jay of the difference between "healthy" and "unhealthy" speculation. Speculation *per se,* he said, was neither good nor bad. Useful speculation, he pointed out, can occur following a period of severe and prolonged depression when it "correctly anticipates and forecasts industrial recovery and business revival." On the other hand, "unhealthy" speculation occurs "when it has reached the stage where it is bidding up prices, either of securities or commodities, with the aid of cheap credit, when production has reached its practical maximum and the further release of credit merely results in driving up prices."[6] He denied that "unhealthy" speculation had prevailed during the preceding eighteen months because the period was characterized by idle shops and unemployment. Miller attached no particular significance to the rise in prices earlier in the year; the increase in economic activity was in his opinion not sufficient to awaken any concern. The adverse effects of ordinary stock exchange speculation would be minimal since there was "a large margin of plant facilities and labor available for production in the country."

Looking back over this same episode several years later, Miller summarized the reactions of the Board to the price increase in the spring and summer of 1922, as follows:

> the significance of this particular episode is that the Federal Reserve, to the extent it gave a good performance at that time, gave it because it was not concerned with stability of prices. Prices were moving rapidly upward, but I think the judgment of the Federal reserve may be properly said to have amounted to about this, that it did not interpret the upward movement of prices as inflationary in character, because close tab on the situation showed that while prices were moving upward, so was production and trade, and sooner or later production would overtake the rise of prices, demand would be satisfied, and prices in turn would trend downward. . . .[7]

In the November, 1922, *Federal Reserve Bulletin* the Board declared that it considered the current increases in output as more fundamental than price changes:

> Early in 1922 prices joined production in the upward movement, and the combined effect of the two was to increase the volume of business. As a factor influencing the economic wealth of the Nation *greater output may be regarded as more fundamental than price changes,* but the readjustments in prices during 1921 helped to bring about increased production . . . Price readjustments which stimulate production have a different significance from price advances which continue after industry has reached its productive capacity and when further advances register merely competitive bidding.[8]

The Board identified two kinds of price changes: 1) price changes which stimulate production; and 2) price advances after productive capacity has reached a ceiling. It is only the second of the two that they definitely regarded as undesirable, what we sometimes refer to as "pure price inflation." If we persist, as indeed many critics still do, in attributing at this time the goal of price stability to the Federal Reserve, we must understand that the Board frowned only upon *unwarranted* price variation. It did not favor in any literal sense price stability. It would be more correct to describe the policy as one of output maximization (full employment) with minimum price variation. So that no misunderstanding can arise as to the priority of the two objectives, Federal Reserve officials during this particular period paid more attention to changes in output than to changes in prices. There is certainly little truth in the charge that the Board by its commitment to the real-bills doctrine thought and acted as though qualitative credit control alone would guarantee price stability.

Although the Board made no changes in discount rates before February, 1923, it indicated by its behavior that the credit policy actually pursued during the last half of 1922 amounted to a shift from one of monetary ease to one of mild restraint. To what extent was this a deliberate shift?

Prices remained relatively stable between August and December. Output continued to increase; the index of production increased from 94.2 (1919 = 100) in June to 116 in December. Total deposits rose by $1.7 billion and bank credit by $1.4 billion. An important change occurred in the composition of bank credit. Loans began to increase substantially for the first time since 1920. The increase in economic activity led to a $400-million increase in currency in circulation which was not offset by Federal Reserve action. Federal Reserve Banks allowed government securities to run down by a little over $200 million, but the net effect was practically nil for there was an increase of bills bought and other securities of $173 million. The gold stock added $141 million to reserves, and bills discounted increased $227 million. Reserves remained at roughly the same level as during the first six months of the year. Interest rates began to turn upwards in September and October. By December the rate on prime commercial paper had returned to the level attained in the previous February.

At a meeting of the Federal Reserve governors' conference in October, 1922, Governor Strong reported that the New York bank had begun to liquidate its investments "at a rate which would at least offset the effects of these further gold imports, the idea being that we had no power to arrest an expansion of bank loans and deposits caused by gold imports, except by offsetting that gold by liquidation of our own investments."[9] He also introduced a resolution to decrease open market investments in proportion as their rediscounts and gold imports increased. The resolution carried but without the provision about gold imports. The governors of the Federal Reserve Banks and Board members thus demonstrated that they still did not understand the relationship between open market sales and the volume of rediscounts.

It should be apparent that neither the Board nor the Reserve Bank governors had formulated in the latter half of 1922 what could be correctly labelled a deliberate and coordinated policy of mild restraint. Federal Reserve officials allowed (not deliberately) the increased demand for reserves resulting from the large currency outflow to exert its full effect on the money market. Furthermore, they focused their attention on the volume of Federal Reserve credit and not on the behavior of member bank reserves or the money supply.

Between November, 1922, and January, 1923, the wholesale price index remained unchanged. The index of output in the basic industries did not increase in November and December but moved sharply upwards (4½%) in January. Towards the end of February the Federal Reserve Board approved an increase in the discount rate for the New York and the Boston banks which prompted Governor Strong to argue that output and employment were nearing a maximum and that additional supplies of credit would only mark up prices without increasing production. In a letter to Governor Norman of the Bank of England quoted by Lester Chandler, Strong explained the reasons for his action:

1) Market rates got to be about 1 per cent above our rate. 2) Stock Exchange loans at top figure, and advancing, with an active bull speculation. 3) Our loans in New York Bank up from low of last year by $300,000,000 or more. 4) After declining in January, rapid increase in our note issue. 5) Production in practically all lines at maximum and nearly at capacity in most industries. 6) Railroad car loading up to capacity. 7) Inventories generally increasing. 8) Prices in nearly all lines steadily advancing on top of largest percentage increase in like period since Civil War (barring late war). 9) Rather general labor shortage. 10) Convincing evidence that any further supplies of our credit to the banks would accomplish no more than to mark up prices, with no increase in production, and probably support an extending speculation.[10]

At least five of the ten reasons enumerated by Strong refer specifically to the fact that output and employment were nearing a maximum. The increase in the rediscount rate in February is consistent with the application of the quantitative test. Further expansion of bank credit was not expected to increase output, only to raise prices.

The application of the quantitative test is referred to explicitly in the March, 1923, *Federal Reserve Bulletin:* "During the past year price advances have been effective in calling forth larger output, and the expansion of production has been supported by the larger use of credit."[11] It is repeated again in May at the time when the production index reached its maximum: "The fact that the recent growth of credit has been accompanied by a further increase in the physical volume of production is favorable evidence of the economic effectiveness of the credit in use."[12] Also, "These increases in production and employment have thus far economically justified the increases in the total volume of bank credit. For credit extension does not result in overexpansion so long as the additional credit yields proportionate results in the larger production and marketing of goods."[13] Wholesale prices increased approximately 2% between January and March. There was no further change in April but a significant decline in May. Output dropped slightly in February, increased 4% in March, faltered temporarily in April, and rose again in May. Therefore, for the first five months of 1923 output expanded about 5.5% attended during all but the last month by a 2% rise in prices. The data seem to reinforce the Board's statements.

This review of the events during 1922 and the first half of 1923 shows that using the quantitative, and not the qualitative, test provides a plausible explanation for the Board's failure to respond to the unusually rapid rise in prices in early 1922 and to its approval of the rate increase in February, 1923. The policy of restraint initiated at that time continued throughout the remainder of the year. There were no further increases in the rediscount rate. However, the Board did table on April 7 the application of the Chicago bank for a rate increase to 5%. The Board thought that the wisest course of action was to liquidate all Reserve Banks' holdings of government securities.

Although an informal committee of Federal Reserve governors had been organized as early as May, 1922 to coordinate the purchases and sales of government securities, formal recognition was not given by the Board to such an organization until March 22, 1923, with the establishment of the Open Market Investment Committee. The first meeting of the new Committee was held in Philadelphia on April 13, 1923. It gave careful consideration to the Treasury's desire to liquidate all of the holdings of government securities by the individual Federal Reserve Banks. The Treasury was concerned over the uncoordinated nature of Reserve Bank sales and purchases of securities and urged the Board to have the banks divest themselves of their holdings.

Adolph Miller proposed the following resolution, the outcome of discussion between the Board and the Secretary of the Treasury:

> It is the sense of the Federal Reserve Board that Federal reserve banks which are carrying a portfolio [of] a considerable volume of open market investments should not increase their discount rate under present conditions until they have substantially effected the liquidation of their open market investments. . . . It is furthermore the opinion of the Federal Reserve Board that there is nothing in the immediate business and credit situation that requires the advance of discount rates for merely psychological reasons.[14]

The resolution was adopted, but C. S. Hamlin interposed the objection that the same results would obtain whether the rediscount rate was raised or not. He explained correctly that the sale of earning assets would accomplish the same results indirectly and would only postpone the necessity for an increase in rates:

> withdrawing money from the market would tend to raise open market rates charged to customers and that this would widen the gap between

Federal Reserve discount rates and customers rates thus forcing us to shorten the gap by raising our rates, unless we were prepared to stand by and lose all control over the situation, and that if withdrawal of money from the market made the Banks increase their rediscounts, we should then have to raise our own rates if we felt any credit control or restriction was necessary.[15]

Although Hamlin grasped the significance of security sales, many of his colleagues on the Board and within the System did not.

In May, the Open Market Investment Committee voted to approve the sale of $50 million of securities. Upon learning of the decision, Governor Crissinger of the Federal Reserve Board wrote immediately to the Committee:

The Board notes with some surprise that in the resolution of May 23, 1923, the committee limits the sale of government security holdings of the various Federal Reserve banks to $50,000,000, which is prorated among them. The limitation of the sale of these securities to the above amount is not in accordance with the policy of the Board. The Board sees no reason why there should be any limitation.

Your attention is being directed to the Board's determination that these government securities should be disposed of as rapidly as possible until all are out of the banks . . . It appears to the Board that the time is propitious for the disposition of all these securities, and the Board trusts that you will immediately take action to dispose of the governments, having due regard, of course, to market conditions.[16]

What is not clear is why the Board decided on this sale of securities. Was it acting merely to satisfy the desires of the Treasury? Or did the Board want a policy of additional restraint? It is reasonably certain from Hamlin's remarks that some members of the Board did not understand that the security sales would lead to an increase in open market rates and hence the necessity to increase eventually the discount rate. This conclusion is reinforced by statements in the *Tenth Annual Report* which show how little significance the Board attached to a change in the composition of Federal Reserve credit as distinct from its volume. The authors of the *Report* seem to identify such a policy as one of neutrality:

The reduction of open-market holdings by reserve banks, therefore, did not result in the withdrawal of support, but in a change in its character. The fact that the reduction of the open-market holdings during 1923 was accompanied by an increased amount of discounting by member banks in a volume approximately equal to the funds withdrawn by the reduction of open-market holdings showed that the total volume of reserve bank credit outstanding was not in excess of the demand for such credit. [17]

The wording of this statement suggests that sales of securities unmatched by an increase in member bank borrowing shows that Federal Reserve credit is excessive. But this is not so. If the sale of securities generates a reserve deficiency, member banks adjust either by borrowing from the Federal Reserve banks or by liquidating loans and securities. The method they employ depends primarily upon relative cost considerations. Presumably they will borrow from the Federal Reserve if borrowing is the cheaper method. If, however, commercial banks liquidate loans and securities, that does not mean that the volume of Federal Reserve credit is excessive. It means that disposing of earning assets is the least expensive method of adjusting to a deficiency of reserves brought about by the sale of government securities on the part of the Federal Reserve.

The Board was searching for a will-o'-the-wisp, a test for the adequacy of a given volume of Federal Reserve credit without regard to the behavior of interest rates. Deposit expansion was regarded as simply the residue of Federal Reserve policy, not a goal. There could be no monetary policy *per se,* that is, policy directed at the money supply, until the Board diverted its interest from the adequacy of a given volume of Federal Reserve credit to the determinants of member bank reserves and the money supply. What many Federal Reserve critics fail to recognize is that the 1923 *Annual Report* did not aim at providing a money supply criterion but a criterion for identifying the "efficient" use of commercial bank credit as well as Federal Reserve credit. Credit and not money was still its principal concern. Within this context the Board proposed the quantitative test for adequacy of bank credit expansion:

> Thus, under immediately prevailing conditions, it is the changes in member bank loans and investments rather than any item in the reserve bank statement that roughly measure the rate of increase in the use of bank credit. This rate of growth of bank credit, compared with the rate of expansion for production and trade, affords, in the absence of such a test as the reserve ratio . . . an important indicator of changes in credit conditions. [18]

Misunderstanding of open market operations did not extend throughout the Federal Reserve System. Nevertheless, the pockets of understanding were few, and fortunately for the behavior of the

System at this time they contained much of its leadership and initiative. It is worthy of noting that although Federal Reserve officials were unanimous, or nearly so, in desiring open market sales there was no unanimity on the effects such action would have.

CHAPTER 6 The Strong Policy: The 1923–1924 Recession

1924 WAS particularly eventful for the Federal Reserve System. For the first time, Lester Chandler has stated, System officials pursued an anticyclical policy to counteract the recession in economic activity which had begun in the spring of 1923.[1] They also took the initial step towards restoring an international gold standard by helping Great Britain to return to gold. Although the policy may have been initiated for purely domestic purposes, it is a mistake to assume that external considerations did not exert a powerful and decisive influence on the timing of Federal Reserve action. Charles O. Hardy, Milton Friedman, and Anna Schwartz have denied that foreign economic considerations were decisive in the policy decisions of 1924 and 1927.[2] But, in fact, the desire of the Federal Reserve Bank of New York to establish a rate spread between New York and London to encourage capital outflows and reduce gold imports was indeed the chief determinant of policy. It was not, however, the only one.

As explained in the preceding chapter, open market policy was centralized in a five-man committee of Federal Reserve Bank governors established in March, 1923, to coordinate buying and selling of government securities. The Open Market Investment Committee, as it was called, had no explicit legal foundation and consequently depended for its success upon voluntary cooperation of the individual members. Decisions of the Committee were subject to review by the Board. Because of the importance and strategic position of the New York bank in the nation's money market and the persuasiveness and influence of its governor, Benjamin Strong, it is not always possible to find out who, within the Committee, supported what reason for action undertaken. Frequently the Committee agreed to an action even though it could not reach agreement on the reasons behind the action. One might say that in grading Federal Reserve performance, the reasons given in support of a policy are seldom trustworthy and therefore are largely irrelevant, especially if the reasons conflict. Nevertheless, it is important to distinguish between action undertaken for the right reasons and action undertaken for the wrong reasons. We cannot evaluate policy in the sense of imputing responsibility unless we acknowledge this distinction and make some effort to identify the extent of the knowledge underlying a policy decision. This can be done for open market policy during 1924 and in a later chapter for 1927.

Was There a Countercyclical Federal Reserve Credit Policy?

The quantitative test applied by the Board in 1922 and 1923 was supposed to be a guarantee against a specific form of inflation, that is, price increases unaccompanied by changes in output. It was meant to be only a temporary substitute for the gold reserve ratio as a test for an excess supply of, or demand for, credit. When the international gold standard was fully restored, decreases in the gold reserve ratio would again be expected to provide the criterion for central bank action. But these expectations derived perhaps more from abstract considerations than from any serious examination of central bank experience. Arthur I. Bloomfield has shown that during the heyday of the gold standard when reserve ratios increased central banks were under no similar compulsion to take measures of the opposite kind. He said: "I can find no clear-cut evidence that any central bank ever lowered its discount rate following gold inflows from abroad because of an explicit desire to play, or even because of an awareness of, the 'rules of the game.' "[3]

It is not clear what using the quantitative test implied about Federal Reserve behavior during a period of price deflation and contraction of output. One might contend that this test did not explicitly call for a reduction in discount rates when output began to decline. The volume of bank credit would adjust to the decline in demand provided that it did not initiate a further unfavorable output response. The argument can be put quite simply. The decline in production reduces the demand for bank credit. Almost immediately a quasi-automatic adjustment of the supply of bank credit occurs through repayment of loans by business firms to banks. Demand deposits contract, and excess reserves increase. The money market tends to ease. The process, of course, can be aggravated if either the banks' or the public's demand for liquidity increases, or if the banks contract by refusing to renew maturing loans. But as long as a liquidity crisis can be staved off, the supply of bank credit in the form of loans will contract *pari passu* with the contraction of demand.

The Federal Reserve's behavior during the second half of 1923 is consistent with the application of the quantitative test to a downswing. According to the National Bureau of Economic Research the recession in business began in the late spring of 1923. The Board's Index of Production in Basic Industries declined 10% between June and September. Although there was a mild upturn in October, the Index by the end of the year stood 17 points, or approximately 13%, below the previous high in the preceding May. Wholesale prices were down about 5% from the peak reached in March, and the Federal Reserve Index of Factory Employment was 4% lower than it was in the spring. Money market rates began to ease during the fourth quarter when the rate on prime commercial paper in New York fell from 5.38% in October to 5% in December. Yields on three-to-six-month Treasury notes and certificates declined from 4.22% to 3.88%. While business activity was receding, the Federal Reserve continued to exert mild pressure. After selling $127 million of government securities in June, the Open Market Investment Committee withdrew from the market and did not re-enter it again before December. Member bank indebtedness amounted to over $750 million throughout the remainder of the year, and total bank credit of the member banks remained roughly constant. Loan expansion came to a standstill in the third quarter but resumed again at a much slower rate in the fourth.

There is no indication that any Board member or other Federal Reserve official was apprehensive about the decline in output and prices during 1923. It may be significant that Governor Strong was away in Colorado from mid-February until October recuperating from an attack of tuberculosis. But there is no reason to believe he would have attempted to reverse the policy actually pursued. When the Board reviewed its policy in the February 1924 issue of the *Federal Reserve Bulletin,* it gave no hint that Board members regarded the 1923 adjustment as anything but normal; they certainly did not view the situation as serious enough to require remedial action. Instead they described the adjustment in these terms:

> The decreased demand for credit for industrial and agricultural purposes during the last quarter of 1923, as reflected in the downward movement of commercial loans and money rates, followed upon a recession in productive activity and wholesale prices which had begun six months earlier. On the recession in 1923 changes in the volume of production and of credit followed the same sequence as on the advance in 1922. This sequence is in accordance with experience of recent years.[4]

This statement is consistent with the passive application of the quantitative test to a downturn in production. It also reveals that the Board simply failed to identify except in retrospect the turning point in economic activity.

The program of security purchases begun at the December 3, 1923 meeting of the Open Market Investment Committee was designed originally to rebuild a depleted investment portfolio. For reasons described in a previous chapter, securities in the special investment account declined from $618 million to $92 million between June 7, 1922, and October 31, 1923. With considerable uncertainty prevailing with respect to the future course of business, the committee decided, in Governor Strong's words, that it would be expedient to acquire "a suitable volume of Government securities of short maturities . . . so as to be in a position to exert an influence from time to time by the purchase and sale of such securities in the open market."[5] The reasons for the turnabout in policy are fairly clear though there may be some dispute about their relative importance. The committee had four broad objectives: 1) to provide an arsenal of securities as a precaution against future emergencies; 2) to lessen the extent of the recession in business activity; 3) to check gold movements and aid in the recovery of sterling; and 4) to create a favorable market for the flotation of "important" foreign bonds. Each of these reasons exerted a perceptible but varying influence on individual members of the Open Market Investment Committee and the Federal Reserve Board. Initially at any rate, the first objective, rebuilding the investment portfolio as a weapon against future contingencies, was extremely important. The report of the Open Market Investment Committee to a joint conference of governors in November, 1924, acknowledged its primacy:

> The first results at which the open market program of purchases aimed have been achieved in that we now possess a considerable portfolio of Government securities available against any emergency. Moreover, the danger of inflation now appears to be more remote than it did a year ago, because of the diminution of gold imports.[6]

Concerning the second objective, neither J. H. Case nor Randolph Burgess, officials of the New York bank, recommended large purchases of securities to improve the level of business activity. Case informed Governor Strong that a recession in business in early 1924 was not improbable, but continued gold imports coupled with Secretary Mellon's suggestion to reduce taxes obviated the need for additional purchases before January. Burgess agreed. He thought that the time for action had passed. The behavior of output between May and September warranted additional purchases, but he said "more recent data are contradictory with a sharp recovery in the stock market and increase in many phases of industrial activity."[7] Under these circumstances Burgess thought it unwise to pursue a policy of large purchases. His opinion was dictated by the unsettled state of business and not a failure to appreciate the countercyclical role of open market operations, as is apparent from the following statement:

> There would be very general agreement to the principle that the Reserve Banks should purchase securities at periods when liquidation in business seems to be going faster than fundamental conditions warrant, and that obversely we should sell securities when business is moving forward so rapidly that the tendency has become unduly speculative in nature. I think there would be agreement to the proposal that the action of the Reserve Banks in these directions should take place early rather than late in the course of the movement which it is designed to check, because early action is much more effective. The present problem is to determine in what type of movement we now find ourselves.[8]

He hesitated to recommend stronger action because he thought two "powerful" stimuli were already contributing to easier credit conditions: gold imports and less active business.

In mid-January, 1924, a larger than normal decrease in currency in circulation and a decline in bank loans were symptomatic of the continued business recession. However, Burgess declared in a memorandum to Case that:

> It is my belief, therefore, that while the situation clearly contains a threat of serious inflation, the time has not yet come to sell securities, particularly in view of the limited amounts now held, but that we should continue to acquire more as far as we can do so without making easier a market already very easy.[9]

The best time for additional purchases, he thought, would be February and March when the regular seasonal pick up in business tended to tighten the money market, though he didn't rule out the purchase of a small quantity before then. The Committee agreed that it was desirable to continue to pay out gold certificates to maintain gold reserves at the 1923 level. If the Committee had thought the business recession needed immediate remedial action, it could have allowed gold inflows to inflate the reserve ratios, easing the way to a cheap money policy. However, the Committee must have been equally concerned with the potentially inflationary threat of gold inflows and easier money generated by the decline in business activity.

A resumé of the business situation prepared by Burgess and Case for Governor Strong for the February 8 meeting of the Open Market Investment Committee showed an improvement in business. There was a 4% rise in the prices of basic commodities, an increase in the price of stocks and the amount of stock market loans, and "heavier" buying in iron and steel and certain other industries. The two men concluded:

> These changes in the business situation appear to make it less desirable to press the purchase of securities than it was a month ago. In general it would seem to be dangerous to be making further advances to the market at a time when stock speculation is rising, commodity prices are rising, and the fundamental conditions are toward easier money. Advances to the market at this time would be apt to stimulate exactly that dangerous speculative tendency, against which the possession of a portfolio is designed as a weapon.[10]

On February 25, the Committee authorized an additional $100 million of purchases. Not before April 22 did the Committee acknowledge the existence of a definite downturn. The indexes of business available for March showed a considerable decrease in production. The report of business conditions prepared for the meeting of the Committee stated:

The prospect for the future, therefore, appears to be for somewhat less active industry and great caution in business enterprise. There therefore appears to be in the business situation no impediment to carrying through a program of building up a portfolio by the Federal Reserve Banks . . . In view of these conditions it seems probable that buying can be carried on safely during the next two or three months, but at progressively lower rates. In order not to drive the market down rapidly it will be necessary to buy slowly and cautiously.[11]

It is interesting to note the negative way in which the case for additional purchases is made, that is, the business situation contains no *impediment* to such a program.

When the Board met on April 26, it considered the application of the New York directors to reduce the discount rate to 4%. Although Miller and Hamlin were in favor of the reduction, Edmund Platt and Secretary Mellon expressed some doubt about its advisability; but that was soon dissipated, and the Board approved the action two days later.[12]

During the first week in May, George Harrison, an official of the New York bank, told the conference of governors that the Open Market Investment Committee had not been able to purchase the full $250 million of securities which had been authorized because of the "scarcity of offerings."[13] He said that the continued influx of gold from abroad posed the danger of credit and price inflation and that the best safeguard against any such danger is the possession of a large portfolio of salable securities. Miller estimated that unused capacity in the country amounted to from 15% to 20% of total productive capacity and pointed out that you could have a "pretty considerable bulge in industry before you have any very considerable price disturbance."[14] He said that in the light of what he knew in May it would have been wise for the New York bank to have reduced the rediscount rate in February. Governor Crissinger concurred, but he thought the rate should have been reduced even earlier, in mid-January.

There were strong differences of opinion among the governors of the Federal Reserve Banks about the probable consequences of a rate reduction. Governor Harding of the Boston bank said that he did not believe a reduction would stimulate business; at most, he said, it might stimulate purchases of securities and stock market speculation. Governors George W. Norris of Philadelphia and J. U. Calkins of San Francisco agreed. Calkins went even further and stated that a reduction of 1% at the New York bank would have "no very marked effect." Miller admitted that he could see no reason to suppose a rate reduction would lead to increased borrowing, but he concluded from testimony by the governors that it would lead to a lowering of costs. The attitude of the governors of the individual Federal Reserve Banks seemed to be that rates should follow, rather than lead, the market.

The attitude of some Reserve Bank governors toward buying more government securities is especially revealing. Governor James B. McDougal of the Chicago Federal Reserve Bank and member of the Open Market Investment Committee favored purchases solely to meet the expenses and dividends of the individual Federal Reserve Banks. Governor Norris of the Philadelphia bank who was also a member of the Open Market Investment Committee opposed the acquisition of additional securities because he thought that it would be a violation of Federal Reserve Bank policy to pour money into the market at that time.[15] Adolph Miller defended the purchase of securities on the grounds that it was necessary to control an excessive upward movement later.[16] Hamlin agreed with both McDougal and Miller. The importance which he attached to both of these objectives is noted in his Diary on May 20, two weeks after the meeting of the governors' conference:

> CSH at meeting of Board points out that the Federal Reserve System is almost literally bleeding to death; that its earning assets are dwindling and that some at least of the Federal Reserve banks can not earn expenses and dividends; that the open market operations are increasing slightly but not in any proportion to the falling off in rediscounts; that he felt the open market committee was being deterred by the Treasury from increasing its investments in Government securities; that we needed at least 500 millions Government securities to enable the banks to regulate credit, in case any future speculative activity should arise.[17]

These reasons are repeated again in a resolution which Hamlin introduced at a Board meeting the next day to increase earning assets from $800 million to approximately $1 billion, action on which was deferred. His failure to suggest using open market operations to remedy the downturn in business at that time was not simply an oversight. It discloses how little importance officials outside of New York placed on a program of purchases to counter a business recession, a fact too often overlooked because of the tendency to exaggerate the New York bank's influence.

Governor Strong came before the Board on May 22 and requested, pending the approval of the Open Market Committee, authority to purchase securities for the account of the New York bank. The Board granted his request. Hamlin reports Strong as having said that "he rather inclined to lower New York rates to 3½%; that while this might have little or no effect upon domestic conditions, it might bring about much borrowing from abroad; that it was a great opportunity for the U.S. to become the money market of the world."[18]

When the Open Market Investment Committee met on May 29, they gave their approval to purchase up to $150 million at once, and for the New York bank to purchase an extra $100 million over and above that assigned to the Committee. Burgess advised Governor Strong that there was no immediate danger of inflation and speculative activity and that additional security purchases would be desirable. Moreover, he asserted that the continued inflow of gold at higher rates than the preceding year "emphasized the importance of a buying program."[19]

Referring back to the objectives outlined on p. 80, the influx of gold was becoming a matter of serious concern to Federal Reserve officials, the natural effect of which was to ease credit and contribute further to reversing the business recession. The gold inflow simply obviated the need for more security purchases. What, then, is the explanation for Burgess's remark that the gold inflow only emphasized the importance of a buying program? It must have been a fear of future inflation posed by the threat of continued gold imports. As a precaution against this, additional purchases were necessary. Furthermore, purchases of government securities would tend to supplement the money market effects of the gold inflow by reducing open market rates and making gold imports less attractive. The Open Market Investment Committee explained the effects of these purchases, as follows:

> The indirect result of relieving member banks from their indebtedness was to allow incoming gold and returning currency to affect the market directly. We simply removed for a time the buffer of rediscounts which the reserve banks held between gold imports and the money market. The time was coming when the buffer of rediscounts would have been eaten away in natural course by the incoming gold and by a longer period of loan liquidation. We have simply hastened the natural effect of gold imports. The results have, we believe, justified the program. First, we have secured an adequate weapon against any gold inflation. Second, this has been done without business disturbance or price inflation but with considerable benefit to business. Third, the program has aided the readjustment of world finance.[20]

The Committee voted again in mid-July to increase securities in the investment account from $400 to $500 million and expressed a willingness to increase them still further if conditions remained the same. These purchases were completed in early September when the account totaled $500 million.

A summary of monthly net acquisitions of bills bought, bills discounted, U.S. government securities, monetary gold stocks, and currency in circulation from December, 1923, to December, 1924, are set out in Table 1. Clearly the most striking fact revealed by

Table 1

Monthly New Acquisition of Bills Bought,
Bills Discounted, Monetary Gold Stocks, Currency in Circulation,
U.S. Government Securities from December, 1923, to December, 1924*
(*$ million*)

Year and month (*1*)	Bills discounted† (*2*)	Bills bought (*3*)	U.S. Government securities (*4*)	Gold stocks (*5*)	Currency in circulation (*6*)
1923					
December	63 (857)	47	20	35	180
1924					
January	−335	−64	17	46	−395
February	10	− 9	35	34	83
March	−50	−61	101	39	8
April	−35	−78	45	57	3
May	−17	−37	31	39	11
June	−80	−42	97	31	− 83
July	−56	−21	75	31	− 37
August	−31 (263)	25	37	10	46
September	− 3	43	33	−12	33
October	−37	123	9	− 2	62
November	− 2	66	− 2	17	105
December	99	106	−42	−26	57

SOURCE: *Banking and Monetary Statistics* (Washington, D.C.: Board of Governors of the Federal Reserve System, 1943).

* Last Wednesday of the month figures.

† Figures within parentheses are total amounts of member bank indebtedness.

Table 1 is that between January and May purchases of government securities failed to offset the decline in reserves brought about by the reduction in bills bought. Bills bought declined by $249 million while security purchases increased by $229 million. Between

March and May, when purchases were the heaviest, the net effect on reserves was negative. We can infer from the table that a reversal of policy of the Open Market Investment Committee was not evident until March. Nevertheless, it was June before the Committee pursued a more vigorous and persistent expansionary policy, precisely one year after the downturn in business identified by National Bureau methods. The Board in the July *Federal Reserve Bulletin* attributed all of the easing of credit to the inflows of gold and not to the purchases of securities:

> The recession in business activity has been accompanied since April by a decreased demand for credit for commercial purposes, and this, together with the continued influence of gold imports, has brought about an unusual ease in the money market.[21]

The effect on interest rates is readily discernible in Table 2. There is a sharp break in the rate on three-to-six-month Treasury notes and certificates and prime commercial paper between March and April. Prime bankers' acceptances declined from 4% to 2.5% in June.

Table 2

Short- and Long-term Open Market Rates in New York City, 1924
(*Percentages*)

Year and month	Prime commercial paper	3–6-month treasury certificates and notes	Prime bankers' acceptances	U.S. Gov't. bonds	Stock exchange time loans 90 days	Average rate on new stock exchange call loans
January	4.88	3.76	4.06	4.30	4.88	4.31
February	4.88	3.54	4.06	4.28	4.75	4.37
March	4.88	3.57	4.00	4.28	4.63	4.12
April	4.63	3.38	4.00	4.23	4.50	4.22
May	4.50	2.99	3.25	4.15	4.00	3.33
June	4.13	2.44	2.50	3.98	3.25	2.19
July	3.50	1.92	2.00	3.94	2.75	2.10
August	3.25	1.90	2.13	3.91	2.63	2.00
September	3.13	2.14	2.19	3.92	2.75	2.10
October	3.13	2.41	2.19	3.87	2.75	2.35
November	3.25	2.58	2.38	3.90	3.25	2.51
December	3.63	2.57	2.94	3.96	3.50	3.63

SOURCE: *Banking and Monetary Statistics* (Washington, D.C.: Board of Governors, 1943), p. 450.

The reduction in bills discounted in the first six months of 1924 by some $400 million was not, therefore, the net result of open market purchases but an increase in the gold stock by $245 million and a decrease in currency in circulation by $240 million. The New York bank lowered the discount rate for the first time on May 1 and followed it by two successive reductions in June and August. Substantial easing during the first five months of 1924 would have occurred even without the $200 million purchase of securities. The same effect probably could have been achieved by lowering the rate on acceptances and bankers' bills so as to have encouraged sales to the Federal Reserve. Governor Strong admitted that in 1924 open market rates were low relative to the rates at which the System was prepared to buy acceptances.[22] As a result very few bills were offered. Between July, 1923, and April, 1924, the buying rate on prime bankers' acceptances at New York was 4¼%. Open market rates on prime bankers' acceptances at New York during the same period declined from 4.13% to 4%. The increasing spread between the two rates probably discouraged sales to the Federal Reserve. If Federal Reserve purchases of acceptances were as sensitive to rate levels as Governor Strong believed, an adjustment of rates at the Federal Reserve might have bolstered up the volume of bills bought and eliminated the need for security purchases. Governor Strong and other members of the Open Market Investment Committee were probably unduly influenced by the newly discovered relationship between member bank indebtedness and open market purchases and sales. An increase in securities purchased, *ceteris paribus,* tended to reduce member bank indebtedness and to ease credit. By concentrating on only two components of Federal Reserve credit to the neglect of the third (bills bought), System officials exaggerated the effect of security purchases.

Both the wholesale price index as well as the production index touched bottom in June, the month that the Federal Reserve commenced a dynamic, as distinct from a more or less defensive, anticyclical policy. Purchases of government securities amounted to $215 million between June and August. There are three possible explanations why the System failed to initiate more positive action sooner: 1) Federal Reserve officials did not recognize the seriousness of the downturn until the late spring of 1924. Then the abrupt drop in May in the Index of Production in Basic Industries by almost 10% and another sharp decline in June of 9% left little doubt as to the existence of an industrial recession and the necessity for remedial action. Factory employment declined 4% in May alone. The decline in prices was negligible. 2) The Open Market Investment Committee considered it an appropriate time to acquire a portfolio so that control of inflation could, if necessary, be exercised at a later time. According to Hamlin, the Committee met on May 29 and decided that a further reduction in rates was not of "prime importance." It thought larger purchases could be made at that time without "unduly disturbing the market, but "that it was imperative to get into the market now to exercise control later in case of threatened inflation."[23]

3) In addition to domestic reasons for the 1924 action, Benjamin Strong advanced the following external considerations:

> To facilitate a change in the interest relation between the New York and London markets, without inviting inflation . . . By directing foreign borrowings to this market to create the credits which would be necessary to facilitate the export of commodities, especially farm produce . . . To render what assistance was possible by our market policy toward the recovery of sterling and the resumption of gold payment by Great Britain.[24]

This refers back to the last objective of the Open Market Investment Committee as set forth on p. 80. The desire to establish a rate differential explains the action taken by the New York bank on June 12 to reduce the discount rate to 3½%, one-half percentage point below the discount rate at the Bank of England. Simultaneously, the rate on 90-day bankers' acceptances in New York fell below the rate on three-month bankers' bills in London, the effect of which was to reduce the exodus of short-term funds from London. Sir Henry Clay stated in his biography of Montagu Norman that "In June New York had put its rate below London with the deliberate intention of helping London back to the Gold Standard."[25]

Governor Strong had outlined his ideas on stabilization strategy to Secretary of the Treasury Mellon in a long memorandum on May 27. He explained the necessity for restoring price levels before gold payment was resumed and the need for maximum cooperation between the New York Federal Reserve Bank and the Bank of England. This could best be achieved, he thought, if the burden of the readjustment fell mainly on the United States and not Britain by putting the New York rate below that of London.[26]

The summer of 1924 seemed a propitious time for pursuing the two goals simultaneously: domestic economic stability, and an early return of the world to an international gold standard. The crucial significance of the latter objective has been set forth vividly by one of Strong's associates at the New York bank:

> That was the time when in my opinion a great man had a great idea; the man was Governor Strong and the idea was that the Federal Reserve System had a responsibility that went far beyond our domestic situation at that time alone. The idea was further that this country could never hope for a permanent groundwork of prosperity until the world was back on a gold basis, and the world could never get back on a gold basis until we helped it. One way we had to help was by making conditions here favorable to the return of the world to gold. [27]

Strong revealed in the 1926 Stabilization Hearings that the guide to the size of government securities purchases was the desire to eliminate the indebtedness of the New York City banks to the Federal Reserve, but this is completely unconvincing since most of the indebtedness had been eliminated in June.[28] Table 3 shows the amount of accommodation extended monthly by the New York bank to sixty-seven member banks in New York City.

Table 3

Monthly Borrowing of Sixty-seven Member Banks in New York City at the Federal Reserve Bank of New York, 1924

($ million)

Month	Amount of borrowing	Month	Amount of borrowing
January	59	*July*	6
February	71	*August*	9
March	50	*September*	10
April	4	*October*	12
May	18	*November*	5
June	8	*December*	31

SOURCE: *Eleventh Annual Report of the Federal Reserve Board* (1924), p. 330.

Since the price index turned up in July and the production index leveled off in July and August, there is no evidence that the Federal Reserve considered additional purchases necessary to promote economic recovery. The least that we can say is that motives for purchases during the summer of 1924 were mixed. Cyclical control was an important one, but so were other factors. The success of the policy pursued was the result of an accidental harmony of monetary goals and not—as Keynes, Harrod, Chandler and others would have us believe—the ushering in of a new and successful era of managed money!

The Federal Reserve made no earnest effort at active intervention to reverse the tide of declining production during the 1923–24 recession until March of 1924. There is no evidence that suggests that Federal Reserve officials recognized the cyclical turning point in 1923. In fact it was July, 1924 before the *Federal Reserve Bulletin* showed that the Board had any recognition of the cyclical downturn and what the Federal Reserve had done, or was preparing to do, about it. In the April issue there is no mention of the large purchases of government securities in March. The reader is left to discover this vital fact for himself amidst the array of statistical data. One could infer from the Board's failure to explain its action that it did not begin to think seriously about the business recession much before the New York directors made application for a reduction in rates at the end of April. It seems that the Open Market Investment Committee and not the Federal Reserve Board provided the leadership initially. But Federal Reserve officials honestly thought that buying government securities would reduce member bank indebtedness and possibly ease credit. They failed to foresee what impact these purchases would have on bills bought. And in fact the easing of credit during the first five months of 1924 was owing more to gold inflows than to open market purchases.

Although the Board behaved as though the recession had not even started till spring 1924, the *Annual Report* of February, 1925, acknowledged that the downturn in economic activity began in the spring of 1923 and continued until mid-1924. There is no hint that earlier awareness by the Board might have brought easing action sooner. Nor is there anything in the famous *Tenth Annual Report* which is inconsistent with the Board's behavior. It admitted that credit should be eased during the recovery stage though there is no concrete policy statement during the downswing. The *Report* specifically states:

> It seems equally obvious that if industry and trade are in *process of recovery after a period of reaction,* they should be given the support and encouragement of cheaper credit by the prompt establishment at the Federal reserve banks of rates that will invite the use of Federal reserve credit to facilitate business recovery.[29]

Adolph Miller, one of the authors of the 1923 *Report,* expressed doubts a few years later about the efficacy of easing money in a downswing: "I think it is a pretty well-established fact that we can not by monetary operations arrest business recession. We can do something to stimulate the flow of money into use when business is 'picking up' and something to check the flow when it is proceeding too rapidly, and thus exercise an influence on the pace of business."[30]

Harold Reed, a contemporary critic of the Federal Reserve, has taken the policy of the Open Market Investment Committee during this episode as evidence that it abandoned the quantitative test for the adequacy of bank credit.[31] According to his interpretation of the test, Federal Reserve credit should be restricted, not expanded, when the production index declines. But what Reed failed to see was the basic asymmetry of the quantitative test. Its chief purpose was to furnish a guarantee against inflation. Although Federal Reserve credit was supposed to be restricted when output reached a maximum, there was no corresponding implication that when output began to decline Federal Reserve credit should be reduced. That was the fundamental mistake of the "liquidation" policy pursued during 1920–21. By 1924, most Federal Reserve officials admitted as much. Benjamin Strong and Adolph Miller said so explicitly. This policy assumed that a reduction of Federal Reserve credit occurs through loan contraction, the creation of excess reserves, and the subsequent reduction in member bank indebtedness. Again, the basic asymmetry is briefly: the Federal Reserve deliberately contracts credit to restrain inflation after capacity output is reached and adjusts passively to a contraction of output.

C. O. Hardy, who was also an astute Federal Reserve critic, denied that the action of 1924 implied an abandonment of the 1923 tests, and he cited the passage in the *Annual Report* quoted above.[32] The meanings of the terms contained in this passage, "recovery" and "period of reaction," are obscure. If interpreted literally, the statement could be taken to mean that credit should be eased only after the trough in business activity was reached, that is, a policy similar to the one actually pursued in 1920–21 and ultimately rejected by Federal Reserve officials. Hardy has given a different interpretation to the phrase "process of recovery after a period of reaction" as equivalent to the downswing phase of the cycle, but this interpretation is inconsistent with some remarks made by Adolph Miller and quoted above.

A preferable interpretation of the quantitative test implies a policy of active ease *after* the downturn has occurred. A contraction in output resulting in a declining demand for bank credit leads eventually to a decrease in loans and demand deposits, an increase in excess reserves, and a reduction in member bank indebtedness. The behavior of the commercial banks in easing credit depends, therefore, on the volume and speed with which they work off their indebtedness to the Federal Reserve. A large residue of member bank indebtedness left from the preceding boom tends to forestall the "automatic" response of the banking system to a decline in loan demand. The change in the Federal Reserve's attitude to this residue was heralded by Chandler as the major change in System thinking between 1920–21 and 1924. According to Chandler, within two years Federal Reserve officials came to understand the relationship between credit availability, interest rates, and the volume of member bank indebtedness as well as the interdependence of rediscounting and open market operations. Neither relationship was adequately understood in the 1920–21 episode when Federal Reserve officials were influenced strongly by their doctrinaire attitude toward government securities held within the banking system.

Why, then, should the tempo of the banking response to a recession be conditioned by the size of the member bank indebtedness left over from the preceding boom? Because its size was the result of collaboration between the commercial banks and the Federal Reserve. The Federal Reserve accepted responsibility for the volume of indebtedness in the upswing. Why shouldn't it also recognize its responsibility for reducing member bank indebtedness during the downswing? This could hardly be interpreted as interference with the "natural" market forces. In fact the pre-1914 mechanism did not shackle the banks with any such recovery-retarding residue. System officials did not realize before 1924 that the Federal Reserve by its action in the boom created an obstacle to a speedy credit response in the downswing. The sale of securities in the upswing simply delayed the money market's response to a change in the demand for bank credit. When the monetary effects of this "artificial" impediment were fully realized, the Federal Reserve took steps to remove it. Getting the banks out of debt to the Federal Reserve can, therefore, be regarded as an attempt to speed up the "natural" response of the banking system to a contraction of loan demand. To regard it as part of a deliberate policy to stabilize business conditions is misleading. In one sense Friedman is correct in that the Federal Reserve might have imparted more instability to the money supply than had existed in the pre-1914 days. It probably did so during the 1920–21 depression. But that was because Federal Reserve officials did not understand the full implications of the tools which were designed for their use. Lack of knowledge, not lack of courage, was the real explanation for the deficiencies in their policy. Once they recognized the restrictive effects of a large volume of member bank indebtedness, the errors of 1920–21 were not repeated.

CHAPTER 7

The Quiet Years: The Application of the Qualitative Test, 1925–1926

THE YEARS 1925 and 1926 have been described as relatively "quiet" in the behavior of the economy and, specifically, in the administration of Federal Reserve monetary policy.[1] Viewed only on an annual basis gross national income in constant dollars increased 4½% in 1925 and 5½% in 1926, a highly satisfactory performance by almost any criterion. Stanley Lebergott estimated unemployment in 1925 to be 4% of the civilian labor force and 1.9% in 1926.[2] These estimates compare with 3.2% in 1923 and 5.5% for the recession year 1924. Thus the annual data for both unemployment and real national income testify to the correctness of the label "quiet" years and "years of steady progress."

Federal Reserve monetary policy during this period is interesting chiefly because it reveals the conflicting attitudes within the System toward growing stock market speculation. Opinions differ about the importance the Federal Reserve attached to the growth of stock market credit. E. A. Goldenweiser concluded that "consciousness of the System's concern with speculation had not yet developed and the expansion of stock-market credit was permitted to proceed with little interference by monetary authorities."[3] C. O. Hardy also thought Reserve officials were generally unsympathetic to any effort to control the use to which member bank funds were put as long as the provisions of the Federal Reserve Act were observed.[4] Walter Stewart, the Board's director of research and statistics during this period, emphasized the critical importance of these years when he said: "I feel, in general, that the mistake of blaming the reserve system for 1920 is now less dangerous than the mistake of praising it for 1925 and 1926."[5] Yet he did not advocate strong action to curb the flow of bank credit to the stock market.

An Abortive Recovery?

The Board's production index finally turned up again in September, 1924, after having remained in the doldrums throughout the summer. The recovery in industrial production, once it got underway, was unusually rapid. The Index of Production in Basic Industries, the only index available to the Board at that time, was 35% higher in January, 1925, than it had been in the preceding August and was equal to the peak level attained in May, 1923. During the corresponding period wholesale prices rose 7%, an amount just sufficient to regain the ground lost during the recession. Open market rates paralleled closely the movements in the production index. The spread between the 3% rediscount rate at New York and open market rates practically vanished.

Federal Reserve officials were opposed in November to any increase in discount rates. Governor Strong thought that an increase would probably injure Europe, for Great Britain was preparing to return to the gold standard. C. S. Hamlin feared that the psychological effect of a rate increase might damage confidence and thus inhibit the recovery. The Federal Advisory Council found no evidence of unusual speculation or inflation. Although opposed to any change in the discount rate, the Council did, nevertheless, recommend a reduction in the portfolio of government securities and acceptances so that the rediscount rate at the New York Federal Reserve Bank could be made more effective. It was their opinion that "extreme care" was indicated in New York "where the activity in the security market has already taken substantial proportions."[6] Both stock prices and the volume of shares traded had begun to move up rapidly.

On December 2, the Board rejected a resolution introduced by Adolph Miller calling for the Federal Reserve Banks to adjust their rates to be 0.25% above actual open market rates, sufficiently above the latter to be effective. The Board maintained that, if approved, the resolution would mean an immediate increase in the discount rate. Hamlin, James, Cunningham, and Governor Crissinger were opposed to Miller's motion. Vice-Governor Platt was the only member who supported it.[7]

When the Open Market Investment Committee assembled on December 19, Governor Strong said that he was considering the question of an increase in the discount rate. He thought that it would be more appropriate at that particular time to sell some securities in order, in his words, to test the market out. Walter Stewart also recommended the sale of securities. Sales from the investment account amounted to $44 million in December. The Committee decided to sell an additional $150 million in January to offset the normal seasonal decrease in currency in circulation. The large inflow of currency of $307 million was more than sufficient to offset both the sale of gold and securities. Member bank indebtedness declined by $50 million to a total of $275 million. Open market rates remained stable.

The economy appeared, to some optimistic observers, to be poised in January, 1925, for a new spurt of expansion. The index of production was nearly 10% higher than it had been in December. However, these oversanguine expectations failed to materialize. The recovery lost its momentum, and a very mild downturn set in that continued through August. Factory employment dropped in July, 1925, to what it had been in May of the preceding year. The decline in the Board's Index of Production in Basic Industries was sharper in 1925 than it had been in 1923. If measured by the revised index which was not available until May, 1926, the decline was less severe.

In February Federal Reserve policy gradually became mildly restrictive. Gold sales totaled $130 million and sales of securities amounted to $109 million, the immediate effect of which was to raise member bank indebtedness by $138 million and to reduce member bank reserves by $70 million. Open market rates tightened. On February 26, the New York Federal Reserve Bank raised the discount rate to 3½%. The increase merely reflected the change initiated by the Open Market Investment Committee and concurred in by the Federal Advisory Council. The action temporarily halted further speculation on the stock exchange. The number of shares traded daily decreased from 2 million in Novem-

Table 1

Monthly Index of Common Stock Prices, Average Number of Shares Traded Daily and Renewal Rate on Call Loans, November, 1924–September, 1925*

Date	Common stock price index	Average number of shares traded daily (*000*)	Renewal rate on call loans
1924			
November	113.4	2,080	2.42
December	119.7	1,788	3.49
1925			
January	125.8	1,744	3.32
February	127.5	1,688	3.60
March	123.9	1,651	3.97
April	123.4	1,088	3.86
May	127.8	1,607	3.82
June	131.0	1,313	3.97
July	135.0	1,353	4.09
August	136.0	1,458	4.19
September	139.0	1,711	4.62

SOURCE: *Federal Reserve Bulletin* (Washington, D.C.: Federal Reserve Board, 1925).
* 1917–1921 = 100

ber, 1924 to a little over 1 million on April 25. According to Table 1 share prices declined in both March and April.

The dual criteria set out in the famous *Tenth Annual Report* (p. 65) gave conflicting recommendations of the appropriate monetary policy to pursue during early 1925. Applying the *quantitative* test, no changes in policy were called for because neither capacity output nor full employment had yet been reached. In fact, since production declined after February a slight easing should have occurred. Be that as it may, the significant feature of the episode beginning in November, 1924 and continuing through August, 1925, was the unusually rapid increase in loans on securities—$600 million during the first nine months of 1925. The rate of increase in the share of total loans taken up by loans on securities was greater in 1925 than in any other pre-1929 year, as shown in Table 2. Reserve officials became increasingly concerned about whether or not Federal Reserve credit was being extended for purely speculative purposes and contrary to the Board's regulations.

The expansion of bank credit did not appear to be related in the

Table 2

Total Loans, Loans on Securities, and Share of Total Loans Given Over to Security Loans for All Member Banks, 1919–1928
(*$ billion*)

Year	Total loans	Loans on securities	Percentage of loans on securities to total loans
1919	15.4	5.4	35
1920	19.5	4.9	25
1921	18.1	4.4	24
1922	17.2	4.5	26
1923	18.8	5.0	27
1924	19.2	5.4	28
1925	20.7	6.7	32
1926	22.0	7.3	33
1927	22.9	8.2	36
1928	24.3	9.1	37

SOURCE: *Banking and Monetary Statistics* (Washington, D.C.: Board of Governors of the Federal Reserve System, 1943), p. 79.

manner described in the *Tenth Annual Report* to the improvement in production. The rise in call loan rates as shown in Table 1 had an ancillary effect of reducing bankers' balances (interbank deposits) of New York City banks by about $175 million in January, 1925 thus tending to tighten credit further in the principal money market. Since the behavior of these balances exerted a significant influence on the banking situation during this period, some explanation of the role they played should be given.

Commercial banks throughout the country had not yet developed the habit of holding excess reserves at the Federal Reserve Banks. Balances above the amount required by law increased in the form of interbank deposits rather than as excess reserves at the Federal Reserve Banks. Nevertheless, whenever the rate paid on these deposits tended to fall below the rate on loans to the stock market, banks in the interior of the country withdrew their deposits and invested the proceeds in direct loans to the stock market. The stock market thus developed a sensitivity to changes in the composition of member bank reserves between required and excess.

Harold Reed, a contemporary Federal Reserve critic, maintained that there had been no sharp reversal in 1925 of the easing policies inaugurated in 1924.[8] He compared the behavior of Federal Reserve credit along with gold stock and currency movements for October, 1924, to February, 1925, and concluded that since member bank reserves increased by about $32 million there was evidently no change in Federal Reserve policy. He assumed that total reserves rather than the composition of Federal Reserve credit was the relevant indicator of monetary policy pursued. Moreover, he argued that the $200-million decrease in government security holdings was matched by equivalent increases in bills discounted and acceptances, and, in his words, "may very well have indicated no more the desire to lessen the total volume of reserve credit than the belief that it would be preferable for earning assets to consist more largely of paper, the acquirement of which is supposed to reveal principally member-bank, rather than Reserve Bank, initiative."[9] What Reed failed to consider was the view of some Federal Reserve Bank officials that the effect of increasing member bank indebtedness was to raise open market rates and to reduce the availability of credit. He may have been right about the effect of Federal Reserve action although in error about the reasons which prompted its behavior. The real problem is not whether or not there was a *sharp* reversal of policy during the winter of 1924–25 but why there should have been a policy of restraint at all. The reason Federal Reserve officials failed to initiate easy money measures when the fall in basic industries' output was about equal in intensity to that in the latter half of 1923 is very simple. They responded exactly as they had before.

The Priority of International Considerations

Employment and output picked up in the middle of the third quarter and increased very rapidly in the final three months of 1925. The index of production rose 10%; factory employment was higher than at any time since April, 1924. Despite the improvement, the production index in December, 1925, was still 5% below the preceding January level. The favorable response of output was accompanied by a 4% decline in wholesale prices attributable mainly to a decline in farm prices. Total bank credit expanded by $1.4 billion in the second half of 1925. This increase was almost twice the amount of the increase during the first six months. During the winter months of 1925 loan expansion at member banks slackened considerably. Commercial loans of reporting member banks actually decreased in November and December by about $35 million while loans secured by stocks and bonds increased by over $230 million. Loans on securities continued to constitute the largest portion of the loan increase. Considering that over 90% of the expansion of bank credit in 1925 took the form of loans on securities, it is not surprising that some Federal Reserve officials expressed more concern about stock market speculation than about the level of economic activity.

The Federal Reserve Bank of Boston applied in early October, 1925 for an increase in the rediscount rate from 3½% to 4%. Disagreement and uncertainty within the System led to a postponement of action until November. The directors of the New York bank opposed any increase in rates. They preferred to use "direct action" or moral suasion to reduce stock exchange loans. At a Federal Reserve Board meeting on October 16, Walter Stewart admitted that some stock speculation resulted from the use of Federal Reserve credit, but he said that there was absolutely no reason for increasing discount rates. Production was slowly increasing with prices practically stationary.[10] He agreed with the New York directors that direct action was preferable. The Board, on the other hand, seemed to be equally divided on the necessity for a rate increase. Vice-Governor Platt, Miller, and Hamlin were in favor; James, Cunningham, and Governor Crissinger were opposed. Hamlin's opinion was conditioned, as he specifically said, by the behavior of the stock market.[11]

When the Board met on November 6 to consider the application of the Boston bank to increase its rate, the opposition to a rate increase had mysteriously vanished. Cunningham was the only Board member who opposed it. At the same meeting he introduced a resolution saying that the Board would approve a rate increase to 4% for New York on the grounds that rate increases should be initiated by the New York bank. The resolution was defeated by a narrow vote of three to two: Cunningham and Miller voted yes; Governor Crissinger, James, and Hamlin voted no.[12] Hamlin considered the introduction of the resolution improper procedure, for the question before the Board, he said, was the application of the Boston bank, not New York.

The rate dispute flared up again at the end of November when the Board reviewed the report of the Open Market Investment Committee. The Committee felt that conditions warranted an increase in discount rates but not the sale of government securities. Miller objected to the report saying that at least $100 million of government securities should be sold. And he introduced a resolution calling for the immediate sale of $50 million. The motion failed at first on a tie vote: Miller, Cunningham, and Platt in the affirmative; Hamlin, Crissinger, and James in the negative. They finally approved the report but only on the condition that the Open Market Investment Committee reconvene to reconsider its policy in the light of changed conditions.[13]

The Committee reconvened on December 1. Governor Strong argued that no change in policy was necessary. He gave the following reasons: 1) stock speculation was under control; 2) stock prices were not far from their 1913 level; 3) an increase in the discount rate would put up customer rates and bring about deflation; and 4) it might also result in gold inflows and interfere with Great Britain's efforts to stabilize the new gold value of the pound. He said that it was Miller's desire to promote deflation pure and simple. Other members of the Committee agreed with Strong, and no change was made in open market policy.[14] But the next day the Bank of England increased its discount rate to 5%, and the situation changed.

The New York bank sought and obtained an increase in the rediscount rate on January 8, 1926. No explanation is made for the rate increase. The domestic situation had not changed perceptibly, so that there can be no other reason for Governor Strong's action than the change in the rate at the Bank of England. That is not to say that the Board approved the action for the same reason.

The Setback in the Stock Market

The stock market suffered a sharp and severe setback in March, 1926. Table 3 shows that the index of stock prices fell from 101.8 in February to 95.8 in March. New York member banks' loans to brokers and dealers dropped $650 million between February 17 and March 10 and a further $300 million by the end of the month. Production and employment remained high until April, then began to decline. At a meeting of the Open Market Investment Committee on March 20 Governor Strong said a business recession had started and that the Committee ought to be prepared to purchase government securities if required.[15] The next day James introduced a resolution at a meeting of the Board to give the Committee the authority to increase the investment account to $300 mil-

Table 3
Monthly Index of Common Stock Prices,
1925–1929 (1926 = 100)

Month	Year				
	1925	*1926*	*1927*	*1928*	*1929*
January	85.1	101.8	105.6	134.4	185.2
February	85.9	101.8	107.9	132.3	186.5
March	83.6	95.8	109.1	137.9	189.1
April	82.8	92.9	111.1	145.9	186.6
May	85.4	93.2	114.2	152.1	187.8
June	86.9	97.2	115.4	145.3	190.7
July	89.3	100.0	117.2	144.2	207.3
August	90.5	102.9	122.0	148.3	218.1
September	92.6	104.3	127.7	156.6	225.2
October	95.6	101.6	126.7	159.1	201.7
November	98.7	103.1	129.6	171.1	151.1
December	100.3	105.4	133.1	171.1	153.8

SOURCE: *Seventeenth Annual Report of the Federal Reserve Board* (1930), p. 214.

lion. It passed by a vote of four to three. Governor Crissinger, Secretary Mellon, Hamlin, and James voted for the motion; Platt, Miller, and Cunningham against.[16] On March 22 Governor Strong recommended to the governors conference that securities be purchased for the specific purpose of easing the money market. Miller and Platt of the Board did not believe that such a policy was necessary. In Miller's judgment there was no recession. Hamlin reports that Secretary Mellon said that there was undoubtedly a recession in business, though no one could tell how long it would last.

On April 22 the New York bank lowered its rediscount rate from 4% to 3½%. Purchases of government securities amounted to some $70 million between March and June and were matched by a corresponding reduction in rediscounts. Money market rates eased slightly. Hardy explained the rate reduction, as follows: "any one who was at all cognizant of the business and financial situation in 1926 could hardly doubt that the most important cause of the rate manipulation of that year was the stock market recession and not the trifling recession of business activity."[17] On this occasion stock market considerations may have been decisive in initiating action to ease credit.

The Policy of Restraint Renewed

In May, 1926, the Board had available for its own use, though it was not published for another twelve months, a revised index of production made up of sixty individual series measuring production in thirty-five industries including both manufacturing and mineral. The new index, as distinct from the old, contained measures of output in the automobile, petroleum, rubber tire, plate glass, and the boot and shoe industries. The economy during the first seven months of 1926 reached a high degree of output stability, though well below capacity and with an unsatisfactory level of factory employment. The production index turned up sharply in August and September (a 6% increase) only to fall back again in the final quarter. The new index remained relatively constant at an average level well above any figure attained in 1925 with the exception of the month of December and equal to peak output prior to the 1923–24 recession.

Between June and September the System pursued a policy of mild restraint. The Open Market Investment Committee sold some $90 million of government securities and made no effort to offset the equivalent flow of currency into circulation. Member bank indebtedness increased by $160 million. On August 13 the New York bank raised the discount rate to 4%. This increase was a deliberate act of credit restraint at a time when there was no readily apparent reason why the economic situation should have been a cause for concern. Why, then, was the rate increased? According to Hamlin, Governor Crissinger told the Board that he had received a telephone call from George Harrison of the New York bank who said that the New York directors "were in doubt as to increasing discount rates and wanted to know if the Board would sustain them if they voted to increase."[18] He also said Governor Strong favored an increase of 1%. The Board agreed that if rates had to be increased that this was a good psychological time to do it. Goldenweiser also favored the increase but intimated there was no reason for it on purely commercial grounds. Hamlin explained his views, as follows:

> I do not believe in increasing rates possibly penalizing business and crop movements in order to control the New York Stock Exchange. In present conditions there is a spread 1 to 1½ per cent between customer rates and our discount rates, and it would be wise to take up this slack.[19]

What Hamlin failed to see was that the Board was partly responsible for the tightening of customer rates.

The expansion in output which the Board anticipated in August failed to materialize and by the end of December the index of production had fallen 7%. Neither the Board nor the Open Market Investment Committee contemplated any changes in either open market policy or the discount rate.

CHAPTER 8

The 1927 Recession: An International Test of Credit Policy

THE CONTROVERSIAL easing policy of 1927 is revealing not only because it represents the second attempt by the Federal Reserve to pursue a countercyclical monetary policy but also because the System added a third credit criterion to the two that were already laid out in the famous *Tenth Annual Report* (see p. 65). The maintenance of the gold standard abroad became for a time the predominant test for the expansion of bank credit in the United States. Action taken to safeguard the international monetary standard was not necessarily either the best-designed nor the best-timed policy for domestic stability even though an easy money policy seemed desirable from either perspective. Federal Reserve officials were well aware that the international stabilization test might conflict with the qualitative test, that is, a policy of substantial ease could very well lead to an expansion of bank credit for purely speculative purposes. But they were prepared to accept the consequences. Adolph Miller bitterly opposed open market operations on the grounds that purchases of securities would tend to fan the flames of stock market speculation. Likewise, the officers and directors of the Federal Reserve Bank of Chicago disapproved, but they were ordered ultimately to comply with the Board's request to reduce the discount rate from 4% to 3½%.

The timing of open market operations in 1927, like the 1924 episode, was geared more to obtain a rate differential between New York and London than to stimulate economic activity. When the international objective had been accomplished, the function of open market policy was to maintain the new structure of rates. So international monetary stability as well as domestic economic stabilization became, for a time, joint goals of monetary policy.

The Pace of Business Activity

Industrial production fell 6% in the final quarter of 1926 but recovered sufficiently during the first three months of 1927 to dispel any doubts in the minds of System officials that a business recession was underway. Although factory employment improved a little in February and March, the January figure was lower than at any time since November, 1924 and still 5% below what it was the year before. Wholesale prices had declined 3% between January and April. After remaining steady in May, they increased 3½% in the five-month period ending in October.

During the first four months of 1927, the Federal Reserve System made little use of the instruments of monetary policy. The rediscount rate remained unchanged at 4% and security purchases were made only for the purpose of replacing maturing issues. Nevertheless, their policy can be characterized as one of "passive" ease. A large inflow of gold and the normal seasonal decrease in currency in circulation exerted their full effects on the money market. In January alone the inflow of gold amounted to about $62 million, greater than that for any single month in the previous five years, and the decrease in currency in circulation totaled $228 million. These two factors made possible a reduction in member bank indebtedness by approximately $200 million. In February another $50 million of gold flowed in, and bills discounted declined by an additional $90 million. Altogether, then, in the first two months of 1927 some $300 million of reserves were provided to the member banks: $100 million from gold imports and roughly $200 million from the currency inflow. Member banks used the bulk of their newly acquired funds to reduce their indebtedness at the Federal Reserve Banks by $275 million. The rate on prime commercial paper declined from 4.5% in December, 1926, to 4.13% in April, 1927. Treasury notes and certificates moved up in April; however, long-term bonds continued their secular decline moving down from 3.56% in December, 1926, to 3.35% in April, 1927.

In early February the business directors of the Federal Reserve Bank of New York wanted to decrease the discount rate, but the Board was opposed to any changes in discount rates at that time.[1]

When the Open Market Investment Committee met on May 9, Governor Strong stated that sales of government securities to offset gold imports should be discontinued. Any more sales would reduce the investment portfolio to a little over $100 million (Table 1), an amount in the Committee's words "too small to afford security against possible future developments . . . It is clear, therefore, that the Committee must from now on give careful attention to meeting this gold problem, either by increasing its portfolio in anticipation of future developments, or by adopting other measures."[2] The minutes of the meeting state that the proposal was made "after consideration of the fact that somewhat lower interest rates ordinarily operate to check gold imports; in fact, that was one of the effects of purchases of securities made in 1924."[3]

Table 1

Holdings of United States Securities in Special Investment Account, January 5–August 31, 1927
(*$000*)

Date	Amount
January 5–March 9	200,000
March 16	176,324
March 23–April 27	201,344
May 4	199,794
May 11	136,312
May 18	152,112
May 25	188,477
June 1	222,447
June 8	316,050
June 15	244,256
June 22	250,448
June 29	250,498
July 6	250,498
July 13	250,498
July 20	265,214
July 27	265,998
August 3	286,498
August 10	299,393
August 17	317,956
August 24	326,031
August 31	353,467

SOURCE: *Fifteenth Annual Report of the Federal Reserve Board* (1928), p. 74.

When the Board met to consider the action of the Committee, Adolph Miller objected, giving as his reason that it would tend to produce inflation. The Federal Reserve Board voted nevertheless to postpone until the following day action on a resolution to bring the investment account up to $250 million. At a special meeting on May 13, Miller again protested that increased purchases might encourage speculation on the stock market. He argued that if such action was deemed desirable, it would be better to wait until the fall when it might stimulate business. He introduced a substitute motion to the effect that no further sales should be made, and that the previous motion to buy up to $250 million of securities should be disapproved. It failed to pass. Voting in favor were Miller, Governor Crissinger, and Cunningham; opposed were Secretary Mellon, Hamlin, Platt, James, and the Comptroller of the Currency.[4] Vice-Governor Platt then moved to approve the original resolution. All of the members voted in favor except Miller.[5] In June the Open Market Investment Committee bought an additional $100 million to offset an equal reduction in the reserves of the New York banks brought about by the purchase of gold by the Bank of France. The immediate impact of these purchases was observable in the short-term government securities market where the rate dropped from 3.33% in May to 3.07% in June. Other rates either moved up slightly or not at all. Securities in the Investment Account between April 27 and July 20, 1927, are set out in Table 1.

In its *Annual Report* for 1927, the Federal Reserve Board characterized the situation in the spring as somewhat uncertain, though by June it had crystallized into a "more clearly defined recession."[6] What clearly defined the recession, if anything, was not the 2% drop in production, for a much sharper dip had taken place between September and December, 1926. Neither was it the behavior of prices, for the wholesale price index had remained unchanged since April. The improvement in production during the first three months, however, did not bring any noticeable improvement in factory employment. The employment index declined about 4% between November, 1926, and January, 1927. The failure of factory employment to improve during the first and second quarters probably convinced some Federal Reserve officials that a business recession had begun. During the last four months of 1926 production had fallen 6% and factory employment 2%. This decline did not provoke the Federal Reserve to take any positive action. We can rule out the price index as a significant factor in determining the course of monetary policy in 1927. The increased ease in the money market during July and August occurred at a time when the wholesale price index was rising for the first time in almost two years.

The Priority of International Considerations

The principal problem of interpreting the easing action taken in July and August, 1927, is whether it was initiated to protect the international gold standard or to foster economic recovery at home. The Board was perhaps too ingenuous in supplying a rationale for its action when it wrote that gold imports to the United States since 1922 had the effect of hindering Federal Reserve Banks from making their credit policies effective:

> For this reason it has been a matter of great importance to the Federal reserve system to restore those influences upon international gold movements under which traditional central bank policies have been developed and tested by experience. Important among these influences are the relative levels of money rates in the different money markets and the exchange values of the currencies. The effectiveness of these factors in determining the flow of gold between countries depends primarily upon the existence of a fixed relationship between the value of currencies and gold. The year 1927 has witnessed important progress in reestablishing such relationship.[7]

Gold imports in the first quarter of 1927 had helped, not hindered, the credit policies of the Federal Reserve by bringing about a condition of ease in the money market when the future movement of production was still uncertain. But what generated alarm was the possibility that the gold inflow might continue.

Lester Chandler has already supplied us with an excellent description of the easy money policy initiated by Governor Strong and approved by most of the members of the Federal Reserve Board.[8] The now famous meeting in New York in early July between Governor Strong, Governor Norman of the Bank of England, Hjalmar Schacht, President of the German Reichsbank, and Charles Rist, Deputy Governor of the Bank of France, was the occasion for another of Strong's bold experiments in central bank cooperation. According to Hamlin Governor Strong failed to take the members of the Federal Reserve Board, with the exception of Governor Crissinger, into his confidence. Although Strong invited the Reserve Bank governors who were members of the Open Market Investment Committee to attend the formal sessions of the conference of central bank officials he neglected to invite the other Board members. Hamlin noted in his Diary on July 25:

Governor Crissinger told me that there was a formal conference in New York . . . the day after they left Washington. Governor Crissinger said all the Governors representing Open Market Committee were there, and others; that it was in every sense a formal conference altho Governor Crissinger did not know this until he got there; that Governor Norman unbosomed himself and told in what a critical position the Bank of England was as regards gold, that it must put up its discount rate to the injury of business, commerce etc., unless the Federal Reserve Bank of New York should reduce its rate. Governor Strong was very short sighted in ignoring the Federal Reserve Board (except Governor Crissinger) in this conference. It will give some of the members, already sore, a reason for continuing so.[9]

Governor Strong's behavior on this occasion indicated poor judgment in failing to keep the Board fully informed as to his intentions.

We know very little about the details of the agreement reached at this meeting. But some additional light is thrown on the outcome in two cablegrams between Governor Strong and Governor Norman sent on August 8 and 9, 1927, which refer to purchases of sterling bills by the New York bank:[10]

August 8, 1927

No. 32/27

I understand from Harrison who is away that the object of these purchases was to avoid gold coming here which the rise in sterling now accomplishes. Please advise just what is accomplished by our purchasing now.

STRONG

August 9, 1927

No. 122/27

ONE Your No. 32/27 paragraph 3. During our discussions in New York I remember there were two objects of these purchases

a) to avoid gold shipments from Europe to New York

b) to reduce gradually your funds now employed by us which funds were acquired simply to accommodate Moreau

TWO Certainly rise in sterling is now accomplishing first object but I think it desirable also to accomplish second.

NORMAN

In a letter to E. A. Goldenweiser dated October 13, 1949, Rist, who was present at the meeting in 1927, said:

You make a correct reference to the meeting of Governors in 1927. You probably know that the decision to lower the discount rate was taken directly in a conversation between Montagu Norman and Benjamin Strong, by themselves. All the rest of us had to do was to approve it later. Once more in this case English monetary policy was decisive for the rest of the world.[11]

Chandler's conclusion is substantially though not entirely correct:

There can be no doubt that the international situation was a major reason for the 1927 easy-money policy, that Strong was motivated by an altruistic concern for European countries, especially Britain, and that at least the timing of the policy was related to the conference with foreign central bankers in early July. But it would be grossly misleading to say that the policy was initiated solely because of the international situation and solely for altruistic purposes. Domestically, a mild recession seemed to have started.[12]

There are at least two objectionable aspects of his statement: the description of Strong's motives as altruistic, and the fact that the timing and magnitude of the purchases of securities might be explained as action to counteract the recession. To Strong as well as to Governor Norman the gold standard imposed certain responsibilities. Acting in accord with the so-called rules is not "altruism" even though it might not yield an immediate advantage. To interpret Strong's action as sheer "altruism" is to disregard his nostalgia for the gold standard apparatus and the traditional mechanisms of control.[13] What convinced at least some members of the Board that Strong's policy was correct was that it would redound immediately to the advantage of the United States by stimulating the demand for our farm crops in Europe. C. S. Hamlin at a Board meeting on September 6 attempted to explain his earlier vote by arguing that a reduction in New York rates relative to London "helped English purchasing power for our exports thus benefiting agriculture."[14] But he admitted that the underlying reason in the minds of the Board and the Open Market Investment Committee was an international one. He disapproved of this saying that he felt that the Board should not establish a rate "solely for International reasons such as this," and that rates should be reduced for "local reasons—a desire to help farmers move their crops; that while they might receive no benefit from such lower rates yet it made it possible for the banks to give them lower rates following such reductions."[15] According to Hamlin, James agreed with him but other members of the Committee felt that the farmers would not get lower rates. Of course, the main issue was not terms of credit to the farmers and Hamlin clearly recognized this. In his Diary on July 27 he penciled in the following remark: "CSH in speaking said he rested his opinion primarily on domestic grounds but he agreed with Governor Strong as to what he said on [the] foreign situation."[16]

It also seems clear that the only opposition to the policy arose over the possibility that it might encourage speculation in the stock market. But the view prevailed that this should not stand in the way of an otherwise desirable policy. The minutes of the meeting were read to the members and approved without objection. Included was the statement:

> The most important consideration at the meeting was undoubtedly the fact that the differential between the rates in New York and rates in London was not today sufficient to enable London, and therefore the rest of Europe, to avoid general advances in rates this autumn unless rates were lowered, and that the consequences of such high rates as would result in Europe would be unfavorable to the marketing of our export produce abroad and would have an adverse effect generally on world trade.[17]

Following the July 27 meeting of the Open Market Investment Committee, discount rate reductions from 4% to 3½% were announced by the Federal Reserve Bank of Kansas City on July 29; St. Louis on August 4; and Boston and New York on August 5. At first the Chicago Federal Reserve Bank refused to reduce its rate on the grounds that it was not necessary. Hamlin reports that Governor Crissinger wished to put in a rate of 3½% at Chicago on August 12 but he, Platt, and the Comptroller of Currency objected.[18] After the Chicago bank refused again to lower its rate on August 26, the Board held a special meeting on September 6 to consider the Chicago rate dispute. The Board voted four to three in favor of forcing Chicago to reduce its rate to 3½%. Governor Crissinger, James, Cunningham, and the Comptroller voted aye; Hamlin, Miller, and Platt were opposed.[19] Hamlin said that he "somewhat doubted its power to put in a uniform rate in order to help New York help the English situation."[20]

The controversy surrounding the conflict with the Chicago bank had far-reaching implications. It represents another important step, the first of which was asserting control over open market operations, in the evolution of the Board's influence over the instruments of monetary management. Hamlin surmised incorrectly that as a result of this incident Secretary Mellon called for the resignation of Governor Crissinger. In a cable to Norman, Governor Strong denied that Crissinger's resignation had anything to do with the Chicago rate controversy:[21]

No. 8827

September 16, 1927

Crissinger's decision to retire made before Chicago rate controversy arose and delay in announcement was due to necessity of awaiting President's and Mellon's return but was an unfortunate conjunction.

STRONG

Purchases of securities *followed* to make the new rates effective. Between July 27 and August 31 purchases amounted to $88 million. The response of open market rates was immediate. The rate on Treasury notes and certificates dropped from 2.96% in July to 2.7% in August. The sharpest break of all came in the rate on prime bankers acceptances which fell from 3.56% in July to 3.13% in August. The decline was sufficient to widen the interest rate differential between New York and London, to accelerate the outflow of funds, and to improve sterling exchange.

Thus the major goals of the easy money policy were achieved by the end of August. Member bank indebtedness, however, remained above the $400-million mark through November. Purchases of securities in September and October were just sufficient to offset the increase in currency in circulation. Rates remained fairly steady except for the abrupt increase in Treasury notes and certificates from 2.68% in September to 3.08% in October. Not only the timing of the decrease in discount rates and the increase in open market purchases but also their magnitude as well was determined by international considerations. There seems to be little doubt that the behavior of interest rates—not prices, not reserves, not the money supply—was the prime target variable of monetary policy.

Both production and factory employment continued to decline. Wholesale prices increased 3% between July and September and remained stable the rest of the year. Yet there was no further easing of rates; in fact there was some slight increase during November and December. The rate policy was confirmed by the Open Market Investment Committee on November 2. A preliminary memorandum prepared October 18, 1927, stressed the importance of maintaining the appropriate rate relationship with Europe to reduce the flow of gold to the U.S.[22] Governor Strong presented a report outlining the policies the Committee ought to pursue through March, 1928. He suggested that: 1) rates for money be maintained at about present levels; and 2) further gold imports be prevented. The following considerations he put forward to guide the Committee:

a) amount of borrowings for Federal Reserve Banks by Member banks
b) general level of market rates
c) movement of foreign exchange rates as an indication of possible gold imports.[23]

To effect these proposals he advocated offsetting gold movements by either sales or purchases of securities; for example, a temporary purchase of securities if money market rates tended to advance in the latter part of the year, and the sale of securities to offset the return flow of currency in January. The suggestion that gold exports should be offset by open market purchases was not inconsistent with maintaining the international gold standard. The so-called sterilization of gold exports was part of the policy of protecting the gold standard with a differential between rates in the United States and abroad.

To understand the behavior of the Federal Reserve, it's important to distinguish between two types of monetary action: 1) that undertaken to establish or to maintain the international gold standard intact, that is, to preserve a system whereby foreign currencies are kept convertible into gold; and 2) that dictated by the so-called "rules of the gold standard game." The former of these two considerations was overriding in determining monetary policy in 1924, 1927, and again later in 1931. (Fortunately the action taken in 1924 and 1927 coincided with the goal of domestic stability. Unfortunately the action taken to raise the rediscount rate in 1931 did not.) In both 1924 and 1927 Federal Reserve officials were confronted with the political necessity of not intentionally reproducing the violent swings of prices of the inflation-deflation cycle of 1919 and 1920. But at the same time they felt a strong commitment to European monetary reconstruction which meant in fact a return as soon as possible to a system of fully convertible gold currencies. It was the apparent conflict of these two objectives which led simultaneously to gold sterilization to isolate the domestic economy from the undesirable effects of gold flows and to open market purchases in 1924 and 1927.

The effects of the policy of credit ease were: member bank

reserves increased by about $140 million between May and December, 70% of which took place in November and December. Total member bank credit expanded $2.6 billion; $1 billion represented credit expansion in the fourth quarter alone. The increase for the year as a whole was divided about equally between loans and investments. Sixty per cent of the increase in investments was in other than U.S. government securities. Total loans at reporting member banks remained fairly constant through April, rose $265 million between May and August, and increased an additional $660 million during the final four months of the year. Of the total increase since September, approximately 70% represented an increase in loans on securities. There was a $200-million increase in security loans in December. This upsurge in bank lending was reflected in the advance of stock prices and security speculation. The advance in stock prices was sufficient to drive the dividend yield on stocks below the bond yield. The evidence is impressive that Federal Reserve credit supplied by open market purchases furnished the basis for the loans to the stock market as well as the advance in stock prices.

In conclusion, it is incorrect to chalk up this episode, as John K. Galbraith does, to an "act of generous but ill-advised internationalism."[24] Galbraith merely underestimates the strength of international considerations in determining monetary policy in the nineteen-twenties.

CHAPTER 9

The Stock Market Mania: 1928

DURING THE first week of January, 1928, President Coolidge made a totally unexpected announcement. He issued a statement to the press in which he said that, after conferring with Treasury officials, he was satisfied that there was nothing alarming about the speculative activity in the stock market. When asked by Governor Young about Coolidge's statement, Secretary Mellon replied that he could not remember any talk with the President about this matter.[1] Hamlin was worried that the President's remarks might encourage stock market speculation and necessitate an immediate rate increase. E. A. Goldenweiser advised the Federal Reserve Board on January 9 that although the situation was grave there was no evidence that speculation was interfering with either agriculture or commerce. Nevertheless, a meeting of the Open Market Investment Committee scheduled for New York on the following Friday, January 13, was changed to Washington, D.C., on the recommendation of Gates McGarrah, the New York Federal Reserve agent, who telephoned and said "there was dynamite in the situation and intimated [the] Board had better not go to New York or it might precipitate matters."[2] Members of the Federal Reserve Board expressed their willingness to approve the sale of securities in preference to raising the discount rate.

Their reluctance to raise immediately the rediscount rate to control stock market speculation can be explained by two important considerations:

1) The increase in the volume of bank credit brought about in 1927, though unusually large by comparison with previous years, had not been accompanied by a sizable increase in business activity. Industrial production in January was still substantially below the level of March of the preceding year, and wholesale prices declined slightly. Factory employment was lower than at any time since 1921. The fear of delaying or retarding the recovery was every bit as real as the fear of condoning the excesses of speculation. A memorandum prepared for the use of the Open Market Investment Committee, clearly in response to the problem, stated that the main question of monetary policy was "how the present credit expansion can best be controlled if possible without adversely affecting business."[3] Furthermore, because of the recent gold outflow, credit policy could be determined "much more independent of the European situation than was the case last summer."[4]

2) There was some question about the authority of the Federal Reserve to regulate the New York Stock Exchange unless it could be shown to be detrimental to commerce, business and industry. Senator Glass defended persuasively this point of view. Governor Young and C. S. Hamlin met with Glass on January 22 at which time Glass reportedly said that the Congress did not intend that the Federal Reserve should regulate the stock market unless it was affecting business adversely. The Board in his opinion had neither the power nor the duty to do so. He reiterated his earlier views (1919–20) that a slight increase in the discount rate would probably not affect the stock market and that the initiative for proposing rate changes rested with the individual Federal Reserve Banks unless the Board believed it was clearly wrong.[5] The influence Carter Glass exerted on monetary policy would be difficult to assess. It was perhaps greater in the design of new banking legislation than in the administration of monetary policy. Previously, he had been Secretary of the Treasury. In 1928, however, he exercised his influence as the most powerful member of Congress in matters pertaining to the Federal Reserve System and general banking and currency legislation. Hamlin merely echoed Glass' sentiments when he voted on January 24 to approve the application of the Chicago Federal Reserve Bank to increase rates. He explained his action thus:

he did not want to increase the danger of chilling the slight improvement in business for the mere sake of putting an end to New York speculation; that we should not overrule the judgment of the Chicago directors—who had the right to establish the rate—unless we were clearly satisfied that their judgment was wrong . . . that he regretfully had reached the conclusion to vote to approve the increase.[6]

Goldenweiser described the Board members' attitude to the Chicago rate increase in a confidential memorandum dated January 28, 1928. It provides us with an excellent cross-section view of the Federal Reserve Board with which to compare the evolution of Board policy at a later date:

The only one definitely in favor of the advance was Mr. Platt, who had been opposed to the reduction, and likes to see rates outside of New York above those in New York. Mr. Miller was rather inclined to oppose the advance at this time, but felt that since the question had been brought up by the Chicago Bank, there was not adequate reason to refuse approval . . . The Governor [Young] said that he would be willing to wait with rate advances, but in case a vote was taken today he would vote for it. Mr. Hamlin expressed his reluctance and yielded largely on his general principles of bank autonomy. The Secretary also was opposed to the advance because he felt that brokers loans were not sufficient reason for raising rates. Nevertheless, he did not want to oppose Chicago, and felt that rate advances would inevitably come before long, and that we might as well have them over with. He does not seem to think that it is very important, as rates to business men do not change much. Mr. Cunningham was very much excited—opposed the rate because he did not wish business penalized for excesses in the stock market, which had been caused to no small extent by the system's open-market policy. He stood out to the last; voted against the approval and asked for the privilege of filing a statement.[7]

George James who was absent favored the increase. What clearly emerges from Goldenweiser's account of the Board meeting is the obvious reluctance of individual Board members to approve an increase in rates at that time. The initiative came entirely from the Chicago Federal Reserve Bank. Bearing in mind the embarrassing episode with the Chicago bank in September, the Board understandably was unwilling to make another strong show of its authority.

The New York bank hesitated to raise its rate before February 3 because of an abnormal flow of funds from the interior of the country which had led to a decline in member bank indebtedness in spite of the sale of securities. The bank thought the increase in rates at other Federal Reserve Banks might stem the flow.

Sales of securities between January 12 and February 1, 1928, amounted to approximately $150 million. Further sales were discontinued in early February and did not resume again until the second week of April. The Open Market Investment Committee recommended on March 26 additional sales of securities to curb an unnecessary expansion of credit but not to increase discount rates. All of the appointed members of the Board approved including Governor Young, Platt, James, Cunningham, and Hamlin except Adolph Miller who argued correctly that sales of government securities would eventually necessitate raising the discount rate. Miller explained his negative vote as follows:

> 1) The absence of any evidence of expansion of borrowings for commercial purposes beyond what is seasonal and proper in character;
> 2) The uncertainty still characterizing the business outlook following the recent recession of the autumn and winter;
> 3) The adverse influence on business recovery that increased money rates may be expected to exert; and
> 4) The almost certain influence that further firming of money conditions such as is contemplated by the program of the Open Market Committee and a policy of further sales of securities to the open market may be expected to have in advancing money rates.
>
> I am of the opinion that the adoption or the approval by the Board of a policy of further firming money conditions will be inadvisable until the whole situation with respect to the probable future course of trade and industry is clearer. The present status of the stock exchange loan account of the banks is not, in my opinion, sufficient justification for a policy of further firming of money at this time.[8]

On April 18 the Federal Reserve Board met to consider the application of the Boston bank for an increase of rates to 4½%. The grounds given for requesting an advance were the increase in member bank indebtedness and a fall in the bank's gold reserve ratio—referred to as "local conditions." According to Hamlin, Miller said that he would never vote to control stock market speculation by an increase in the discount rate. Secretary Mellon replied: "he did not feel [that the] Board could overrule the Boston directors who expressly based their decision on the local situation."[9] When Mellon called for the vote, Miller, without explanation, voted to approve the motion! James alone dissented. Between March 26 and April 27 the Open Market Investment Committee sold $119 million of securities. By the end of May the securities in the special investment account amounted to only $82 million. At a governors' conference on May 1, Miller told the assembled governors that open market sales should be stopped and control exercised, if necessary, through the discount rate. Sales continued, nevertheless, until the middle of July after which the Committee withdrew from the market.

Effects of the Restrictive Policy

The impact of the Federal Reserve's restrictive policy of both security sales and discount rate increases during the first six months of 1928 is evident from the behavior of open market rates and the level of member bank indebtedness. Neither the money supply nor member bank reserves increased. Between January and June, 1928, the loss of $276 million of gold was approximately offset by a corresponding decrease in currency in circulation. Sales of securities of approximately $415 million plus the reduction in bills bought of $164 million explain the increase of member bank indebtedness of more than $500 million. In June member bank indebtedness exceeded $1 billion, a sum greater than at any time since 1921. Sixty per cent of the increase had occurred in April and May mainly as a result of a decrease in the gold stock of $128 million and security sales amounting to $158 million. Interest rates moved up slowly at first, then accelerated in April. The rate on new call loans to the stock market averaged 6.3% in June. Credit restriction affected only slightly the yield on government bonds which increased from 3.18% in January to 3.29% in June, hardly sufficient to exert strong pressure on the long-term market. The rate on the three-to-six-month Treasury notes and certificates in June was 3.9%—the highest level reached since November, 1923. Short term rates, excluding Treasury bill rates, were not high, at least before May, by comparison with the three previous years.

In a narrower sense one of the objectives at which System officials aimed was a slackening in the rate of expansion of bank credit used to support stock market speculation, namely brokers' loans. At the end of June credit extended to brokers by reporting member banks in New York City for their own account was some $300 million below the January figure; credit extended to brokers by out-of-town banks increased by only $100 million. However, loan funds supplied by non-bank lenders increased by $750 million. The mobilization of corporate cash balances resulted in a $440 million reduction in interbank deposits, one effect of which was to reduce required reserves.[10] Stock prices actually declined in February but increased an additional 15% before the end of May. (Table 3, Chapter 7, p. 103).

Total bank credit at all member banks declined by $550 million in the first two months of 1928 but expanded rapidly thereafter. Between March and June the increase totaled $1.3 billion, all but $160 million of which represented an increase in loans.[11] Excess reserves were negligible and cannot explain any part of the increase. Moreover, there was no reduction in the security portfolio. Adjusted demand deposits of member banks increased by only $49 million whereas net demand deposits, from which required reserves are computed, actually declined by $45 million. Cash in vault declined $77 million and capital accounts increased by some $221 million. It was these three factors that contributed to the expansion of bank credit in the form of loans: 1) a change in the composition of deposits, an increase of time deposits of $521 million; 2) a reduction in cash in vault; and 3) an increase in the capital accounts. Goldenweiser prepared a memorandum for his files at the end of September in which he attempted to summarize in his own mind the main effects of the restrictive monetary policy:

> The effect of higher money rates in this country has been to slacken somewhat the issue of securities and probably reduce the rate at which plant was over-expanding. Business has not suffered, except probably by some reduction in building—which is probably wholesome . . . No evidence that higher money rates have drawn money to New York, at least from other banks.[12]

He concluded that "It would seem that the general credit situation is in a sound condition."

A Leakage in the Apparatus of Control

A fundamental weakness in the apparatus of monetary control appeared during the first half of 1928. The credit restriction policy had the effect of increasing and not reducing the flow of funds to the stock market from non-bank lenders. During the first six months the increase amounted to $750 million. To use a metaphor of Sir Dennis Robertson, money began to well up from the earth on such a scale as to thwart the purposes of the monetary authority.[13] A less restrictive policy by the Federal Reserve might well have reduced the flow of funds from non-bank sources and increased the efficacy of the policy of direct pressure (moral suasion) to reduce bank lending to the stock market. Most critics have indicted the Federal Reserve for its timidity in not tightening sufficiently. It could equally well be maintained that Reserve officials tightened too much and too soon and that their principal fault lay in not initiating earlier the policy of direct pressure. There was no warrant at all on grounds of economic stabilization for the abrupt shift in policy of December, 1927. Neither the behavior of prices nor production indicated the necessity for a sudden about-face. Wholesale prices remained steady through April. Industrial production had increased 5% in February, but still fell short of the highs reached in the last quarter of 1926 and the first quarter of 1927. Factory employment in June, 1928, was lower than at any time since 1924. Therefore, there would appear to be little support for Chandler's statement: "The objective of promoting stability of prices and business activity justified the first move toward credit restriction in early 1928."[14] The Board attributed the poor showing of the employment index partly to improvements in productivity but mainly to the recession in industry. Considering that factory employment was lower than at any time during the preceding three years, there was no overriding reason on purely stabilization grounds for invoking a strong policy of restraint in the early months of 1928. The policy was effective in retarding any further improvement in the index of industrial production which remained unchanged between February and June. Factory employment continued low, and wholesale prices continued stable.

It was bank lending to the stock market rather than the performance of the economy as a whole that was behind the change in Federal Reserve monetary policy at the beginning of 1928. The Board acknowledged that the "firm money policy" of the System was adopted in view of the continued growth of security loans.[15]

Acceptance Rate Policy and Easier Money

New York advanced the discount rate from 4½% to 5% on July 13. Five days later the Open Market Investment Committee recommended no further sales of securities. The Board gave its unanimous approval. The special investment account was down to about $75 million. In July the Committee's attention was drawn by its staff to the problem of the effects of continued credit restraint on the level of business activity. Especially noteworthy is the attention paid to the length of the lag in monetary policy. The report on the credit situation prepared for the Committee stated:

If the present high interest rates are continued for several months it seems probable that business activity may be affected six months or a year from now. The evidence for this probability may be summarized briefly.

1) Charts of business volume and interest rates since 1900 show that continued high rates have almost invariably been followed by business declines after a lag of six months to a year.

2) A reasonable explanation is found in the restriction of new enterprises by high money rates.

a) High money rates discourage speculative building construction—as indicated by declines in building six months to a year following high money rates.

b) High money rates tend to discourage new financing, which would lead to business activity six months to a year distant.

3) Present business conditions may be peculiarly susceptible to restriction of credit.[16]

The report concluded, however, that high money rates had not been in effect long enough to have exerted any "noticeable adverse effects." The rates' purpose was presumably to check "unsound uses of credit" and was regarded merely as a temporary expedient.

The Committee was apparently influenced by these arguments, for they concluded that continuation of present high rates would not be "wholesome" and "the Reserve System should be prepared, if and when conditions warrant, to exercise its influence to modify these conditions."[17] In their opinion preparation for the autumn movement of crops would be an appropriate time to reconsider current policy.

The Committee repeated in August the views it had expressed in July. In a letter to George Harrison of the New York bank, Governor Young outlined the position of the Board with respect to open market purchases to ease credit:

The Board would not care to agree to the purchase of Government securities, except as a last resort. We understand from the discussion had with your committee that you favor easing through the bill market, if possible, and through the Government security market only if unavoidable. With this understanding, the Board approves the purchase of Government securities by the Committee but limits the amount to $100,000,000.[18]

On August 16 by a vote of three to two the Board approved purchases of $100 million only if necessary to offset seasonal requirements.[19] They preferred to acquire acceptances rather than government securities. According to Hamlin, Governor Harding of the Federal Reserve Bank of Boston believed that no more government securities should be purchased to ease the money market "but that acceptance rates should be lowered and acceptances bought; that the proceeds from sale of acceptances filter into the money market more slowly than purchases of Government Securities."[20] Although acceptance rates remained unchanged between August 22 and November 21 the volume of acceptances increased over $300 million. In November the total amount of bills bought was greater ($471 million) than at any time since March, 1920. The buying rate on acceptances, established on July 26, was 4½%—0.5% below the rediscount rate.

Most open market rates continued to rise in the third quarter, but there was substantial easing in the fourth. The rate of prime commercial paper after reaching a peak in September declined in October and November. The Treasury certificate rate dropped sharply from 4.7% in October to 4.26% in the two succeeding months. The rate on call loans, however, continued to advance. It averaged 8% on new loans in December. Between August and November member bank indebtedness declined $237 million but increased $368 million by the end of December. The increase in member bank borrowing in December was not however reflected in the behavior of open market rates. Purchases of acceptances leveled off in December. The increase in indebtedness was attributable mainly to the $300-million increase in currency in circulation. Member bank reserves increased only slightly. At the end of December, Miller informed the Board that the spread between the discount rate and the call loan rate was 10% and might tempt member banks to borrow for a profit. He proposed a resolution asking the banks what they intended to do about it. All of the Board members approved except Governor Young. The Comptroller did not vote.[21]

The industrial production index began to pick up again in July and rose 4½% during the third quarter. It remained fairly constant in the fourth quarter while wholesale prices declined slightly. Total bank credit of member banks declined in the third quarter but increased $750 million again in the fourth. Nevertheless, the overall rate of expansion was curtailed in the second half of 1928. Loans increased by $850 million. Investments decreased by $230 million. Adjusted demand deposits increased in the second half of the year but were slightly less than a year before. For the year as a whole total bank credit of member banks expanded $1.4 billion, 90% of which was in the form of loans. Non-bank lenders mobilized an equivalent amount for speculation in Wall Street. The expansion did not lead to an increase in the deposit component of the money supply. Member bank reserves were about the same at the beginning of the year as at the end.

During the second half of 1928, the Board relaxed its policy of continuous restraint. The effect of the System's acceptance policy was to ease credit conditions somewhat—perhaps by more than could be foreseen at the time. The Federal Reserve acknowledged that its reluctance to change the rate on acceptances after July 26 had the effect of easing credit in the last months of the year:

> In 1928 . . . the increase in acceptance holdings of the reserve banks during September, October, and November was sufficient to provide all of the autumn increase in the demand for funds, and in addition to permit member banks to reduce their borrowings, with the result that money rates declined for a time during a period of heavy seasonal demand for credit. The relatively favorable rates on acceptances as compared with other types of loans had resulted in an unusual growth of this form of bank credit, and the high money rates prevailing in the open market rendered them unattractive to investors.[22]

The Board concluded in the *Annual Report* for 1928 that there was no evidence that the increase in rates was having unfavorable effects on trade and industry. The Open Market Investment Committee was informed in November that the effect of the bill purchase policy was to ease credit by reducing member bank indebtedness by about $100 million at a time "when the demand for credit for speculative use is as strong as ever before."[23] And that it was too early to judge whether the business situation and the behavior of the stock market was "upon a sound economic basis" or represented "boom psychology."

No additional changes in either discount rates or open market operations occurred between August, 1928, and July, 1929. This period has been the source of considerable controversy. Why was the Board reluctant to approve an increase in rates? Seymour Harris concluded that one of the reasons was a fear of the consequences to Europe, namely the fear of jeopardizing the gold standard by creating domestic difficulties in some European countries as well as encouraging the inflow of gold.[24] Probably a more important reason was the alleged necessity to accommodate the seasonal demands of business. Harris criticized Reserve officials for apparently placing seasonal factors above "the requirements of controls."[25] Monetary authorities viewed the problem as one of satisfying seasonal demands without exerting additional pressure on either open market rates or the availability of credit. If reserves and not Federal Reserve credit had been the prime target, it would have been a simple matter of supplying the needed reserves through open market operations. Nevertheless, Reserve officials framed the question in terms of how much Federal Reserve credit would be required to accommodate seasonal demands. And then they decided on the technique for supplying it. If member bank indebtedness increased, they argued, this would put additional pressure on open market rates whereas lower bill rates might encourage the purchase of acceptances. Reserve authorities dismissed the first on grounds that it was inappropriate. The choice then lay between acquiring bills or government securities. They decided on July 26, 1928, to raise the rate from 4¼% on acceptances to 4½%, 0.5% below the discount rate which had been advanced to 5% on July 11. This decision was unfortunate because it gave the commercial banks the initiative in determining the quantity of bills presented to the Federal Reserve Banks. If the differential proved to be too wide, the Reserve Banks would acquire more bills than could be justified on purely seasonal grounds. In fact this is precisely what happened. A policy designed ostensibly to meet seasonal pressures had the effect of reducing the degree of pressure exerted on open market rates. The acceptance policy as it was administered turned out to be a policy of involuntary ease.

Why, then, did the Board prefer the purchase of acceptances to open market operations? The Board's preference for an acceptance rate policy was based upon a mistaken opinion. Some members, notably Hamlin and Miller, held the view that the method of injecting reserves determined the use to which the reserves were put. Governors Harding and Young held that the proceeds of acceptances seeped into the call money market much more slowly than the proceeds of security purchases. A lowering of bill rates, they maintained, cheapened credit to meet legitimate business needs but did not increase the flow of credit immediately to the stock market. Paul Warburg, who met with the Board on January 5, agreed with Governor Young.[26] Hamlin and Miller should have known better. Their persistence in the path of error, at least in

Hamlin's case when the same policy was pursued in the second half of 1929, was not due to ignorance. He reported a conversation which he had in June, 1929 with Deputy Governor Case of the New York Bank who, Hamlin said, insisted: "that whatever the source funds getting into the market were used by banks in the same manner, whether procured by bills or Government Securities."[27] The error once again discloses the failure of Board officials to recognize the crucial role of reserves and, indirectly, the money supply as one of the principal objects of monetary control. Furthermore, it reveals that faulty knowledge, not inept administration, was once again the source of the monetary strategy pursued.

CHAPTER 10

The Miller-Hamlin Policy of Direct Pressure: 1929

BY MID-1928 the monetary authorities found themselves hopelessly entangled in what can be called a classic monetary dilemma. That is, action to control stock market speculation was actually: 1) increasing, not decreasing, the supply of funds feeding the stock market; and 2) advancing open market rates to levels that might affect business adversely. The behavior of output, employment, and commodity prices provided little warrant for the restrictive policy begun in January. The purpose of Federal Reserve policy was clear enough—to control stock market speculation by controlling the flow of bank credit through sales of securities and increases in the rediscount rate, without hindering output. What was not adequately appreciated, however, was the effect of increasing open market rates, including the call money rate, on the supply of funds furnished by non-bank lenders. The volume of new funds flowing to the stock market amounted to about $2.6 billion between January, 1928, and September, 1929. The stream was continuous without any signs of letup in its rate of increase.

Recognition of this convinced at least one member of the Board that further tightening of rates would only prove futile. Hamlin wrote in his Diary on March 22, 1929, that "if a 6% rate would not check loans for others there was no reason, in [his] mind, for a rate increase."[1] This extraordinary mobilization of both idle and active balances to finance stock market speculation requires detailed investigation to determine how the demand for money was affected by stock market speculation. Corporate treasurers had the incentive not only to activate idle balances but also to economize the use of existing active balances. Without knowing the determinants of corporate cash balance behavior during this period, we cannot stipulate the consequences of a more restrictive policy on the supply of funds, particularly during the first six months of 1928. Would a more restrictive policy have simply increased further the funds supplied the market by non-bank lenders? Would a less restrictive policy have encouraged the banks to expand directly loans to brokers? Would a policy of direct pressure inaugurated a year earlier have been effective? We don't know. The answers to these questions, at least for the time being, must remain conjectural.

On January 3, 1929, the directors of the New York Federal Reserve Bank voted to raise the minimum buying rate on acceptances to 4¾%, 0.25% higher than the rate established on July 26, 1928. Governor Young of the Federal Reserve Board was angered by this action, not only because he disapproved of the increase, but also because he thought that the action required the prior approval of the Board in Washington.[2] Governor Harrison defended the New York bank's procedure, saying that it was the one followed for years without question or disapproval of the Board. Governor Young protested and referred Harrison to the Board's policy as set out in an X-Letter dated January 5, 1926.[3] But this incident is more significant because of the light it throws on the views of Governor Young. In a conversation with Goldenweiser on March 6, 1929, Governor Young had explained the role of monetary policy during the preceding six months and the reasons for his disapproval of the New York bank's action to raise acceptance rates:

> In the autumn and up to the end of the year, he [Young] was chiefly concerned in having credit remain reasonably cheap for business. In order to accomplish this he was in favor of extending credit freely through discounts at the prevailing rate and also was in favor of buying as many acceptances as possible. On January 3, the Governor thought that the New York bank gypped him by raising the bill rate contrary to his wishes and not letting him know about it until after it had been given out. He seems to think that things might have worked

better if the bill rate had not been advanced, in which I feel confident he is mistaken—that [the] higher bill rate has helped to work off the bill portfolio . . . In view of gold imports and the small volume of securities in the open market investment account, the liquidation of the bill portfolio has been particularly desirable. That, however, is my view and not his. He feels that everything that has been done since the turn of the year has been a part of a rate-raising program—the advance in bills was the first step. The Board's various warnings have been in the same direction . . . The Governor said that he still believed that events shape rates rather than rates influencing events. He said that I do not agree with him in that respect . . . I think that fundamentally what he has in mind is not that the Federal reserve banks can't do it, but that his instinct is that on the whole the Federal reserve banks will do best if they adjust themselves to events, rather than trying to shape them. I have sympathy with that position, but there are times when leadership is essential.[4]

Apparently Governor Young was relying upon the stock market to break itself without any active intervention on the part of the Federal Reserve. Opposed to this policy of doing nothing were the officers of the Federal Reserve Bank of New York and a majority of the Federal Reserve Board. The Open Market Investment Committee met on January 7, 1929; it decided that the investment portfolio should not be changed unless there was a decrease in member bank indebtedness sufficient to ease money market rates. The total amount of securities in the special investment account had not altered since November 12, 1928. A memorandum prepared for the use of the Committee identified three factors worthy of serious consideration in the event a policy change was contemplated: 1) the effectiveness of any action taken in controlling the unusually rapid expansion of credit; 2) the effect upon domestic business; and 3) the effect upon the world monetary situation and indirectly on world trade.[5] The committee was, therefore, not unmindful of the international consequences of rising open market rates in the U.S. *vis à vis* Europe.

Beginning in mid-January Adolph Miller seized the initiative within the Federal Reserve Board by formulating the now famous policy of "direct pressure," that is, a policy of moral suasion to prevent an increase in member bank indebtedness for the purpose of financing Wall Street speculation. He submitted a letter on January 24 to the Board on the proper use of the credit facilities of the Federal Reserve Banks.[6] After much discussion and subsequent revision, the letter was approved by the Board and circularized to all the Federal Reserve Banks on February 2. In it the Board described its reaction to the increased activity in the stock market, as follows:

1) The firming tendencies of the money market which have been in evidence since the beginning of the year—contrary to the usual trend at this season—make it incumbent upon the Federal reserve banks to give constant and close attention to the situation in order that no influence adverse to the trade and industry of the country shall be exercised by the trend of money conditions, beyond what may develop as inevitable.

2) The extraordinary absorption of funds in speculative security loans, which has characterized the credit movement during the past year or more, in the judgment of the Federal Reserve Board, deserves particular attention lest it become a decisive factor working toward a still further firming of money rates to the prejudice of the country's commercial interests.

3) The resources of the Federal reserve system are ample for meeting the growth of the country's commercial needs for credit, provided they are competently administered and protected against seepage into uses not contemplated by the Federal reserve act.

4) The Federal reserve act does not, in the opinion of the Federal Reserve Board, contemplate the use of the resources of the Federal reserve banks for the creation or extension of speculative credit. A member bank is not within its reasonable claims for rediscount facilities at its Federal reserve bank when it borrows either for the purpose of making speculative loans or for the purpose of maintaining speculative loans.

5) The board has no disposition to assume authority to interfere with the loan practices of member banks so long as they do not involve the Federal reserve banks. It has, however, a grave responsibility whenever there is evidence that member banks are maintaining speculative security loans with the aid of Federal reserve credit. When such is the case the Federal reserve bank becomes either a contributing or a sustaining factor in the current volume of speculative security credit. This is not in harmony with the intent of the Federal reserve act, nor is it conducive to the wholesome operation of the banking and credit system of the country.[7]

This letter reveals no dogged adherence to the real-bills doctrine, though, of course, there is still evidence of its influence. Paragraph 4 states that the Federal Reserve Act does not stipulate the use of resources for the extension of speculative credit nor that a member bank is "within reasonable claims" when it borrows for such a purpose. The Board did not say that Federal Reserve credit will *always* be denied to banks who borrow to make speculative loans. That such credit was not in fact denied is only too apparent from the Federal Reserve's behavior between 1925–28. The crucial proviso appears at the end of the second paragraph. Activity in the stock market "deserves particular attention lest it become a decisive factor working toward a still further firming of money rates to the prejudice of the country's commercial interests." The Board's chief concern was the high level of open market rates and their effects on business activity and not the quality of credit *per se*. They make it quite plain that anxiety in January, 1929, was due to the "firming tendency of the money market" brought about by the increased demands for speculative credit. What they failed to realize was how much their own policies were contributing to the restraint. The Board was extremely reluctant to penalize legitimate business by high open market rates which they believed might very well react unfavorably on industry and trade. Yet, they did it anyway!

The Board was sharply divided over the merits of the policy initiated by Miller. Governor Young preferred to do nothing. Vice-Governor Platt thought that control through the discount rate would be more effective. Secretary Mellon was not very enthusiastic about an increase in rates, but he thought an increase was inevitable. However, James, Cunningham, and Hamlin were strong supporters of the policy of direct pressure. Goldenweiser described Cunningham's position as follows:

> Mr. Cunningham is keenly aware of the bad effects of high rates on business. He talks about a staggering blow and remembers the bonds he lost in 1920. On the whole, he makes the best statement for moderation, because he frankly thinks in terms of the hardship of high rates for the small business man. He refuses to attack the problem from any point of view except that.[8]

Governor Harrison told the Board members on February 5 that the directors of the New York bank would prefer not to increase the discount rate until all other means of control had been tried, namely an increase in the bill rate and conversations with member banks to prevent excessive borrowing. He said that he had no recommendation to make at that time, but that it was a very serious period in our credit history. When he turned to discuss the Board's letter of February 2, he stated that the New York bank had done about as much as it was practical to do through direct action and that the continuation of such a policy would have little effect on the total volume of credit outstanding. It would only lead to a "shuffling process" whereby loans would be shifted among banks and securities sold.[9] Hamlin relates that Governor Harrison informed the Board on February 7 of the New York bank's intention to advance the discount rate. Hamlin thought that all of the Board members except Governor Young and possibly Platt were opposed to any rate increase at that time.[10]

Immediately after the Board dispatched its letter to all Federal Reserve Banks initiating the policy of direct pressure, Governor Norman of the Bank of England visited New York and Washington to stress the seriousness of maintaining the international gold standard in the face of relatively high rates in New York resulting, he thought, primarily from Wall Street speculation. In his opinion New York should have advanced rates more quickly for the express purpose of breaking the market so that rates would go down again shortly thereafter. The hidden assumption in this line of reasoning was, of course, that the stock market could be broken without precipitating a serious recession in business. Some Board members, including Hamlin and Governor Young, were convinced that Harrison had a commitment to Norman to engineer a rate increase, but Goldenweiser dismissed the idea of any such agreement. Rather he thought that Harrison simply "desired to play the world game."[11] On this occasion, as in the past, the policy which the New York bank thought suitable on domestic grounds did not conflict with international considerations. Unlike before, however, the Board not only rejected the cure recommended by the New York bank but also rejected Norman's view that the stock market could be broken without bringing on a serious recession in business. Board members did not ignore the international consequences of their actions, for in the *Federal Reserve Bulletin* for April, 1929, they stated the Board's desire "to see money rates at a lower general level has been due in part to its realization of the bad effects of continued high money rates on domestic business, and in part to its unwillingness to draw gold from abroad, with consequent advances in money rates in other countries, some of which are suffering from industrial depression."[12] The key to the Board's policy of direct pressure was its desire for a mild liquidation of bank credit to the stock market which might reduce the pressure on open market rates.

Reviewing Federal Reserve policy many years later, Adolph Miller contended that the Board's policy during the first half of 1929 was successful, and he advanced three reasons to support his appraisal: 1) between February and May, 1929 brokers' loans by reporting member banks declined $650 million; 2) money rates increased sharply; and 3) stock prices fluctuated within a comparatively narrow range. He insisted that the Board was not guilty of faulty judgment and that the Congress had in passing the Banking Act of 1933 ratified Board policy during the early months of 1929.[13] This is indeed a curious and mistaken logic implying that congressional action of some sort at a later date constitutes ratification of an administrative board's decisions.

C. S. Hamlin, who was also a strong advocate of direct pressure, was convinced in late March that the policy was working and was having the desired success. On March 22 he entered the following in his Diary:

> CSH pointed out that, while Brokers loans had increased 125 millions since February 7, the total New York discounts had fallen off 70 millions and the reserve ratio had increased from 76 to 83%. This CSH said showed that direct pressure was working.[14]

On the same day he said that Governor Harrison of the New York bank informed the Board that they might ask the Stock Exchange to limit arbitrarily credit to brokers but that he (Harrison) personally was opposed to such a move at that time. Hamlin stated further: "We left no doubt in Governor Harrison's mind the policy of direct action without any increase of discount rate must go on for the present at least."[15] Both Governor Young and Secretary Mellon agreed with Miller and Hamlin's policy of direct action but thought discount rates would have to be raised eventually. Opinion, however, within the System was not unanimous. Frederic H. Curtis, chairman and Federal Reserve agent of the Reserve Bank of Boston, filed a report which stated that conditions in New England were worse rather than better as a result of direct action. On April 19 Hamlin and Miller again reaffirmed their belief in the Board's policy and pointed out the decline in Federal Reserve credit by $300 million as evidence. Hamlin admitted that the decline may have been due to gold imports and the decrease in currency in circulation. Miller even stated what kind of evidence he felt would refute the case for direct pressure. He mentioned specifically an increase in Federal Reserve credit and a rise in the ratio of loans for speculative purposes to commercial loans. The reduction in Federal Reserve credit according to Hamlin pointed to a reduction and not an increase in rates unless it was the duty of the Board to liquidate drastically the stock market. Neither Hamlin nor Miller saw the function of the Board as extending to the regulation of non-bank lending. The control of Federal Reserve credit was the immediate target variable of monetary policy. As long as Federal Reserve credit declined, there was no justification for an advance in rates![16]

Galbraith's colorful description of Federal Reserve policy during the early months of 1929 is seriously misleading and scarcely does it justice. He castigates System officials for not doing anything on the grounds that they didn't want to.[17] Of course, what the Board did might be described as doing nothing but the charge that they did not want to act to curb stock market speculation can not be supported. They might be charged with excess enthusiasm for the wrong policy, but any fault in their behavior arises out of their lack of knowledge, not their lack of purpose. Galbraith dismisses the whole episode with a quip: "Finally the Board decided to write a letter and issue a press release. It could do no less."[18] They refused to do more because they were convinced their policy of direct pressure was a success. One is compelled to argue that in their zeal to pursue a policy of direct pressure, they glued their eyes to the wrong gauge.

During the first six months of 1929 the net increase of bank credit at member banks was negligible. Loans and investments declined by $290 million during the first quarter and increased by $320 million in the second. Loans went up by $500 million while investments declined by approximately $470 million. Reserves fell by $70 million, and member bank indebtedness increased by over $100 million. Two hundred million dollars of gold flowed in, but this was not sufficient to offset the huge decline in bills purchased of $375 million. Hence, the increase in the volume of rediscounts and the decline in reserves. Open market rates increased appreciably. The rate on prime commercial paper advanced from 5.38% in January to 6% in June. The rate on Treasury certificates and notes moved up only slightly but varied within the period between 4.39% and 5.09%. The yield on government bonds continued to rise slowly. Call money rates rose rapidly. Between January and March call money rates increased by almost 3 percentage points, the day-to-day variation being much greater.

It is perfectly apparent that the policy of direct pressure inaugurated in February failed to prevent the continued rise in open market rates. If anything, it probably tended to raise them further. Stock prices, however, remained fairly stable. The index of stock prices was lower in June than it was in January, and brokers' loans for the banks' own account and for out-of-town banks declined a total of $525 million. But the decline in brokers' loans at banks was offset by a corresponding increase in non-bank lending of approximately the same amount.

The Dispute with the New York Bank

The opposition of the New York bank to the Board's policy of direct pressure was persistent and unrelenting. At the time of the Board's announcement of the new policy Governor Harrison said that the directors of his bank did not favor an immediate increase in the discount rate. Instead they preferred to exhaust the other alternatives first, that is, to increase the bill rate and to admonish those banks whose records showed excessive borrowing.[19] However, Governor Harrison and the other executive officers probably desired an immediate increase in the discount rate.

At the beginning of January the New York bank had increased the minimum buying rates on bills to encourage the seasonal runoff in its bill portfolio. They repeated this action on four successive occasions, increasing the buying rate from 4½% on January 1 to 5⅜% on March 25. The immediate effect was to reduce the bill portfolio by the end of March by an amount $150 million less than in the same month of the preceding year. The results, therefore, were equivalent to a similar amount of sales of U.S. government securities. This action to raise bill rates represented a positive program to restrict credit while operating under the Board's restraint of no increases in the discount rate and while the policy of "direct pressure" was in effect.

The controversy between New York and Washington did not break out openly, however, until February 14. Governor Harrison telephoned Washington saying that the directors of the New York bank had unanimously established a 6% rate subject to Board approval. Board members wanted to delay action until the following day, but the directors informed the Board through Harrison that they would not leave the New York bank until the Board acted one way or the other. Hamlin described this dramatic confrontation as follows:

> Then Governor Harrison said his directors were going to give out a public statement of the action of his Board. Governor Young read him regulation X4140, August 22, 1924 of Board forbidding this and saying if the Directors did this they must do it on their own responsibility . . . Finally Governor Young suggested that we disapprove the

application at once. The members did not want to do this as [they] felt New York had no right to try to impose a condition of immediate decision. Finally at about 6:45 P.M. the Board voted to disapprove action and stated that the existing 5 per cent rate was to remain in force. *All* voted aye. I feel that [the] New York directors felt that they were bigger men than old Grant and thought they could bluff the Board into a favorable decision. The Board however called their bluff and taught them a lesson they never will forget.[20]

The Board was unanimous in disapproving the New York bank's request. Even although Platt and Governor Young voted to disapprove, they both stated explicitly that increases in rates were only a matter of time.

Throughout March, April, and May the Board continued to reject a barrage of requests for discount rate increases on the part of the New York bank. By far the largest number of requests originated with New York, but intermittently the Philadelphia, Chicago, and Boston banks petitioned for changes. These were all promptly rejected. The grounds for denying the requests remained the same: direct pressure was working successfully. Governor Harrison attempted to persuade Secretary Mellon of the necessity for a change in rates. He recounted a telephone conversation with Undersecretary of the Treasury Ogden Mills on April 25 in which there was a veiled threat if the New York bank did not get its way:

I pointed out that while I hoped and would use every effort to persuade our various directors not to resign, thinking that would be most unfortunate at this time, nevertheless there would come a time, after this present episode had been settled, when some of the directors would possibly consider resigning, in the belief that their services and judgment is [sic] being more or less arbitrarily thwarted by a relatively small minority in Washington.[21]

But Secretary Mellon by that time had already been persuaded that an increase in rates was necessary.

Opposition within the Board to the Miller-Hamlin policy of direct action developed slowly. Vice-Governor Platt supported the policy until March 20 after which he voted in favor of rate increases for New York; Secretary Mellon joined him on April 18. Finally on May 16 Governor Young voted to approve a rate increase. None of these men ever had very much faith that moral suasion could do the job alone, but they were willing to experiment and to await the results. On the other side Miller, Hamlin, and Cunningham remained firmly convinced that the policy of direct pressure was working well. James and the Comptroller of the Currency voted with the majority. By the last week in May, however, the stage was set for a compromise.

On May 22 Governor Harrison and Gates McGarrah, Federal Reserve agent, went to Washington to discuss the rate controversy with the Federal Reserve Board. They told the Board that because of the policy of direct action member banks in New York City were very reluctant to borrow from the Federal Reserve Bank for any purpose, preferring instead to pay 7% for outside funds. The two men recommended advancing the discount rate immediately to 6% with an understanding between the member banks and the Federal Reserve Banks that legitimate demands made upon them would be accommodated.[22] According to Hamlin both men maintained that a Federal Reserve Bank could not refuse to accommodate a member bank whose reserves were depleted by security loans to customers which in effect constituted a denial of the validity of the Board's policy of direct pressure. Thinking ahead to autumn, they suggested an easing program towards the end of the summer either through security purchases or lowering of the bill rate. Adolph Miller said that if he approved a 6% discount rate it would only be with the understanding that the bill rate would be lowered by July.[23]

The following day, May 23, the Board again denied New York's request for an advance in the discount rate. During the remainder of the month both Board members and officials of the New York bank discussed among themselves the necessity for a compromise. McGarrah wrote to Governor Young on May 31 outlining the views of the New York directors:

> It is the belief of the directors of the bank that the Federal Reserve Board policy of seeking the control of credit without an increase in the discount rate and otherwise as generally understood, has created much uncertainty throughout the country, and that the bringing of the Federal Reserve Board and this bank into harmony with respect to a program which will remove uncertainty is essential to the restoration of confidence and the development of a situation where a relaxation of credit in the interest of the country as a whole may be more quickly permitted. They believe that at the moment the agreement upon a mutually satisfactory program is far more important than the discount rate.
>
> In view of recent changes in the business and credit situation, we believe that a rate change now without a mutually satisfactory program might only aggravate existing tendencies.
>
> With this in view, and the interest of trade, industry, and agriculture, we believe that it may soon be necessary
>
> 1) To establish a less restrictive discount policy in order that

member banks may more freely borrow for the proper conduct of their business.

2) To correct the widely understood intimation of the Federal Reserve Board that collateral loans are not a proper function of legitimate banking.

3) To be prepared to increase the Federal Reserve bank portfolios if and when any real need of doing so becomes apparent.[24]

He concluded by saying that the New York directors would refrain from any rate action until some agreement could be reached on future policy.

The Board met on June 1 to consider the advisability of reducing the extent of direct pressure and initiating a policy of gradual ease to prepare for the regular seasonal increase in credit demands. Miller and Hamlin advocated an increase of $100 million in Federal Reserve credit through bill purchases. Miller argued that if the $100 million reduced the volume of member bank indebtedness, the 5% discount rate was adequate. If this amount did not, he favored an increase in Federal Reserve credit.[25] The last was, of course, a *non sequitur*. Bill purchases, like purchases of government securities, add initially to excess reserves, and the net addition may be employed either to take down rediscounts, to increase excess reserves or to act as a base for further credit expansion. Miller's confusion on this point is difficult to explain. Hamlin expressed similar confusion. They apparently thought that Federal Reserve credit injected into the bill market flowed through only one pipeline to satisfy the "legitimate" needs of business. The error stems from their failure to appreciate the relationship between reserves and bank credit.[26] As noted earlier, Case, deputy governor of the New York bank, had explained to Hamlin in June that the use to which funds were put was independent of the source of reserves, but obviously it made no impression on him. All of the Board members, with the exception of Governor Young, approved the easing action in a straw vote.[27]

The Board invited some of the New York bank directors to a meeting in Washington on June 5 at which time Governor Harrison surmised that there was no immediate likelihood of an increase in the discount rate. The discussion was taken up mainly with the necessity for some easing action at the time of the autumn movement of crops. The Board's reply to McGarrah's letter reaffirmed their belief in the efficacy of the policy of direct action, and in the event of a mid-year increase in the demand for bank credit they favored:

a temporary suspension of a rigid policy of direct pressure, which, however, should not be abandoned, but rather tempered in order to permit member banks that have not found it practicable to readjust their position in accordance with the Board's principle, to avail themselves of the rediscount facilities of the Federal Reserve banks for the purpose of avoiding, as far as possible, any undue strain or any unnecessary increase in the cost of credit in meeting the seasonal needs of agriculture, industry and commerce.[28]

They preferred easing through bill purchases if the volume of member bank indebtedness became excessive.

Following the Board's letter dated June 12, the immediate course of action pursued by the Federal Reserve Bank of New York was to allow the member banks to rediscount more freely than during the period when the Board's direct pressure policy was in effect.

In early August Harrison appeared before the Board and recommended an easing policy which combined an increase in the discount rate with purchases of either bills or securities. He explained that raising the rediscount rate and leaving the bill rate unchanged to ease credit was not absurd. The high discount rate would lead banks to repay their indebtedness, and the disparity between rates would encourage the flow of bills into the System.

At a meeting of the governors of the Federal Reserve Banks on August 7, Governor Young introduced among several alternative courses of action the possibility of an increase in the rate in New York and a simultaneous lowering of the bill rate. According to Goldenweiser seven or eight of the governors were in favor while Governors Seay, Black, and Martin were definitely opposed. Of those governors who approved they did so with the understanding that there would be no immediate rate change outside of New York. Goldenweiser's description of the attitude of the individual Board members is revealing:

James and Cunningham were against a rate advance. Miller was willing to have the rate go up in New York, provided the other banks would not advance it; the Governor was in favor . . . and Hamlin appeared to be yielding. It was not clear how Pole [the Comptroller of the currency] and Mellon stood and I was a little surprised at the Governor saying that the majority of the Board were in favor of doing nothing, because I thought he could get a majority, since Platt could always be counted on for a rate advance.[29]

The next day all of the governors approved the plan except Governor Black of the Atlanta Federal Reserve Bank. Goldenweiser summed up the proceedings as follows: "The net result is a loss of leadership by Miller to Young, a great victory to Harrison and a brighter prospect for effective system policy."[30]

On August 8 the Board approved Miller's resolution to allow New York to advance its discount rate to 6% and to reduce the bill rate from 5¼% to 5⅛%. The rate changes went into effect the next day but only at the New York bank. Hamlin was not willing to admit that the Board had backed down, for he wrote in his Diary:

> After the vote CSH said the Board had not reversed itself; that direct action had merely been suspended toward [the] end of June; that sole reason why Board had not before this increased discount rates at New York, was for fear of penalizing business; that this fear, according to testimony of Dr. Miller himself, had ended . . .[31]

Between August 7 and October 23, the Federal Reserve Banks purchased $300 million of acceptances, more than in any corresponding period since 1922. Since currency in circulation and U.S. government securities remained virtually unchanged, the large volume of bills purchased enabled the banks to reduce their indebtedness by approximately $160 million and to add $64 million to their reserve balances. Although the rate on prime commercial paper increased from 6.13% to 6.25% in September, Treasury certificates and notes witnessed a marked drop from 4.7% in August to 4.37% in October.

The expansion of bank credit of all member banks was sharply curtailed during the first nine months of 1929. There was a $300-million decline in the first quarter and a $500-million increase in the second and the third, the net increase amounting to only $200 million for the entire period. In the two latter quarters, loans expanded by over a billion dollars. Securities decreased by $700 million, $430 million of which represented government securities. One of the unanticipated effects of the policy of ease established in August was to counteract the natural tightening effect of security liquidation by the banking system. In the second quarter member banks sold $300 million of government securities. The rate on Treasury certificates and notes increased from 4.8% in April to 5.09% in May, but in June it returned to its former level in April. The same pattern, except at a lower level, is observable in the third quarter. At the end of September rates were 0.5% below the previous peak reached in May. Presumably the banks were able to shift from securities to loans without the risk of incurring serious capital losses.

Two aspects of Federal Reserve monetary policy during the 1928–29 episode stand out clearly from our description: 1) the errors in the knowledge of Federal Reserve officials about how monetary policy works; and 2) the weaknesses in the technical apparatus of control. Members of the Federal Reserve Board failed to appreciate adequately the relationship between call money rates, open market rates, and the response of the non-bank lenders. System officials simply did not recognize any responsibility for the behavior of the supply of credit flowing from non-bank sources. Moreover, many officials did not understand that the method of injecting reserves did not determine the use to which reserves were put. Hence their confusion over security purchases versus lowering bill rates as a method of meeting an additional demand for bank credit. Failure of the monetary authorities to seriously consider using selective credit controls and credit rationing to cut down stock market speculation was more a defect in knowledge than a defect in character.

CHAPTER 11

The Aftermath of the Stock Market Collapse: 1929–1932

"The stock market went all to pieces yesterday."
CHARLES S. HAMLIN

Clearing Away the Debris

ON THE morning of October 29, before the Stock Exchange Clearing Committee announced the call loan rate, the Federal Reserve Bank of New York communicated its willingness to purchase immediately some $100 million of government securities to alleviate money market strain. These purchases which actually amounted to $132 million were effected without the prior approval of the Board and outside the System's regular Open Market Investment Committee account. Governor Harrison disclosed later that he made the decision to acquire securities at 3 A.M. after consultation with a "few" directors of the New York bank.[1] This was done partly for psychological reasons and partly to prevent the tightening of money while stock exchange loans were transferred to many New York banks.[2] Banks and individuals in the interior of the country had withdrawn money at call from the New York Stock Market. Upon learning of Harrison's decision, the reaction of the

Federal Reserve Board in Washington was less than enthusiastic. Adolph Miller was indignant and said that the banks should have been forced to rediscount, and C. S. Hamlin said he "inclined to agree" with Miller but excused the New York bank on grounds that it was a critical emergency.[3] Nevertheless, the majority of the Board favored a rediscount policy of "liberality" and quick action and advised Governor Young to inform each Federal Reserve Bank of the Board's decision. Only Board members Cunningham and James expressed serious reservations about this policy, and they both urged caution. The Board did not contemplate any further action at that time.

The initiative for additional open market purchases did not come from the Board in Washington but from Governor Harrison and the New York bank. He entreated the Board to reduce the high level of member bank indebtedness by purchasing $200 million of government securities immediately. The Board denied his request and granted the Open Market Investment Committee only emergency or stand-by authority. However, between October 30 and November 20 the Committee purchased securities at the rate of $25 million a week, operating under the old instructions approved by the Board on September 24. Again on November 25 Harrison repeated his request for authorization to purchase $200 million of securities. On this occasion he added, perhaps as a veiled threat, that if the Board agreed to his request the New York bank would not buy securities for its own account as it had done on October 29 and 30 without obtaining their prior approval. Since the Open Market Investment Committee did not have a formal legal status, the ultimate jurisdiction over the operations of the Committee had not been settled. Board members sanctioned the request in a narrow four-to-three vote—Cunningham, James, and Miller voting no.[4] Together these three board members formed a strong minority who consistently opposed easing action by means of open market operations. Although purchases during the month of December amounted to $155 million, no additional purchases were made thereafter until the second week in March, 1930. Member bank indebtedness declined in November about $80 million from the previous high attained in the final week in October, but it still remained over $900 million. During the second half of November, member bank reserves decreased by $232 million. For the month as a whole, the decline was about equal to the increase for the week overlapping the crash.[5]

Federal Reserve action in December brought down the level of rediscounts from $912 million on November 27 to $632 million on December 31, a reduction of $280 million. The amount of member bank indebtedness was still some $265 million higher than it was during the easy money episode of May–August, 1927, and about $400 million above the corresponding amount during the 1924 easy money period.

The response of the System between October 29 and December 31 can be divided roughly into two phases. During the first phase the New York bank on its own initiative acquired government securities, and the Federal Reserve Board endorsed a liberal discount policy primarily to ensure orderly liquidation of stock market credit. The rapid withdrawal from the stock market of funds supplied by non-bank lenders created a vacuum which, to avoid a banking crisis and the shutdown of the stock market, the Federal Reserve stepped in and filled. The New York bank reduced the discount rate from 6% to 5% on November 1 and to 4½% on November 15. This action taken by itself did not represent any substantial easing. It is true that open market rates broke sharply in October and declined significantly through December. But it would be an exaggeration to attribute the marked decline in open market rates either to the relatively small amount of securities purchased or to the reduction in discount rates. More probably the decline was the consequence of the drastic reduction in the demand for credit for speculative purposes.

The first phase of the postcrash policy ended when the Open Market Investment Committee and the Federal Reserve Board finally approved easing credit through open market operations. The Board shifted its attention from the problem of preventing a banking collapse to the problem of counteracting the recession. The Board's response to the stock market crisis was in the classic tradition, and purchases of securities in November did not mean a change in policy, only continuation of an earlier policy. It is indeed doubtful whether combating the recession gained the attention of the Board members before the end of November. They rejected Harrison's proposal to acquire $200 million in the early part of November and, even when approval was finally given, the Board was divided sharply on the merits of the policy. If combating the recession had been uppermost in their deliberations at an earlier stage, it is difficult to explain their reluctance to have acted sooner or more aggressively.

Although the index of industrial production had fallen 6% between June and October, factory employment remained high. The precipitous fall in production did not take place until November and December. The index dropped 12% in November and 8½% in December. The decision to purchase $200 million of securities was made, therefore, before the end of November and without knowledge of the extent of the decline of industrial activity. Hamlin had recorded in his Diary on October 29 that both he and James had expressed the fear that the stock market crash "would bring about a real business depression but the others did not seem to think so"; but neither pressed the point further.[6] There was no comparable decline in industrial production during a single month since the establishment of the Federal Reserve System, not even in 1920. Hence, there was no previous experience by which the Board could judge the importance of the event. The Board's response in December was not analogous to its response in 1924 and 1927 because the magnitude and timing of Federal Reserve action on those two previous occasions was the result mainly of international considerations and not the severity of the recession at home. The improvement of production in January and its see-saw behavior through May provided ample reason for regarding the adjustment of business activity as comparable with the 1924 and 1927 downturns. There was no specific reason for viewing it otherwise. It is indeed tempting to contend that the further large reduction in member bank indebtedness in January was entirely fortuitous and resulted from the more than normal inflows of currency in circulation. Currency in circulation declined $351 million and rediscounts fell $225 million. Part of the increase in reserves offset the decline of $134 million in bills purchased and gold exports. Nevertheless, the net reduction in indebtedness at a time when the production index turned upwards engendered skepticism among the Reserve Bank governors about the merits of a more vigorous policy of "affirmative ease" advocated by Governor Harrison.

On January 28, the Open Market Policy Conference met and voted to continue the status quo; that is, to refrain from further purchases of government securities. Eight out of the eleven governors opposed Harrison's policy of affirmative ease. However, they did not object to lower bill rates to accommodate business. Most of the governors of the individual banks thought that further loan liquidation was desirable and that the Federal Reserve should not intervene to hasten the reduction of money rates which in their judgment would follow of their own accord. Governor Norris of the Philadelphia Federal Reserve Bank explained the majority view as follows:

The majority opinion was that what has already been done has set in motion a trend which should result in lower rates. Between a reduction of discounts and large purchases of securities, and a reduction of rates to business there is always a lag and that lag is likely to be greater at this time because the appetite of the bankers has been whetted during recent months and they are slower about coming down.

We (speaking here for the majority opinion) feel we should not interfere in that movement either in the direction of halting it or attempting to expedite it, unless the situation clearly calls for some action and we cannot see that it does. On the contrary, we feel it is better that the situation should clear up further, that the extent and duration of this recession should be more ascertainable than at the present moment, and that it is inexpedient for us to exhaust at the present time any part of our ammunition in an attempt to stimulate business when it is perhaps on a downward curve and we had better wait until we feel that we have reached a stable basis when the administration of some stimulant may have a distinct and good effect rather than to exhaust our ammunition now in what may be perhaps a vain attempt to stem an inevitable recession.[7]

The majority rejected the view expressed in the preliminary report to the Open Market Investment Committee, drawn up by officials of the New York bank, that credit had not been eased sufficiently to encourage business enterprise. Short-term rates received a disproportionate amount of attention to the neglect of mortgage and bond rates.

When the Board met two days later they accepted the Committee's proposal and moved to approve a 3¾% bill rate. James and Cunningham voted no, and Miller abstained. When asked by Secretary Mellon if he did not believe in some easing, Miller, according to Hamlin, replied yes, but that it should be done very cautiously. On the same day New York requested approval for a discount rate reduction of 4%. The Board denied New York's request, the motion having lost on a tie vote: Miller, James, and Cunningham once again voted no, with Platt joining in.[8]

The opposition within the Board to any additional easing action, except through the bill rate, can be explained by the strong skepticism which existed with respect to cheap money as a stimulus to business activity. This skepticism was held not only by those who persistently voted no to easing policies but also by those who on the whole favored them. Cunningham, James, and Miller let their skepticism lead them to dissent, whereas Harrison, Hamlin, and perhaps a few others maintained a certain animal faith even while seeming to agree with the skeptics. (See previous passages describing the Board's official position concerning the role of lower interest rates in promoting recovery.[9]) In the *Tenth Annual Report,* the Board had argued that lower interest rates might stimulate business once recovery got under way but did not say that cheaper money would necessarily shorten the downswing.

Adolph Miller was plagued by doubts about the efficacy of rate changes. His position is set forth very clearly in the Stabilization Hearings for 1928 wherein he reaffirmed his belief in the view reflected in the *Tenth Annual Report:* "The view I have entertained since 1922–23 was that in the incipient stages of a business recovery a low rate may exercise a stimulating effect."[10] But he was careful to distinguish between the ability of low interest rates: 1) to arrest a business recession; and 2) to stimulate business once recovery set in. He testified:

> I think it is a pretty well-established fact that we can not by monetary operations arrest business recession. We can do something to stimulate the flow of money into use when business is 'picking up' and something to check the flow when it is proceeding too rapidly and thus exercise an influence on the pace of business.[11]

When the directors of the New York bank gave as their reason for lower rates that it would stimulate business, Hamlin asked Miller at a Board meeting if all economists agreed that lower rates would not stimulate business. He replied that *most* were of that belief, but not all.[12] This is indeed an interesting and significant answer for Miller to have made to the Board considering that he was a professional economist who might be expected to give an informed opinion on the status of current thinking in the profession. Like many such statements, Miller's reply was in all probability harmless. Nevertheless, the influence which such statements by a professional economist might exert on the other Board members can not be entirely discounted. At the very least, it should leave open the question whether or not Board members moved too slowly because they lacked courage or because they lacked sufficient knowledge to warrant stronger action. It is plausible that the rapport between policy-making officials of the Federal Reserve System and their critics within the economics profession left much to be desired. The role of the economist, both as formal and informal adviser, at all levels of government was less well developed before the era of the New Deal than after.

Member bank indebtedness declined about $120 million in

February mainly as a result of $34 million of gold imports and an inflow of currency of $98 million. In the early part of the month New York requested a reduction in the discount rate to 4%. Miller objected. He maintained that the decrease in the rate would only stimulate the stock market and that lower rates would not stimulate business. Stock prices had already risen by some 40% since the October low. The Board at first voted to disapprove but Cunningham changed his vote and the motion carried.[13]

In March Hamlin reported that Goldenweiser gave a "very pessimistic" account of business conditions. Miller agreed and added "the depression was much graver than he anticipated and . . . we ought to consider whether the System could not be helpful . . . he would approve a rate reduction to 3½%."[14] Evidently he considered the effect of a rate reduction on stock market speculation to be less crucial than the seriousness of the recession. Since he doubted the effect of lower rates in stimulating business, it is not easy to account for his change of opinion or how the rate change could be expected to exercise its effect. Governor Young suggested giving the New York bank the authority to purchase securities up to $50 million. The Board with the exception of Miller approved. Continued gold imports of $80 million coupled with the additional purchases of government securities led to a reduction of rediscounts by $100 million and a small increase in total reserves. New York had applied for and the Board approved a rate reduction to 3½%. When the Open Market Policy Conference met on March 24, most of the Reserve Bank governors regarded the purchases earlier in the month as "unwise." Some felt that money rates had been eased more rapidly than desirable. Evidently they were satisfied with the degree of ease actually prevailing. Member bank indebtedness exceeded $200 million, but short-term open market rates had declined substantially since October, though they were still above the recession lows of 1924 and 1927. The policy of maintaining the bill portfolio at the January level was successful in February but less so in March.

Towards the end of April, 1930, New York again applied for a reduction in its rate to 3%. But on this occasion Harrison gave as one of the reasons, in addition to the further decline in business and commodity prices, "reviving" the bond market which he said was "historically" and "logically" a precedent to economic recovery. The Board disapproved the request unanimously. Goldenweiser summarized the reasons why they denied the rate decrease as follows:

1) There is no evidence of money not being available to business on reasonable terms, and no reason to believe that further reduction in rates will help to revive business.

2) Further ease in money would probably result in further increasing speculative activity. (New York Bank loans to Brokers are at the highest level on record).

3) Gold movements: Gold is coming from Orient and Brazil—not Europe—[15]

What is puzzling is Hamlin's entry in his Diary that the Board had been considering, in response to other Federal Reserve Banks, "a tightening rather than an easing policy"![16] Miller said he might approve a decrease in the discount rate provided there was a material reduction in the System's holdings of government securities. Still this is even more difficult to comprehend in the light of Goldenweiser's remark that business conditions were getting worse rather than better. The Board, nevertheless, approved several days later a reduction in the minimum buying rate for bills at New York from 3% to 2¾%. New York again resubmitted its request in May to lower the discount rate. This time the Board approved but only by a narrow margin of four to three. Miller, Cunningham, and James continued to vote no. Cunningham "objected vigorously on grounds that a lower rate would not help business or agriculture."[17]

Why the majority of the Board changed its mind within one week is not easy to ascertain. One plausible explanation advanced by Hamlin was the fact that both the Bank of England and the Bank of France had recently reduced to 3% and the existing rate might revive gold imports and encourage further undesirable expansion. He admitted that the reduction of rates abroad influenced his decision. Whether it influenced any other Board member, we can only surmise. Neither changes in production nor employment in April would seem to justify the sharp reversal of policy within a one week interval. In this instance the traditional rules of the gold standard game probably account for the timing of the action. For surely it was recognized that continuing gold imports by easing credit would stimulate recovery. Concern about controlling future expansion was additional testimony that the Board continued to view the recession as mild, recovery not very far away, and present measures adequate. Miller opposed the reduction in the discount rate to 3% because he thought the Board and the New York bank would be too timid to reverse when the time came!

Harrison appeared before the Board on May 14 and argued that a bold open market policy was necessary to put up prices and improve the bond market. The New York directors were still divided on the merits of additional purchases of government securities. They were reluctant to embark upon a program of "credit management." He stated that although short-term rates had come down substantially, long-term rates were still relatively high. In April, for example, the yield on United States government securities was 3.31%, almost unchanged since November. The yield on railroad bonds was 5.11% in November, 1929, and 4.92% in April, 1930. When the Open Market Policy Conference convened on May 21, it concluded that there was no reason for added purchases of government securities. In June the Board voted to allow New York to buy $50 million of securities. The opposition within the Board to security purchases remained strong and was still composed of Miller, Cunningham, and James. If Vice-Governor Platt had not switched his vote the motion to approve would have failed.

The views of the Reserve Bank governors were reaffirmed on June 23 when the executive committee of the Open Market Policy Conference voted four to one against any additional purchase of government securities. Harrison alone favored a more vigorous open market policy.[18]

During the summer both member bank indebtedness and total reserves remained relatively constant. However, short-term rates continued to fall. The rate on Treasury notes and certificates reached a low of 1.53% in August, and the prime commercial paper rate dropped to 3%, lower than at any time since the establishment of the Federal Reserve System. An unanticipated increase of $70 million in the bill portfolio since July 1 accomplished in part what Harrison had sought to accomplish by open market purchases. From April to August the index of industrial production and employment decreased 9%. Despite this serious decline the Open Market Policy Conference voted nine to three again on September 25 to maintain the status quo.[19] To offset gold exports the Open Market Policy Conference requested authority to acquire up to $100 million of securities. On this occasion Governor Harrison agreed with the majority. He saw no reason either to buy or to sell except to maintain the current condition of monetary ease. He was not convinced yet that the situation could be remedied by a heavy dose of easy credit. Curious as it might seem, it was Adolph Miller who recommended substantial purchases of government securities, and Governor Harrison who cautioned against the attendant dangers.

How did the New York and other Federal Reserve Bank governors feel about open market purchases during the first half of 1930? Two indisputable facts emerge from the memoranda, prepared for Governor Harrison, reporting the weekly meetings of the Board of Directors of the New York bank:

1) The general policy of the New York bank was directed primarily towards improvement in the bond and mortgage loan markets. Presumably by improvement they meant rising prices and healthy absorption of securities by the commercial banking system. The New York bank directors maintained that such improvement was "historically and logically" a precedent to business recovery and might stimulate both domestic and foreign investment, the latter being of especial significance.[20] Therefore, since January they had pursued a policy of reductions in both the bill and rediscount rates. There was still some concern about whether or not such action would encourage stock market speculation, but no one considered postponing action on this account.

2) The immediate aim of policy, or the "target variable," was "to keep the member banks in the principal money markets of the country practically out of debt at the Federal Reserve Banks, and to preserve a condition of credit ease in those markets."[21] It was Harrison's opinion that so long as the New York member banks remained practically out of debt, there was no justification for forcing further funds upon the market. To this position he adhered unswervingly throughout 1930 and 1931. The need for additional purchases turned, therefore, upon the behavior of the bill portfolio and the extent of the indebtedness of the New York banks to the Federal Reserve. The New York bank expected to accomplish through reductions in the bill rate what might have been accomplished more efficiently by open market operations. The directors of the New York bank were reluctant to undertake open market operations before they were satisfied that the "risks of prolonged depression" were greater than the "risks of credit management." Some of the directors felt that the acquisition of securities when member bank indebtedness was at minimum levels represented inflation, a danger, however, which could be faced after it became clear that the only alternative was price deflation.[22]

Throughout the rest of May and the greater part of June there was further discussion on the advisability of acquiring more securities. On June 4 and 5, the New York bank purchased $20 million, but later in the month the executive committee of the Open Market Policy Conference rejected the suggestion for further purchases. It is well worth noting that it was the executive committee and not the full Policy Conference which voted against additional purchases. Some critics have maintained that the reorganization of the Open Market Investment Committee to include all of the Reserve Bank governors explains the System's failure to have initiated a more courageous open market policy. In 1930 the Open Market Investment Committee was abolished and replaced by a Committee which included the twelve governors of the Federal Reserve Banks. The name was changed to the "Open Market Policy Conference." The reorganization probably had the effect of weakening the influence of the New York Federal Reserve Bank. An executive committee of the Policy Conference made up of the original five-man Investment Committee (governors of the Federal Reserve Banks of New York, Boston, Chicago, Cleveland, and Philadelphia) was responsible for executing the policy decisions of the Conference. The new executive committee included three members of the old committee—Governors McDougal, Fancher, and Norris.

Upon learning of the executive committee's decision, the New York directors decided to prepare a careful statement of their position and to send it to all of the other Federal Reserve Banks. Although the directors entertained for a time the idea of withdrawing from the Open Market Policy Conference, they preferred persuasion and further discussion to independent action on the grounds "that there is still a real difference of opinion, among those deemed capable of forming a judgment, as to the power of cheap and abundant credit, alone, to bring about improvement in business and in commodity prices." The following excerpts of the letter sent to all Reserve Bank governors outline the position of the New York directors:

> They do not feel that low discount rates or further purchases of government securities will of themselves fix commodity prices or restore business activity . . . They do feel, however, that further purchases of government securities in circumstances such as the present, can do no possible harm and will likely accomplish some good.
>
> As they view the situation it is about this: The United States and most other countries of the world are in the midst of a severe business depression. The decline in business activity has been great as judged by almost every available index. Unemployment is serious. Commodity prices have suffered the most severe and rapid decline since the postwar deflation of 1921, and are now about 12 per cent less than a year

ago. The decline has been most pronounced in the last few weeks. Profit margins are seriously cut, purchasing power has been reduced, and many people are facing unemployment and distress.

Our directors have believed, therefore, that whatever steps the Reserve System may take, whether through discount rates or open market operations, to facilitate a more active and stronger bond market through which capital funds may be made available for new enterprise or distributed to those parts of the world where purchasing power is now seriously curtailed, should be taken promptly and courageously. . . .

In previous business depressions recovery has never taken place until there has been a strong bond market through which new enterprise requiring long time capital may be financed.[23]

The response of the governors of the individual Federal Reserve Banks provides the best evidence that we have revealing the views of System officials outside of New York and explaining why additional purchases were not made in the spring and the summer of 1930. Only two of the Reserve Bank governors agreed with the recommendations of the New York bank: Governor Black of Atlanta and Governor Seay of Richmond. Seay thought that it was a convenient time to accumulate a portfolio, as he put it, "with a view of establishing a measurable control of the credit situation later on . . ."[24] One of the strongest replies attacking the position of New York came from Governor Calkins of San Francisco. It sums up pretty well the objections of the other governors to a policy of more credit ease through open market operations:

1) We do not believe that the creation, promotion, or encouragement of a bond market is within the province of the Federal Reserve System, nor do we believe that any efforts which may be put forth by the System will result in such an improvement of the bond market as to favorably affect general business or foreign trade . . .

2) We believe that to make credit progressively cheaper and more abundant may cause an unfavorable psychological reaction, rather than a favorable one.

3) We believe that the volume of credit forcibly fed to the market up to this time had had no considerable good effect, certainly no discernible effect in the last few months.[25]

Most of the governors and the directors neither believed in nor understood how monetary policy could be used to promote business recovery. The view was still strong within the System that the Federal Reserve should adjust passively to changes in the level of economic activity. Governor Talley of the Dallas bank in a passage remarkable for its loose construction and obscurity stated:

> Directors were not impressed with the arguments which you presented . . . they are unwilling to interpose direct action in a period of reaction to a previous period of action that perhaps, shall I say, was not courageous enough or did not go far enough in its preventive attributes. The thought is simply this—that a direct effort toward ease on the part of the System should not through artificial means transcend the force of the reaction measured by the forces of action at the high point of the force of action in the opposite circumstances . . . We also think that it [N.Y.] should assume responsibility for what it does not do as well as what it does undertake, and that it should have the fortitude to meet a period of reaction and go through an era of readjustment patiently and calmly, acting in accordance with conditions as they are found, instead of undertaking to make conditions as they are desired, with the result of shaking their congestion out on the country. We are still convinced that capital must flow from savings, either represented by an excess of income over expenditure, from profits or from the creation of new wealth, and we are not convinced even by your letter, that it can be supplied with reserve bank credit.[26]

Governor Geery of Minneapolis replied: "It seems to me that there is danger of stimulating financing which will lead to still more over-production while attempting to make it easy to do financing which will increase consumption."[27] Both McDougal and Norris argued that the supply of credit was no deterrent to additional investment under prevailing conditions. McDougal was of the opinion that the strength of the Federal Reserve Banks should be conserved in order to meet future contingencies.

It ought to be clear that the New York bank did not at this time contemplate substantial purchases of government securities. Its objective was limited in scope and did not go beyond the goal set out by Burgess and Strong in the nineteen-twenties—that is, to eliminate the indebtedness of the New York and Chicago banks. In fact, on July 18, Governor Harrison dispatched a letter to all Reserve Bank governors acknowledging their replies and announcing that there was no longer the need for additional security purchases, for the bill portfolio had unexpectedly increased from $65 million to $170 million. He said:

> Thus, the condition which we have desired, and for the attainment of which we believed purchases of Government securities might be necessary, has been achieved during the past ten days in natural course

through developments in the bill market which could hardly have been anticipated.

As we pointed out in our letter of July 3, we believe that the important end to be achieved in present circumstances is that the money center banks should be substantially out of debt and that there should be some surplus funds available.[28]

Thus by the middle of July the New York bank viewed the credit situation as satisfactory and the immediate aims of policy achieved.

In September two officers of the New York bank, Randolph Burgess and Carl Snyder, raised the question about a more aggressive program of purchases. Snyder pointed to the discrepancy between the behavior of the reporting and nonreporting banks and concluded that the latter must have substantially curtailed the amount of credit. He recommended large purchases of government securities to combat the credit deflation. Burgess said that if he were acting alone he would favor putting out more surplus funds as a further inducement to banks to find ways of employing them. Governor Harrison did not agree, saying that additional purchases when member bank indebtedness was at a minimum would be "forced investments, and the dangers of such a policy of 'inflation' were great and the advantages doubtful." Furthermore, he thought that the division of opinion within the System on the merits of additional purchases was too great to warrant any change in monetary policy at that time.

The complacency of Governor Harrison is clearly revealed by the following excerpt from the memoranda of Board of Directors meeting dated September 17, 1930:

The Governor was not convinced that present economic difficulties could be remedied by a heavy dose of easy credit any better than by the small dose which had already been administered and he pointed out that when all of the New York City banks are more or less continuously out of debt at the Reserve Bank over any considerable period of time it means a very easy reserve position.[29]

So it was not merely the Reserve Bank governors' opposition to security purchases, but also Governor Harrison's genuine skepticism as to their desirability which delayed a more aggressive open market policy.

By the end of October a majority of the officers of the New York bank favored a more vigorous policy, but Harrison continued to disagree. On this occasion he advanced a new reason why action should be postponed: although easier money might stimulate a desirable outflow of gold from the U.S., he thought that France would probably absorb most of it and where, in his opinion, "it would be less useful, from a world standpoint, than in this country." He reiterated his views again in March and April, 1931. In his judgment there were still no compelling reasons for adopting a policy of additional credit ease. And he emphasized that his decision did not turn upon the opposition of the other Reserve Bank governors. It seems perfectly clear from Governor Harrison's remarks that the expansion of the Open Market Investment Committee was not the real reason for the inaction and delay as Friedman and Schwartz have alleged.

Reorganization of the Federal Reserve Board

At the end of August, 1930, Young resigned as governor of the Federal Reserve Board to accept an appointment as governor of the Federal Reserve Bank of Boston. He replaced Harding who had died the previous April. Undoubtedly Young's resignation was engineered from the White House. Eugene Meyer was appointed governor of the Federal Reserve Board on September 16 and, together with Ogden Mills and George Harrison of the New York bank, assumed leadership of administration economic policy, if it can be said that there was one. On September 15 Vice-Governor Platt resigned to accept a position in private business, with eight years of his term remaining. Since no more than one Board member may come from a single Federal Reserve district, and both Platt and Meyer represented the New York district, Platt had to resign before Meyer could be appointed. Hamlin described a conversation with Platt in which the subject of his resignation was discussed:

> Had long talk with Platt as to his interview with Secretary Mellon. Platt said that Mellon began by saying he had heard that Platt had had an offer from a group of banks,—that they were all first class men and that he hoped Platt would accept it. Later he would [?] have Platt to understand not directly but by the necessary implication that Hoover hoped he would accept as he had someone he wanted to put in his place.[30]

Hamlin surmised that Ogden Mills had encouraged President Hoover to reorganize the Board in the interest of New York, but that is merely Hamlin's conjecture. On November 28 Cunningham, who had consistently opposed easing action through open market operations, died. So throughout the rest of the year the Board was composed of the four appointed members—the new Governor Meyer, Hamlin, Miller, and James—and the two *ex officio* members, Secretary Mellon and Comptroller Pole.

The reorganization probably weakened rather than strengthened the Board since Meyer, because of his inexperience, was not able to provide leadership, especially in relationship to the New York bank and the Treasury. Thus the influence of Governor Harrison and Under Secretary Mills increased. President Hoover had assumed by his appointive power a direct responsibility for monetary policy, and since he was instrumental in the removal of both Governor Young and Vice-Governor Platt, he bore primary responsibility for providing the Board with competent and courageous new leadership. Instead, Hoover weakened the Federal Reserve Board by failing to fill immediately the vacancies created by the resignations of Platt and Young and the death of Cunningham. Seldom has a President had the opportunity to reorganize the Board by making three appointments within a three-month period and at a time when the country faced a serious economic crisis. Thus while the responsibility for monetary policy remained with the Board through the critical months ahead, the President can be said to be responsible for its vacuum in leadership.

Between August and November member bank indebtedness remained approximately constant. Member bank reserves increased $40 million mainly as a consequence of gold imports. Government security holdings did not change. Nevertheless, open market rates continued to decline with the notable exception of the yield on railroad bonds which had risen from 4.8% in September to 5.1% in November, the same level as prevailed in November, 1929.

There was a rash of bank failures which were restricted mainly to banks having connections with the Bank of the United States the significance of which has been explained by Raimund Goldschmidt as follows: "The failures of late 1930 were such that banking authorities and the public were able to regard them as exceptional cases, having no representative value whatever for the situation of urban banking in general. The first group of failures were restricted to banks having intimate connections with one rather new and very expansive banking house."[31] Both the New York bank and the

Open Market Policy Conference were concerned about these bank failures. The situation was made worse by the unusually low prices prevailing in the bond markets, especially of the high-yield low-quality bonds held by country banks. At a meeting of the Open Market Policy Conference in January Burgess made the suggestion that $1 billion of securities could be purchased to revive the bond market, but this suggestion was ignored.

Both production and employment continued to decline without any observable effects on Federal Reserve policy. The Federal Advisory Council met on November 18, 1930, only to recommend the status quo with respect to discount rates and open market operations except in the event of some seasonal credit strain. In the final week of December the Open Market Investment Committee purchased $33 million of government securities, but an additional $100 million were acquired outside the regular open market account, including resale agreements. The Committee disposed of these securities during the first and second weeks of January, 1931, and did not engage in further operations for the investment account until May.

One of the consequences of the rise in the number of bank failures towards the end of 1930 was a slight but perceptible increase in hoarding. Although industrial production had fallen 2% during 1930, the decrease in currency in circulation which began in the fourth week of December and continued through January, 1931, was some $80 million more than during the preceding year. The amount of currency in circulation on March 25, 1931, was $4.26 billion compared with $4.18 billion on March 26, 1930. Between April and June currency in circulation increased an additional $113 million as compared with a $41-million decrease in the previous year.

Open market rates continued their sharp decline through June. The prime commercial paper rate was down to 2% and the yield on Treasury notes and certificates had fallen to 0.55%. Long-term rates remained intractable. The government bond yield was only 0.5% below what it had been in October, 1929 and the yield on railroad bonds stood about 0.4% above the precrash level. The yield on railroad bonds rose from 4.8% in September, 1930, to 5.7% in June, 1931—an important fact which affected the solvency of some commercial banks as well as other financial institutions. The increase in hoarding coupled with the rapid depreciation of railroad bonds should have been a signal to Reserve officials that more drastic action was called for. The signal was not altogether ignored. Miller seemed to be disposed to additional purchases ostensibly "to force banks to increase their investments."[32] Governor Meyer, according to Hamlin, objected to Miller's suggestions on the grounds that "psychologically it would make people think we had entered on a campaign of inflation . . ."[33]

The hesitation to act during the spring could have been due to the mild improvement in business conditions as indicated by both the Board's index of industrial production and factory employment. The index increased 7% between December and April while factory employment remained stationary. In early March Harrison told his directors that there were no compelling reasons for additional credit ease. Action taken by lowering bill rates and the rediscount rate was successful. However, Carl Snyder, an official of the New York bank, told Goldenweiser that the continued purchase of securities was absolutely necessary and that the only reason for not buying them was the Board's apparent desire to see a large army of unemployed![34] Meyer said at a Board meeting on April 3 that he thought domestic conditions were slowly improving. It was Goldenweiser's opinion that keeping the member banks out of debt to the Federal Reserve was sufficient. He did not think that anything further should be done.[35] At a conference of governors held towards the end of April, the majority of those present expressed disapproval of any policy to make money easier; however, they did sanction the purchase of an additional $100 million of securities. Governors Fancher, McDougal, and Black approved the purchase to check gold imports. Harrison and Governor Meyer thought it would hasten the effects of the gold movement and thus avoid harming European countries. The Open Market Policy Conference purchased $42 million of securities in May which were exactly offset by a corresponding sale by the individual Reserve Banks of securities held outside the System's regular open market account, the net effect being zero.

The danger of increased hoarding was clearly apparent to Hamlin and Governor Meyer by early summer. Hamlin noted in his Diary on June 16:

The Governor [Meyer] pointed out that almost 187 millions of gold had been imported in last 6 months and 84 released for earmark . . . He suggested considering buying say 100 million of Government Securities to restore this to [?] and to offset hoarding. We decided to call a meeting of Executive Committee of Open Market Conference Thursday or Friday. To CSH this hoarding in New York and Chicago is the most serious phase of existing depression and he believes a liberal pouring out of money might tend to stop hoarding. Increase of money in circulation—including hoarded money since last November—375 million; since last April 150–175 largely at Chicago. Evidently much is being hoarded.[36]

Goldenweiser thought that the effect of the increased gold imports was to offset currency hoarding. He told Governor Meyer that the question of further easing had nothing to do with either hoarding or gold imports. Goldenweiser confided that he could not accept the accumulation of excess reserves as a remedy for the business situation.[37] The remainder of the summer was taken up with extending credits to certain foreign central banks. On July 12 the Board approved the resolution of the New York bank to extend to the Reichsbank a $100-million credit until August 15. Some efforts were also made to support sterling exchange.

On August 10 Governor Meyer told the open market committee that the Board would approve a proposal to acquire $200 million or $300 million of government securities in an effort to induce the banks to purchase railroad or other bonds, the principal aim of which was to prevent further depreciation of their prices.[38] The committee of governors rejected the Board's suggestion and as a compromise voted eleven to one to purchase $120 million. Governor Harrison alone among the governors dissented. He thought that nothing short of a bold stroke would be adequate. Young, former head of the Board and now governor of the Boston bank, argued that any necessary action could just as well be undertaken through lower acceptance rates and that his directors were opposed to purchases of government securities except in real emergencies. Miller said that the committee had erred in not recommending stronger action. Goldenweiser described the climate of the meeting in the following terms:

Apparently the members of the conference, more or less under instructions from their boards of directors, were opposed to affirmative easing action and agreed to the compromise more or less in a sense that it would enable the system to offset tightening influences rather than to do affirmative easing. Young was opposed to the easing program and voted against the compromise on the ground that forcing money on the banks at this time would do no good. Meyer was clearly disappointed and inclined to blame it on the fact that the Governors were too much under the influence of their boards of directors and were in substance instructed delegates. Miller said that the system should either do nothing or act vigorously. To his mind yesterday's action represented failure to grasp an opportunity.

There were three Deputy Governors present: Worthington, McKay, and Gilbert. Calkins and Fancher had left before the Board came in. The meeting did look more or less disbanded and as though it was represented to some extent by minor people. This condition gave point to Meyer's objection which he raised to the procedure.[39]

The Board mysteriously delayed a week before approving the recommendation of the governors. No purchases for the System's special investment account were made before the fourth week in December. The purchases approved in August were not carried out immediately because the New York directors felt that would be unwise. They thought member banks would merely pile up excess reserves without employing them in the bond market. Both Governor Harrison and Governor Meyer favored a slight firming of rates. On September 20, the announcement was made that Great Britain was abandoning the gold standard, and Federal Reserve policy shifted from ease to restraint.

The Gold Crisis

Immediately following the announcement that England had gone off the gold standard, the U.S. began to lose gold. Weekly gold exports and changes in currency in circulation are given in Table 1 for the period from September 30 to October 28, 1931. Because most critics of the Federal Reserve usually characterize policy during this episode as blundering, we must be careful to describe correctly the actual course of events. Such criticism implies that the authorities *could* have acted otherwise based on knowledge and experience available at the time—not simply that they *should* have. It makes very little sense to suggest they ought to have acted differently if their actions were consistent with previous behavior and understanding of how the System should function.

The System's response to the gold outflow was that prescribed by the traditional gold standard rules. On October 1 both Adolph Miller and C. S. Hamlin recommended that New York should increase the discount rate immediately from 1½% to 2%. They were fully apprized of the possible effects in the bond market, but they agreed that this should not be allowed to interfere.[40] The actual outflow of gold for the week ending September 30 was only $156 million and the increase in currency in circulation $80 mil-

Table 1

Weekly Gold Exports and Changes in Currency in Circulation: September 30 to October 28, 1931*

(*$ million*)

Date		Gold Exports	Currency in Circulation
September	30	−156	+ 82
October	7	− 99	+185
	14	−218	+ 42
	21	− 87	+ 32
	28	− 48	
TOTAL		−608	+341

SOURCE: *Banking and Monetary Statistics* (Washington, D.C.: Board of Governors, 1943), p. 386.

* Wednesday figures.

lion, hardly sufficient to warrant immediate remedial action or apprehension about maintaining the convertibility of the dollar into gold. The Hamlin and Miller reaction was probably conditioned by imperfect understanding of pre-1914 gold standard experience. The New York bank officials, on the other hand, did not think that an increase in rates was advisable immediately. Governor Harrison told the directors of the New York bank that any rise in money rates at that time would be regrettable because of adverse effects on the bond market. Also he said it might encourage the gold outflow, by creating unfavorable expectations abroad about the future convertibility of the dollar.

On October 8 the Board approved unanimously the New York bank's application to increase its rate to 2½%. Gold exports in the two-week period amounted to $255 million and the increase in currency in circulation amounted to $267 million. The drain on member bank reserves totaled $511 million which was met in part by a $158-million increase in member bank indebtedness and $338-million increase in bills bought, the remainder by a decrease in member bank reserves. The outflow of gold was heaviest in the second week of October when it totaled some $218 million. The New York bank again increased its discount rate to 3½% on October 15.

Three reasons are usually given for this action: 1) The rate increase was simply the orthodox response of the banking authorities to a gold drain under the gold standard mechanism. 2) The rise was the result of negotiations between the Bank of France and the New York bank to induce the French to maintain their balances in the U.S. 3) The real problem was not the danger of gold exports at all but the so-called free gold dilemma, that is, insufficient collateral to back Federal Reserve notes.

The evidence for the first reason derives from two independent sources, a preliminary memorandum prepared by officers of the New York Federal Reserve Bank for the Open Market Policy Conference on November 30:

> In the past three months the United States has gone through an extraordinary financial crisis in which were combined the largest gold export movement in the history of the country and a heavy domestic withdrawal of currency continuing a movement of almost a year's duration. These foreign and domestic drains upon bank reserves were met in the classic way by increases in discount rates combined with a policy of free lending. This is the method of meeting such an emergency described by Walter Bagehot in his *Lombard Street* in the following terms:
>
> > Whatever persons—one bank or many banks—in any country holding the banking reserve of that country, ought at the very beginning of an unfavorable foreign exchange at once to raise the rate of interest . . .[41]

The other piece of evidence is a lengthy memorandum prepared by Governor Harrison describing the actions of the board of directors of the New York bank the day preceding the actual increase in rates, October 8, 1931:

> Governor Harrison reviewed the conditions under which the discount rate of this bank had been reduced to 1½ per cent, and pointed out that the conditions which might logically be expected to lead to a rise in the discount rate were either 1) a revival of business, or 2) a material increase in the demand for Federal Reserve credit and/or 3) a large outward movement of gold. He pointed out that during the past three months there had been a substantial increase in the demand for Federal Reserve credit incident to the export of gold and the hoarding of currency, and that this increase in the demand for Federal Reserve credit had been accompanied by a moderate rise in open market money rates. These developments made an advance in the discount rate appropriate, he said, the principal reason for questioning the advisability of such an advance being the effect it might have on public psychology. Incidentally, he reported that Governor Moret of the Bank of France had expressed concern over the low money rates prevailing in this country and in France, and felt that the discount rates, both of this bank and of the Bank of France, should go up, a

move which Governor Moret thought would increase rather than diminish confidence abroad.

Governor Harrison said that he considered it advisable to advance the rate by a full point, if it were to be raised at all. He said also that if we are going to put up our rate the present circumstances might provide a more favorable time for an increase than the conditions which might prevail after another two or three weeks. As for the probable effects of an advance in the discount rate, a) he doubted whether an increase would stop the gold outflow or the withdrawals of currency from the banks, b) he thought that higher rates by improving bank earnings, might improve the psychology of bankers and increase their willingness to lend and invest funds, c) he was doubtful whether the psychology of the general public would be affected, as hoarding has probably not been induced by concern over bank earnings; d) he felt that reserve bank rates would be more nearly in touch with money market conditions.[42]

Randolph Burgess, who was attending a conference in Europe, cabled the New York bank advising against a rate increase and pointed out that the amount of free gold had not been materially affected by the gold drain. But this advice went unheeded. On October 15 Governor Meyer told the New York directors "that an advance in the rate was called for by every known rule" and that he believed "that foreigners would regard it as a lack of courage if the rate were not advanced."[43]

An analysis of the second reason (pp. 164–165) is given by William Adams Brown Jr. in his two-volume history, *The International Gold Standard Reinterpreted, 1914–1934:*

. . . immediately after September 21, 1931 large sales of dollars took place and large transfers were made to Europe. The demand for francs in particular was overwhelming. During October gold exports from New York to Paris were $324 million, and $63 million in gold was shipped to Belgium, the Netherlands, and Switzerland, but New York was still drawing gold in substantial amounts from Argentina, Japan, and several other countries, so that the net exports for October were $337 million, only slightly larger than the gold movement to France . . . Under these circumstances international considerations of the type that had prevented the wholesale conversion of sterling balances, which were probably not far from $600 million, would be retained in New York [and] become a matter of negotiation between New York and Paris, and it soon became very clear that, in view of her recent experience with sterling, France would have to be offered substantial inducements to refrain from carrying out her long cherished program of conversion of Bank of France divisen [foreign exchange holdings of the Bank of France] into gold. Those which the United States was able to offer were two—first, assurances or guarantees that no policy would be pursued that would endanger the maintenance of the gold standard in the United States; second, an increase in the interest rate that would make the employment of French funds in New York more profitable. The attitude of the American banks immediately after Great Britain's suspension of the gold standard was favorable to an agreement or understanding on these lines. Withdrawal of Bank of France balances on a large scale would have been seriously inconvenient to the New York money market as a whole and to the particular banks holding French balances. These banks made their views felt in Washington where apprehension for the preservation of the gold standard had already created a receptive state of mind. . . .

Between September 19 and October 31 money in circulation increased $404 million, the monetary stock declined $725 million . . . Fear gripped the American market as these changes began to disclose themselves, and it became necessary to give official assurance that the American gold standard was not in danger. For this purpose Randolph Burgess went to Basle at the time of the October meeting of the Board of the Bank of International Settlements. In October also two emissaries of the Bank of France were sent to America to discuss with Federal Reserve Officials and with the Treasury the conditions on which Bank of France balances would be left in New York. Meanwhile, the discount rate of the Federal Reserve Bank of New York had been raised from 1½ per cent to 2½ per cent on October 9 and to 3½ per cent on October 15. A general understanding seems to have been reached by the bankers.[44]

Governor Harrison told his own directors and the Board in Washington that there had been no agreement made with the Bank of France. At an executive meeting of the New York bank on October 26, 1931, Governor Harrison said "that it had been publicly reported that this bank had agreed with the Bank of France to advance its discount rate to 4%, and that, of course, this report was without foundation."[45] And in a letter to Governor Meyer dated December 18, 1931, he again denied that there had been any complicity between the two central banks:

I have from time to time advised you of the conversations which I had with Mr. Farnier and Mr. Lacour-Gayet of the Bank of France during their visit in New York, and indeed you yourself had extended talks with them, so that you are already familiar with the purport of these conversations. Nevertheless, I cannot return the enclosed documents to you without the comment that there is no basis in fact for any statement that we asked the Bank of France not to withdraw its deposits from the American money market or, indeed, that they had "agreed" to do so. Nor is there any foundation to statements which have been made from time to time in consideration of such an "undertaking" the Federal Reserve Bank of New York had agreed to maintain a firm money policy by increasing its discount rate to 4% or by any other action.[46]

The evidence is clear then that there is no basis for the allegations made by Brown that the New York bank's increase in its discount rate grew out of negotiations with the Bank of France to induce the French to maintain their balances in the U.S.

As for the third possible reason for the New York bank's action (see p. 165), it was definitely not a decline in free gold which prompted officials to raise rediscount rates, for the amount of free gold was larger at the end of the period (October 28) than at any time since the movement began. Why, then, did the System not purchase securities to offset hoarding and the huge gold outflow? When asked the same question by Representative James G. Strong of Kansas, Governor Meyer replied:

> Within a few weeks after September 21, $750,000,000 was withdrawn by foreign countries from their balances here and taken in the form of gold. No country in the history of the world has ever been able to stand that kind of drain of gold . . . but in view of the large drafts on this country by foreigners, and, I believe, even some remittances by Americans out of the country from fright, purchases of securities by the reserve banks at that time were impracticable. We could not undertake anything of that character in October without loss of gold. That is my opinion. You will remember at that time we had to raise the discount rate from 1½ to 2½ and 3½ per cent. Purchases at that time would not have had a stabilizing effect. They would have tended to neutralize the effect of the advances in the discount rate, which was an important intrinsic and also an important psychological factor at that time.[47]

Apparently it was the view of some Federal Reserve officials that open market purchases might produce in Europeans a lack of confidence in the American dollar and thereby touch off an increase in domestic hoarding, a view which Brown said was validated when open market operations resumed on a large scale in March.

Contrary to the testimony of Governor Meyer, Goldenweiser told Hamlin on November 5 that the Bank of France had not materially changed its deposits in the U.S. and that the increase in gold in the Bank of France was the consequence of sales of American securities by Frenchmen who took the proceeds in gold and deposited them in the Bank of France.[48]

Gold exports and domestic hoarding subsided in November. But the new wave of bank failures throughout the Middle Atlantic States created a "credit blockade" on the part of the banks whose principal concern now was to increase their liquidity. At a meeting of the Open Market Policy Conference on November 30, Harrison reported that many New York banks were fearful that a substantial increase in rediscounting might impair confidence abroad and renew hoarding at home. Moreover, he did not approve of purchasing government securities on the grounds that it might interfere with the Treasury's plans to market a large short-term issue on December 23. Governor Meyer agreed with Harrison, but Miller thought that the situation should be met boldly by any amount of security purchases sufficient to induce banks to increase the availability of credit and that he would not be averse to lowering required reserves. The Board approved the resolution of the Open Market Committee which stated that although there was no need at present, authority should be given to purchase up to $200 million of securities to be sold at the beginning of the new year. The New York banks opposed a return to the same easy money conditions that prevailed before the gold crisis. They felt that low rates would impair further the solvency of some banks. Governor Harrison doubted whether they would cooperate in extending credit if excess reserves increased under those circumstances. He preferred to wait until the first of the year.

When the Investment Committee met again on January 11, Harrison stated that he had recommended to Senator Glass passage of an amendment allowing government securities to serve as collateral for Federal Reserve notes. He said that the System's free gold was now between $400 million and $500 million and might prove to be a menace in the future. He did not recommend any additional purchases of securities but thought an emergency might arise within two or three weeks requiring such purchases.[49]

It seems clear that at least until the end of December the free gold problem was not the explanation for either the increase in discount rates or the reluctance to purchase a large quantity of government securities. The Federal Reserve's failure to act was owing more to consideration of the impact of such purchases on

European confidence in the dollar and indirectly on domestic hoarding propensities. The increased tempo of bank failures in December and January involving some $500 million combined with the almost negligible return flow of currency in circulation, highly abnormal at that season of the year, created fresh anxiety and led to a change in policy. Before a new policy could be inaugurated, however, it was necessary to clear away some existing obstacles in the form of collateral requirements against Federal Reserve notes.

The immediate occasion for the removal of restrictions on the collateral of Federal Reserve notes was, according to President Hoover's account, the fear expressed by the Secretary of the Treasury Ogden Mills "that we were within two or three weeks of being forced off the gold standard."[50] Hoover arranged a White House meeting on February 8 attended by Governors Harrison and Meyer and General Dawes, president and administrative head of the Reconstruction Finance Corporation, at which it was agreed that legislation would be introduced immediately to permit government securities to be collateral for Federal Reserve notes. Glass, who had previously opposed such action, finally agreed to sponsor the new legislation with Representative Steagall.[51] It was approved by Congress on February 27 without much debate.

Although the new legislation enabled the System to purchase a large quantity of government securities, it cannot be inferred that the amount of free gold was the major deterrent to increased purchases in November and December. Henry Villard, for example, did not criticize the System for its failure to purchase securities before March, 1932, because he assumed implicitly that the free gold problem was the explanation for the System's reluctance to take action and that the Glass-Steagall Act could not have been passed earlier. He argued, however, that the Federal Reserve's unwillingness to adjust the bill rate was less defensible.[52] On the other hand, Seymour Harris thought the Federal Reserve had acted correctly and did not criticize its behavior in 1930–31. He concluded:

> Was a policy of dear money, reflected in an increase in the Bank and buying rates and a failure to purchase securities in large quantities, justifiable? I am of the opinion that reserve policy was correct. A loss of 500–600 millions of gold and the withdrawal of 600 million of notes in a period of a few months certainly justify the action of the reserve banks in requiring the market to obtain its reserve credit expensively.[53]

He thought the mistake of System officials stemmed from their behavior in the previous decade in placing too much emphasis "on the relation of indebtedness to rates and altogether too little on the balances of member banks."[54] Short-term rates occupied a disproportionate share of attention to the neglect of member bank reserves and the money supply.

CHAPTER 12 From Easy Money to the Collapse of the Banking Mechanism: 1932–1933

THE LEVEL of member bank indebtedness was approximately the same in February, 1932, as it had been in October, 1929. Borrowed reserves (excess reserves minus borrowings) amounted to $843 million in the former period and $792 million in the latter. Nevertheless, short-term interest rates were still considerably below their 1929 peak. The rate on prime commercial paper was 3.88% whereas in October, 1929, it was 6.25%. Three-to-six-month Treasury notes and certificates bore interest at 4.37% in the earlier period and 2.42% in the latter. The situation, however, was altogether different in the long-term bond markets. The yield on U.S. government bonds in February, 1932, was 4.11%, substantially higher than the October, 1929, figure. A similar depressed situation prevailed in the markets for municipal and corporate bonds, one important effect of which was to impair or jeopardize the solvency of thousands of commercial banks.

At the very least one might have expected a speedy return to the same degree of monetary ease that had prevailed before the gold crisis in October, 1931. But unfortunately the return to a policy of ease was blocked by a combination of political and technical circumstances. Borrowed reserves had amounted to $162 million in

September, 1931. They did not drop below that figure for another twelve months. And only beginning in October, 1932, did free reserves become positive.

Governor Harrison attributed the failure to purchase securities in January and February, 1932, to the free gold problem and to the delay in the formulation of the government's program for recovery.[1] The references to the free gold problem as a deterrent to further security purchases are too numerous in the Harrison Papers to dismiss, as some authors do, as merely a rationalization for the policies pursued.[2] Harrison thought that the existing situation should be attacked on a united front with the Reconstruction Finance Corporation in the van, presumably to cope with the problem of bank failures. Harrison looked more to the RFC to improve banking conditions than to any action sponsored by the Federal Reserve System.[3] The fact that Governor Meyer had accepted the chairmanship of the RFC in addition to his duties as Governor of the Federal Reserve Board certainly tended to confuse the issue of Federal Reserve responsibility. Goldenweiser shared Harrison's view. In a memorandum prepared on January 7, 1932, he said that he did not believe that the situation could be remedied by forcing reserves on the member banks. Only by restoring the confidence of the bankers and the depositors could conditions be improved, and the chief instrumentality was the RFC.[4] It was becoming increasingly clear that System officials did not recognize any strong obligation to maintain the solvency of the banking system. And in this view they probably had the approval of the administration. Two of Harrison's directors urged doing more while some Reserve Bank governors, notably McDougal of Chicago and Seay of Richmond, desired to do less. McDougal favored letting some securities run off, and Governor Seay recommended making any additional funds available through the discount window. Harrison objected to further decreases in the discount rate on grounds that it might precipitate a large withdrawal of French, Swiss, and Dutch funds. He preferred to postpone doing anything until such time as action on a broader front could be undertaken and until the fate of the Glass-Steagall Act had been decided.

Three days before the Glass-Steagall Act became law Governor Harrison initiated a request to purchase $250 million of securities at the rate of $25 million a week for the purpose of bolstering the sagging level of commodity prices. The preliminary report submitted to the Open Market Policy Conference stressed the heavy borrowing outside of the money market centers as the major cause of continued credit deflation. Borrowing by banks outside of the principal centers amounted to $850 million, an amount considerably greater for this group than in 1929. The Committee approved the purchases in February partly to offset gold losses, partly to reduce the indebtedness of country banks, and partly to bolster the confidence of the public.[5] At least one member of the Federal Reserve Board, Adolph Miller, was prepared to approve an even larger amount of purchases.

When Governor Harrison testified before a House Committee in April, he explained why purchases had not been made more rapidly:

> Now, as soon as we got that protection [Glass-Steagall Act] the system agreed upon the purchase of Government securities at the rate of $25,000,000 a week, which has proceeded now for seven weeks. I may say we should have gone faster; others may say we should not have bought them at all . . . and while I myself am perhaps more sympathetic with speedier action, I understand the views of others who think we might have gone a little slower; . . . $25,000,000 a week is not a small amount, especially when we have to realize the technique of the operation . . . Perhaps we could have gone a little faster without clogging the banks by giving them too much excess reserve. If you give them too much excess reserves when they lack confidence it is just like flooding the carburetor of an automobile.[6]

On the purely technical side, he warned:

> There is always difficulty about the mechanism and the speed with which we operate. First of all, it is not always easy, over a certain number of days, to buy as many Government securities as you might want. They are most popular investments and they are sometimes hard to get, and without completely discouraging the market you sometimes can not purchase them as rapidly as you want them.[7]

When Friedman and Schwartz state that the enactment of the Glass-Steagall Act did not lead to any immediate change in Federal Reserve policy for a period of six weeks, they neglect what the Federal Reserve was doing.

These remarks by Governor Harrison reveal the still imperfect understanding of Federal Reserve officials of the response of commercial banks to a change in excess reserves. What, for example, did Harrison mean by "clogging the banks by giving them too much excess reserves?" The phenomenon of excess reserves on any scale was a new experience to System officials. Presumably Harrison expected the banks to expand bank credit with an increase in reserves. When bank credit failed to expand, Federal Reserve officials were at a loss to explain why. Their confusion on this occasion can be attributed largely to a lack of knowledge of the determinants of the banks' demand for excess reserves.

The conduct of open market operations during the first half of 1932 left much to be desired. Security purchases were neither planned nor executed efficiently. The Open Market Policy Conference made no attempt to distinguish between its "dynamic" and its "defensive" responsibilities. The aims of open market policy remained vague—to raise prices, to retard liquidation, and to increase bank credit. Not before June 16 did Governor Harrison suggest a definite target variable of $250 million to $300 million of excess reserves.[8] In mid-July the Committee authorized the purchase of securities to the extent necessary to maintain excess reserves at the $200-million level. Previous to that, Harrison had acknowledged the importance of increasing excess reserves though he only roughly specified the amount. He indicated at the end of April that it might be desirable to slow up the program when excess reserves of New York banks reached $200 million.[9] And on May 12 he told the New York directors:

> The best yardstick to use, he suggested, would be the figures of member bank reserves—we might decide upon the level at which these reserves should be maintained and then direct our open market policy to that end. When the figures of member bank reserves are sufficiently high to produce adequate pressure upon the banks and to provide adequate credit for business as recovery sets in, we shall probably have done our part.[10]

What was the reason for the stepped-up purchases to $100 million beginning in the second week of April? According to Hamlin's Diary, Governor Meyer expressed the view on March 3 and again on March 18 that the "tide had turned," but at a meeting of the Open Market Policy Conference on April 22 Hamlin observed that Meyer's former optimism had vanished. He, Governor Meyer, and Adolph Miller were satisfied that "a bold stroke was necessary" and that additional purchases of $500 million should be authorized. The governors approved the proposed purchase by a vote of ten to one; Governor Young alone voted no.[11] He did not have much faith that the newly created reserves would be widely diffused and he feared the adverse effect the purchase would have on the confidence of bankers and the public. What, if anything, we may ask had occurred to alter the economic outlook? The index of production dropped two points in March and, although the April figure was not yet in, it would show a further decline of 9% since February. The drop in manufacturing output was even more discouraging; the index stood at 68 in February and 61 in April. Factory employment behaved similarly. But to Governor Harrison an equally important reason for speeding up action was to forestall "radical" financial legislation by Congress which was pending.[12] The Congress was considering passage of a Soldiers' Bonus Bill and the Thomas Bill to issue Federal Reserve Bank notes with 2% government bonds as collateral. Secretary of the Treasury Ogden Mills told the Open Market Conference that the Congress and the Administration had done all they could do in developing remedial action and that the duty rested clearly on the Federal Reserve System. He said that a failure on their part to take vigorous action was "almost inconceivable and almost unforgivable."[13]

Three weeks later, on May 13, Adolph Miller completely reversed himself and announced that the increased purchases were not effective and that he did not favor buying another $500 million.[14] It would be interesting to know the reason for Miller's sudden change of heart. Loans at reporting member banks declined by approximately $268 million in May but this reduction was more than offset by a $268-million increase in securities. Borrowed reserves for all banks declined $240 million but decreased only slightly at country banks. On May 17 the Open Market Policy Conference approved by a vote of ten to two the purchase of an additional $500 million of securities. Hamlin recorded that "at least one half of the members seemed to doubt the success of the operations but almost all seemed to feel that the policy . . . should be carried through."[15] Adolph Miller seemed to have grasped the significance of the increase in excess reserves when he said that "the country was still thinking in terms of safety rather than resumption. A program of resumption was necessary."[16]

During the first two weeks of May some consideration was given by the New York bank to the purchase of long-term securities. Burgess indicated that it was becoming difficult to obtain large amounts of short-term securities. One of the directors, Albert H. Wiggin, chairman of the Chase National Bank, even presented a remarkable memorandum recommending the purchase of other than government securities. Harrison objected saying that there were too many obstacles in the way. By the end of the month excess reserves were at a level, Harrison said, about where they ought to be maintained.

What Is Monetary Ease?

In order to appraise Federal Reserve policy it is important that we understand how System officials interpreted "monetary ease." It should be obvious that the behavior of the money supply formed no part of the meaning of this phrase in the sense that the behavior of the money supply was not a leading "indicator" of credit conditions. Failure to be perfectly clear about the meaning of the expression "monetary ease" has frequently led to a misinterpretation of the aims and objectives of monetary policy. Federal Reserve officials continued to talk about pursuing a policy of ease even though the money supply was contracting, production falling, and prices declining. The term as employed by Federal Reserve officials primarily meant availability of bank credit as well as its cost. But essentially, the term refers to the willingness of the banking system to expand bank credit with a given addition to surplus reserves. The Board explained in its *Nineteenth Annual Report* (1932) that:

During 1932 the Federal Reserve System continued to pursue the policy of monetary ease which it had followed since the beginning of the depression. This policy was expressed through the purchase of United States Government securities in the open market and through the reduction of rates charged for discounts and for acceptances . . . In the autumn of 1931, however, when there was a large outflow of gold following the suspension of the gold standard in England and a large volume of currency withdrawals in this country, discount rates were advanced to 3½ percent at most Reserve banks and to 4 percent at the Richmond and Dallas banks. [17]

It is a mistake to interpret "monetary ease" solely in terms of the behavior of interest rates, for the Board did not consider inflexible long-term rates as incompatible with monetary ease; for example, the *Annual Report* for 1932 states:

At the end of 1932 short-term money rates were at record low levels, but low rates did not extend to the long-term markets, where yields on long-term issues, except those of the United States Government, continued high and flotation of new capital issues were small.[18]

The extent or degree of monetary ease is more difficult to assess. The Board's interpretation seemed to emphasize the method employed rather than the results achieved. In April when Harrison testified before a House Subcommittee he outlined what he considered to be the *modus operandi* of open market purchases. His testimony is instructive, for it reveals the vagueness of Federal Reserve monetary targets and explains to a considerable extent the action taken in March, 1932. He described the way in which open market purchases generate monetary ease in the following manner: "We know that as a rule when we buy securities and reduce the discount rate, the influence is toward ease and expansion of credit *and eventually a rise in the price level.*"[19] The immediate impact was to be judged by the pressure applied to the banks to expand their loans and investments, a relatively narrow sector viewpoint. When conditions are "normal," Harrison stated, the creation of excess reserves puts pressure on banks to make more loans and investments. But he maintained that when these conditions did not prevail "it is a futile thing for the reserve banks to expend their resources for the purchase of Government securities unless the money we put out is going to operate as a basis for expansion of bank credit."[20] That is, there is no reason to increase the volume of excess reserves beyond certain limits. Of course, he was familiar with the fact that excess reserves would supposedly be used initially to take down borrowings and induce bankers to be more liberal in the expansion of bank credit. But his principal concern was the behavior of bank credit, not the money supply. The normal mechanism, he argued, had broken down and excess reserves tended to pile up because the confidence of the banking community had suffered a severe shock—the result of a combination of circumstances: bank failures, panicky depositors, and threats of withdrawals of foreign deposits. Reserves injected through open market operations simply supplied the bankers' demands for increased liquidity. Harrison concluded: "You then have, in spite of the excess reserve, a resistance to its use which the reserve system can not overcome."[21] Granted that his analysis of the increase in excess reserves is correct, still his pessimistic conclusion about the futility of further additions to member bank reserves and the prop they give to the money supply and bank liquidity does not necessarily follow.

One way of viewing open market purchases and their effects is to consider such additions to reserves as meeting the bankers' increased demands for liquidity. Until that demand is satisfied, at prevailing levels of interest rates, credit will not readily be made available by the banking system. In the presence of an excess demand for liquidity, the failure of bank credit to expand with an increase in surplus reserves is understandable. Harrison summed it up thus:

> Well, I myself am a firm believer that if you have two factors, the excess of reserves plus confidence, the principle will probably work. That is, you will have the expansion of bank loans and investments, and you will have the repercussion in price level, provided no other factors interrupt.[22]

He apparently thought that the restoration of confidence was not an appropriate job of credit policy alone. Instead he gambled upon a decrease in hoarding, a let-up in gold exports, and the success of the policies of the Reconstruction Finance Corporation. On a more technical level, he probably concentrated too much of his attention on the situation of the New York and Chicago banks and not enough on the banks outside the two large metropolitan areas. He refers repeatedly to the possibility of a temporary glut of excess reserves but does not explain what he means in terms of banker response:

> There is another reason why you may not be able to go as fast as you might like to go, and that is this: That you run the risk, if you go too fast, of flooding the market or the banks with excess reserves faster than they can use them, or faster than is wise for them to use them. The proper and orderly operation of the open market, I think, is to create a volume of excess reserves gradually, gradually increasing them, and keeping it up constantly, and not have periods when you have got excess reserves one week and none another week.[23]

He argued that a too-rapid rate of increase in excess reserves might lead to an improper distribution of credit. The presumption is that he is referring to the diffusion of reserves throughout the country as a consequence of the initial injection at New York. The Board explained the diffusion process, as follows:

> United States Government securities were purchased for the most part in New York, the principal market for these securities, and the funds arising from the purchases were in the first instance added to the reserve balances of New York banks. Later, however, these funds were distributed, largely through Treasury disbursements of all kinds, including advances by the Reconstruction Finance Corporation to banks and other institutions throughout the country. Funds acquired in this manner by banks in the interior, not being employed locally, subsequently found their way back to New York and other financial centers

through the redeposit of funds by outside banks with their city correspondents.[24]

During 1932, interbank deposits increased over $830 million, indicating that many country banks were redepositing surplus reserves in big city banks instead of using them to take down rediscounts. The increase in excess reserves at New York and other leading cities resulting from this maneuver could not be expected to lead to an increase in bank credit for the very simple reason that they represented a part, a very essential part, of the operating reserves of those banks to be withdrawn immediately in the event of a serious disturbance. An examination of Table 1 shows the distribution of net free reserves among the various classifications of member banks. It is very clear that the heavy indebtedness of the country banks acted as an important drag on the expansion of bank credit. However, these banks were utilizing their surplus reserves to build up liquidity by deposits with correspondents. Presumably, their supposed reluctance to remain indebted to the Federal Reserve Banks was more than offset by their desire for immediate, quick liquidity.

Table 1

Free Reserves, December 1932*

All member banks	245+
New York City	283+
Chicago	163+
Reserve city	19–
Country banks	182–

SOURCE: *Banking and Monetary Statistics* (Washington, D.C.: Board of Governors, 1943), pp. 397–399.

* Average of daily figures.

What Harrison meant by a temporary "glut" of excess reserves can only be surmised from remarks he made subsequently before a joint meeting of the Board and the Open Market Policy Conference on January 4, 1933. On that occasion he said if excess reserves in New York and Chicago increased much beyond the $600 million mark "the chance would be that the banks would cease to pay any interest on deposits, which would undoubtedly increase hoarding."[25] He also suggested that if New York and Chicago stopped payment of interest on bank deposits, "this would tend to scatter the excess reserves now deposited in New York and Chicago throughout the country, and would bring a pressure for using them which did not now obtain."[26] This latter suggestion was unanimously opposed by the Reserve Bank governors on the grounds that it would probably encourage hoarding.

The theory of open market operations elaborated by Burgess and Governor Strong in the mid-twenties furnished no relevant guideposts for action in March, 1932. In the earlier period interest centered mainly on the behavior of the banks in New York and Chicago with respect to member banks' indebtedness and open market rates. The presence of excess reserves beginning in 1931 introduced a new and unfamiliar element into the administration of open market policy. The Open Market Committee when confronted by the presence of excess reserves was forced to reconsider the theory of open market operations. Governor Strong described how the process was supposed to work in his remarks to the governors' conference in March, 1926:

> Experience in the past has indicated that member banks when indebted to the Federal Reserve Bank of New York and in a less degree at other money centers constantly endeavor to free themselves from the indebtedness, and as a consequence such pressure as arises is in the direction of curtailing loans . . . As a guide to the timing and extent of any purchases which might appear desirable, one of our best guides would be the amount of borrowing by member banks in principal centers, and particularly in New York and Chicago. Our experience has shown that when New York City banks are borrowing in the neighborhood of 100 million dollars or more, there is then some real pressure for reducing loans, and money rates tend to be markedly higher than the discount rate. On the other hand, when borrowings of these banks are negligible, as in 1924, the money situation tends to be less elastic and if gold imports take place, there is liable to be some credit inflation, with money rates dropping below our discount rate. When member banks are owing us about 50 million dollars or less the situation appears to be comfortable, with no marked pressure for liquidation and with the requisite elasticity. Under these circumstances no single bank tends to be in debt for any extended period and borrowings are passed around among the different banks . . . In the event of business liquidation now appearing it would seem advisable to keep the New York City banks out of debt beyond something in the neighborhood of 50 million dollars. It would probably be well if some similar rule could be applied to the Chicago banks, although the amount would, of course, be smaller and the difficulties greater because of the influence of the New York market.[27]

Chandler concluded from Strong's statement: "Now that Federal Reserve officials had come to understand open-market operations, their control instruments could be employed with more initiative, precision, and effectiveness."[28] The difficulties with this interpretation are numerous. What Strong described is how open market operations should work during a relatively mild recession, referring specifically to credit availability and the cost of credit in the two leading national money market centers. He was careful to point out that the mechanism quite probably works more sluggishly in other centers, with no benchmarks for the appropriate level of indebtedness there. Strong's explanation is usually referred to as the "reserve position theory." The emphasis of the theory is on the relationship between member bank indebtedness and open market rates. The New York bank in particular tended to view open market operations as a technique for rate manipulation and making credit available in the national money market rather than as a mechanism for controlling the money supply.

Even during the easy money policy of 1924 the indebtedness of the country banks remained above the $150 million level while that of New York and 100 other leading cities fell within Strong's permissible range. A policy of monetary ease in 1927 meant that the combined indebtedness of member banks outside New York City remained above $300 million. So monetary ease in both 1924 and 1927 was thought to be consistent with relatively large net borrowed reserves outside the central reserve cities. The experience with open market operations in 1924 and 1927 differed substantially from that of 1932. Net borrowed reserves amounted to approximately $800 million in February, 1932, all but $23 million of which was concentrated in reserve city and country banks. The degree of ease in the New York and Chicago money market was no reflection, therefore, of conditions prevailing outside the area. Thus the 1924 and 1927 experience was simply not relevant. The one important element in the 1932 situation which was different was the increased demand for liquidity. The diffusion of reserves from the New York market operated not only to take down rediscounts but also to increase excess reserves in New York and Chicago. The reason for the latter effect was the transfer of surplus reserves to New York in the form of interbank deposits on which interest was paid. The level of borrowed reserves by itself probably exaggerates the degree of restraint. The Open Market Committee purchased $850 million of securities between April 6 and July 1. During this period borrowed reserves at reserve city banks declined $192 million to $100 million, and at country banks by only $61 million, to $296 million. Gold exports totaled over $400 million and currency in circulation remained constant.

Harris pointed out thirty years ago that Reserve officials were surprised by the results of their purchases in 1932. According to the Strong-Burgess view, purchases should have lead first to a reduction in rediscounts and then to an increase in reserves, but Harris showed that the large purchases in April had a different effect:

> Member banks outside of the New York District seemed disposed to accumulate balances in New York rather than repay the reserve banks. Purchases of 356 millions of securities were followed by a reduction of rediscounts for the System of but 83 million (or approximately 12 per cent); and rediscounts remained at the high level of more than 500 millions. Moreover, the reduction of rediscounts in the New York District was 26 millions: balances increased by 172, although rediscounts remained at a level (above 100 millions) high in view of conditions. Member banks in New York were afraid to use the additional cash to repay the New York Reserve Bank, and outside member banks in debt either did not obtain the additional cash dumped on the market or else were so frightened that they preferred to remain in debt and move their balances to New York.[29]

The appetite for cash had apparently become so strong that the immediate impact of further open market purchases was to satisfy the banks' increased demands for cash without an expansion of bank credit. For weekly reporting member banks outside New York City the item "Balances with Domestic banks" increased from $774 million on February 24 to $1.15 billion on May 25—an increase of $374 million. Interbank deposits at reporting member banks in New York City increased $304 million during the corresponding period.

At the July 15 meeting of the Open Market Policy Conference, there was some discussion of gradually reducing the volume of security purchases. Governor Harrison stated that the level of excess reserves should be maintained at about the $250-million mark. No substantial purchases were made for the investment account after July 20, 1932. Between August and December excess reserves increased from $270 million to $526 million, an increase of $256 million. However, during this period the gold inflow amounted to $400 million and the increase in Treasury currency outstanding to $125 million. The amount of currency in circulation remained approximately constant thus enabling discounts to be taken down by $169 million and reserves to increase by $362 million. Harrison told his directors on July 7 that the burden of assisting the banks during a crisis should be assumed by the RFC, and its operations liberalized to check further bank closings.[30]

It is instructive to note that during the same period, reserves of the New York banks increased by $246 million while discounts declined by only $30 million—from $93 million to $63 million. The New York City banks had free reserves of $283 million in December. On November 15 the Open Market Policy Conference convened and decided that there was no occasion to acquire more securities at the present time. The question was whether to sell or leave the investment account unchanged.

The Nationwide Banking Crisis

When the Open Market Policy Conference met on January 4, 1933, the governors of the individual Federal Reserve banks expressed their opposition to any further expansion of excess reserves. These reserves, concentrated mainly in Chicago and New York, had risen to over $500 million, and there was growing agitation among Reserve Bank governors to allow some securities to run off.[31] Governor Seay of the Richmond bank recommended the sale of at least $200 million of securities. While not going so far as to specify the actual amount to be sold, Governors Young, Martin, Hamilton, McDougal, and McKinney agreed in the main with Seay's proposal. Governor Harrison did not object, provided that excess reserves were maintained at existing levels. I have already explained (pp. 180–181) that Harrison thought additional reserves might force the bank to suspend payment of interest on demand deposit balances which would probably lead to an increase in domestic hoarding. The governors, however, were unanimously opposed to any program that would further reduce the interest paid on demand deposits.[32] Governor Norris of the Philadelphia Federal Reserve Bank argued that the expansion of excess reserves would only impair member bank earnings. Short-term yields which had been drawn down by monetary policy to all-time lows doubtless aggravated the problem of the maintenance of adequate earnings. Liquidity considerations imposed by the failing confidence of the public in the banking system entailed an additional sacrifice of profits and reduced income which tended to weaken further the solvency of the banking system.

Governor Martin of the St. Louis bank correctly pointed out that the real reason why excess reserves were not being used was that they satisfied the bankers' demands for liquidity in the face of the threat of widespread bank failures.[33] Both Governor Meyer and Secretary of the Treasury Ogden Mills spoke of the dangers of a change in the present policy. They thought the sale of securities might give an impetus to the passage of certain so-called inflationary bills pending before the Congress, and this danger was not to be minimized. According to C. S. Hamlin, Meyer also volunteered the information that the result of the recent presidential election "had not been such as to inspire confidence in the country."[34]

Both the Open Market Policy Conference and the Federal Reserve Board approved a resolution calling for the sale of securities to offset the return flow of currency but not to reduce the level of excess reserves. The target level for excess reserves was set at $500 million. However, total government security holdings in the investment account were not to rise above $1,851 million without calling another meeting of the conference. This latter stipulation may have interfered with the conduct of an open market program both before and after the onset of the national banking crisis in mid-February. The Conference, however, did not meet again until after the declaration of the Bank Holiday by the incoming President Franklin D. Roosevelt.

At an Executive Committee meeting of the New York bank on January 16, Randolph Burgess drew attention to the weakness in the long-term bond market resulting from reports of government security sales. However, Governor Harrison said that "this result almost was inherent in the open market program we have adopted, and offered no reason for abandoning that program."[35] He also added that Burgess might have painted an "unduly gloomy picture of the bond market."

In a memorandum to Governor Harrison on January 19, Burgess summarized the gist of the conversations held at the New York bank by Secretary Mills, Owen Young, Russell Leffingwell, Parker Gilbert, Burgess, and Governor Harrison:

> There was then an extended discussion of Federal reserve open market policy, Mr. Leffingwell and Mr. Mills stating the belief that it had been a mistake to sell any government securities, particularly because of the effect on Treasury credit and the effect on the banking and business situation . . . Some difference of view was expressed as to the effectiveness of additional amounts of excess reserves, some of those present believing that large excess reserves would be effective and others stating a belief that additional amounts would have diminishing effectiveness.

It was also pointed out that the recent policy probably went as far as it would be possible to secure cooperative agreement in the Federal Reserve System.[36]

Hamlin discloses in his Diary on January 20 that Harrison said "a majority of the Governors in their hearts favored a complete reversal of open market policy by letting Government securities run off permanently without replacing."[37]

By the end of the first week in February excess reserves had fallen below the target level of $500 million established at the January meeting of the Open Market Policy Conference. The New York bank acquired $25 million of securities. This action was repeated ten days later when, simultaneously, the bill rate was lowered to 0.5%, because of the restriction on government security purchases.[38] Apparently the ceiling placed on security purchases at the January meeting of the Open Market Committee interfered with plans for additional purchases.

Seymour Harris concluded thirty years ago that as late as the week ending February 1 the "signs of impending disaster were not apparent."[39] Loans and investments of reporting member banks increased by $106 million. However, he continued, in the subsequent four weeks loans and investments fell by $900 million, $700 million of which was concentrated in the New York City banks alone. Table 2 shows member bank indebtedness, government securities held by Federal Reserve Banks, currency in circulation, and excess reserves of member banks weekly for the period January 4 through March 8. It is readily apparent that a serious and critical situation had developed by the middle of February. The governor of Michigan had declared a bank holiday for all banks in that state. This event signaled the onset of a severe banking crisis which was to spread rapidly to all sections of the country and was to culminate in early March in the complete breakdown of a large part of the financial system.

According to Table 2 currency in circulation increased by approximately $200 million during the first two weeks of February. This contraseasonal increase in domestic hoarding led to a small increase in member bank borrowing and to a much larger reduction in excess reserves. Excess reserves on February 15 as indicated by Table 2 were substantially below the $500-million target level set in January. The government security portfolio remained virtually unchanged at $1.8 billion. It certainly appears reasonable to ask why Reserve officials did not initiate immedi-

Table 2

Member Bank Indebtedness, Government Securities held by Federal Reserve Banks, Currency in Circulation, and Excess Reserves of Member Banks: Weekly* from January 4 to March 8, 1933

1933		Bills discounted	Government securities (*$ million*)	Currency in circulation	Excess reserves
January	1	251	1,851	5,383	582
	11	248	1,812	5,302	627
	18	249	1,778	5,315	609
	25	265	1,763	5,324	573
February	1	269	1,764	5,365	499
	8	253	1,784	5,418	501
	15	286	1,809	5,567	340
	22	327	1,834	5,701	401
March	1	712	1,836	6,432	272
	8	1,414	1,881	7,251	129

SOURCE: *Banking and Monetary Statistics* (Washington, D.C.: *Board of Governors,* 1943), p. 387.
* Wednesday figures.

ately an expanded program of purchases to offset the increase in hoarding of currency. Instead there was a rapid expansion in member bank indebtedness and a general tightening of credit. We noted earlier that in January the Open Market Policy Conference had placed a ceiling of $1.8 billion on the amount of securities held in the investment portfolio. To exceed this limit required another meeting by the full committee. Governor Harrison announced at an Executive Committee meeting of the New York bank on February 20 that the excess reserves of the New York City member banks had almost disappeared, and he stated further "authority granted by the Open Market Policy Conference would not permit relieving the market through purchases of securities."[40] Instead he suggested that it would be necessary to supply funds through the bill market.

The question really boils down to why there was no meeting of the conference to obtain authority to increase purchases of government securities. We have already pointed out that officials of the New York bank, particularly Governor Harrison, did not believe the conference would approve additional purchases because of the strong opposition of some of the Reserve Bank governors at their previous meeting in January. At a Board of Directors meeting of the New York bank held on February 23, Harrison explained: "In so far as purchases of Government securities are concerned, our partners wouldn't go along. . . ."[41] And again on February 27, he told the directors that he had been in Washington the day before to discuss the situation with Governor Meyer and Secretary Mills. They both agreed that "it would be futile, at this time, to attempt or to consider further purchases of government securities."[42] Harrison also made it quite clear that he had no intention of recommending purchases unless the Boston and Chicago Federal Reserve Banks agreed to participate. He added: "he had always pressed this point of view in his contacts at Washington, and that his insistence had tied our own open market program to promises of governmental economy, a balanced budget, and a sound currency."[43] His statement appears almost inexplicable outside of the political context. It would appear that Harrison and perhaps Governor Meyer attempted to interject a new criterion by which to judge the necessity for open market operations. Rumors were widespread about President Roosevelt's intention to devalue the dollar and "inflate the currency." Perhaps Harrison expected, but failed to obtain, such assurances from the President-elect. It was the political climate then and not simply the banking situation which exercised a strong influence in shaping Federal Reserve policy. Leadership, if it can be said that there was any, passed quietly to the Federal Reserve Board. And it was ever so firmly declined.

The Federal Reserve Board reviewed the banking situation upon the closing of the Michigan banks. It discussed the desirability of new legislation to meet any national emergency which might develop but concluded that little could be expected during the present session of the lame-duck Congress.[44] On February 22 President Hoover dispatched a letter to the Board requesting advice as to the seriousness of the banking crisis in which he said:

> I should like to be advised by the Board as to whether the Board considers that the situation is one that has reached a public danger and whether the Board considers the Federal Reserve system can protect the public interest, or whether the Board considers any measures should be undertaken at this juncture and especially what, if any, further authority should be obtained.[45]

Governor Meyer replied to the President's request, as follows: "At the moment the Board does not desire to make any specific proposals for additional measures of authority, but it will continue to give all aspects of the situation its most careful attention."[46] Earlier in December Meyer had explained his views about the role of political factors in shaping monetary policy. He told the New York directors when they were considering the sale of securities:

> Reverting to the political aspects of the question, Governor Meyer said that he could not avoid them if we would. Questions of currency, credit, and the price level are the principal questions which influence the body politic at the moment and inasmuch as the Federal Reserve System is intimately concerned with all of these questions, we are tied to the political situation whether we like it or not. To take action now, without considering its broader political aspects, would be dangerous for the Federal Reserve System.[47]

These remarks were even more appropriate in late February than they had been in the previous December. Governor Meyer was unwilling to consider the banking situation apart from the political climate of which it formed a part. By default the initiative for monetary action fell therefore upon the President who did not have the requisite economic advisory machinery for assuming the burden. The inevitable result was inaction, delay, and ultimate catastrophe.

Hamlin recorded in his Diary on February 24 that Secretary of the Treasury Ogden Mills was in a "very disturbed state of mind" and urged the Board to consider carefully if there was anything more that it could do.[48] Adolph Miller, who at the time was also informally advising President Hoover, suggested two measures: 1) the use of clearing house certificates; and 2) a moratorium—but neither was received favorably by the majority of the members of the Board.

At a meeting on February 27 Governor Meyer called the Board's attention to the increase in foreign exchange rates and money market rates and suggested that the New York bank "recognize" the advance in rates. According to the Board's minutes, other members present expressed agreement with Meyer.[49] The kind of "recognition" contemplated meant only one thing—a call to advance the rediscount rate. Secretary Mills, fearing the strain on commercial banks, requested the approval of the Board to permit Governor Harrison to buy $100 million of government securities to offset the drawing down of Treasury deposits. Governor Meyer replied that an increase in government security holdings would be inconsistent in the face of an upward trend in open market rates. He insisted that the rise in rates was inevitable and that the New York market should protect itself against higher rates abroad. Open market purchases, he said, would be ineffective in preventing what he thought was an inevitable readjustment of rates.[50] An unidentified member of the Board advanced the argument that open market purchases might be interpreted in Europe as evidence that the Federal Reserve was supporting the Treasury's financial policies which could have a detrimental effect on the government's credit. The Board did not favor the suggestion of Secretary Mills. It is clear then that both a majority in the New York bank and the Board in Washington rejected open market operations as a tool to deal with the banking crisis.

Obviously disturbed by the Board's unwillingness to act, President Hoover dispatched another letter to the Board on February 28 in which he set forth three specific proposals:

> Since my letter of a few days ago the banking situation has obviously become one of even greater gravity. I naturally wish to be properly advised as to such measures as can be taken to prevent the hardships to millions of people which are now going on. Although the Board is not the technical adviser of the President, yet it appears to me that in the large sense it should be prepared to advise me as to the measures necessary for the protection of the banking and currency system in times of emergency. I would, therefore, be glad to know whether the Board considers it desirable: a) To establish some form of Federal guarantee of banking deposits; or b) To establish clearing house systems in the affected areas; or c) To allow the situation to drift along under the sporadic State and community solutions now in progress . . .[51]

Hamlin relates that there was a meeting on the same night in the Board's rooms in the Treasury to discuss the banking situation and to recommend what the Board might do to stave off the impending crisis. Present were Governor Meyer, Secretary Mills, Governor Black of the Atlanta bank, and officials of the New York bank and the Reconstruction Finance Corporation.[52] Since Hamlin stated that he did not learn of this meeting until the following day when it was announced by Secretary Mills and Governor Meyer, some members of the Board were obviously excluded from the inner councils formulating monetary policy. An official of the New York bank favored a 50% guaranty of deposits by the government, but apparently no agreement could be reached as to the advisability of the Board advocating the use of clearing house certificates and scrip or the guarantee of deposits.

When the Board met the next day, Governor Meyer declared that he would not favor a government guaranty of deposits of whatever amount. Miller was emphatic in urging the Board to devise some means of dealing with the situation, and he pressed his point about the issue of clearing house certificates. He admitted that many local bankers objected to their issue, but he thought that it was futile to rely on local initiative in these circumstances, and that the Board should take affirmative action to break down their resistance. Hamlin agreed to Miller's proposal, but action was once again postponed. Moreover, Miller said the Board was drifting and should have approved the use of clearing house certificates two weeks ago, "that this inertia made him feel that the whole Board should be reorganized."[53]

On March 2 the Board sent a letter to President Hoover outlining its objections to the proposals contained in his previous letter:

> In response to your first inquiry, the Board has requested me to advise you that it is not at this time prepared to recommend any form of Federal guarantee of banking deposits . . . We know that the question of issuing clearing house certificates has been or is being considered in the communities . . . but, for a number of reasons . . . [the Board] have not felt, up to this time, that it would be feasible or desirable for them to resort to such a device . . . Answering your third inquiry . . . so far no additional measures or authority have developed in concrete form, which at the moment, the Board feels it would be justified in urging.[54]

They rejected the Hoover proposals, and they were either unprepared or unwilling to offer any alternatives. The System decided to adjust passively to the credit restraining effects implied by the increase in external and domestic hoarding. Before Hoover had received the Board's letter, however, he wrote again urging them to reconsider some form of guarantee of banking deposits and to impress upon them the extreme gravity of the situation.

When the Board reassembled on March 2, it was their unanimous opinion that a banking holiday should be declared on the following Friday, Saturday, and Monday (March 3, 4, and 5). The Attorney-General advised the Secretary of the Treasury Ogden Mills that the President could invoke the authority granted to him under Section 5 of the Trading with the Enemy Act passed during World War I, if the emergency justified it. However, Secretary Mills said that the matter was not entirely free from doubt and that he would not advise President Hoover to issue a proclamation without the explicit approval of the incoming administration. All of the Board members agreed, nevertheless, that a banking holiday should be declared immediately and that Congress should be called into special session on Monday and not later than Tuesday to enact appropriate legislation. This, of course, required the approval of President-elect Roosevelt, and so Secretary Mills advised William Woodin, the incoming Secretary of the Treasury.

On Friday, March 3, the Federal Reserve Board spent another day discussing the necessity for a proclamation by President Hoover declaring a national bank holiday. Several futile attempts were made to obtain agreement between President Hoover and Roosevelt. New York applied for and obtained approval for an increase in its discount rate from 2½% to 3½%. Also the Board suspended the reserve requirement of the New York bank for ninety days because the reserve ratio had fallen below the legal minimum.

Later the same evening Governor Meyer wrote to President Hoover calling for a Presidential proclamation since the Senate had already adjourned for the day. He warned that the situation had reached such a critical point where immediate action was necessary to prevent a complete banking collapse. It was the emphatic opinion of Secretary Mills that unless Roosevelt agreed to call Congress into special session on Monday, there was absolutely no legal basis for a proclamation by the outgoing President. So convinced was he of the tenuous authority for such drastic action, Secretary Mills requested and obtained permission to include the following statement in the Board's minutes:

> The Attorney-General holds that the authority under the Trading with the Enemy Act is of the thinnest possible kind and at most there is the barest color of authority and that he does not believe the President can do it without the agreement of the President-elect, to be followed by a validating act by the Congress. I think it should be further noted that it was my understanding when I left the President ten minutes ago that Governor Roosevelt felt that in view of the information he had from New York that he did not see the occasion for him to request a national holiday, or, indeed, to assume responsibility for it. I think therefore that in view of the opinion given by the Attorney-General that I do not see how the President can act on the recommendation of the Board tonight unless the whole question is to be reopened. I don't differ with the other members of the Board on the practical situation as it exists now at midnight. There is no formal opinion from the Attorney-General.[55]

The Board minutes show that Adolph Miller left the meeting at about 10:00 P.M. and went to the Mayflower Hotel in Washington to discuss the banking situation with Roosevelt and to deliver copies of the proposed banking proclamation and other papers. Upon arriving at the hotel, Miller was told that he could not see Roosevelt because he was engaged upon his inaugural address. At 12:30 A.M. Governor Meyer's letter urging the declaration of a banking holiday was delivered to the White House. According to the report appearing in the minutes, Governor Meyer's secretary returned to the offices of the Board shortly after 1:00 A.M. and said "when he arrived at the White House, he was informed that the President had retired at 12:00 A.M. [midnight], and that the attendants there hesitated to disturb him. Finally, however, they telephoned to Mr. Richey, one of the President's secretaries, who authorized them to deliver the letter to the President at once."[56]

Hoover took no action, but he was so incensed by the letter that he sent the following reply to Governor Meyer:

Hon. Eugene Meyer
Federal Reserve Board
Washington, D.C.

MY DEAR GOVERNOR MEYER:

I received at half past one this morning your letter dated March 3rd. I must assume that this letter was written on the basis of information received by you prior to 11:30 o'clock last night for the reason that before your letter was sent you had certain information as follows:

a) At 11 o'clock last night the President-elect had informed me he did not wish such a proclamation issued.

b) The Attorney General had renewed the same opinion which he had already given to the Board that the authorities on which you were relying were inadequate unless supported by the incoming administration.

c) That groups of representative bankers in both Chicago and New York, embracing members of the Board of Directors of the Federal Reserve Banks in those cities, were then in conference with the governors of the states of Illinois and New York, and that the governors of these two states were prepared to act if these representative groups so recommended. It appears that the governors did take action under their authorities, declaring a temporary holiday in these two critical states, and thus accomplishing the major purposes which the Board apparently had in mind.

In view of the above I am at a loss to understand why such a communication should have been sent to me in the last few hours of this Administration, which I believe the Board must now admit was neither justified nor necessary.[57]

Yours faithfully,
HERBERT HOOVER

With reference to Paragraph A in the Hoover letter, Hamlin related that Adolph Berle, Jr. told him that Roosevelt did not agree that it was unwise to issue the Presidential proclamation. He was with Woodin the whole evening, and he said that Roosevelt had no objection to Hoover's issuing a statement on his own but did not wish to join with him. And in a letter to C. S. Hamlin, Governor Harrison pointed out that only after Hoover decided not to act did New York's Governor Herbert Lehman, upon the recommendation of the New York Clearing House Committee, decide to declare a holiday for the banks in that state:

In fact, you may remember that late into the night (March 3) Mr. Mills and the President were still discussing the possibility of a national holiday, and Mr. Mills asked me not to leave the bank until I was expressly released by him. Consequently it was not until well after midnight, when Mr. Mills told me that the President had finally definitely decided not to declare a national holiday, that I went uptown to Governor Lehman's apartment.

He and members of the New York Clearing House Committee, representatives of various private banking firms and others formed a group, I should say, of about twenty-five men when I arrived. It was agreed that the Governor would declare a holiday for two days, Saturday, March 4, and Monday, March 6, with the understanding that he would make a statement to the effect that he had done so at the request of the Clearing House Committee and with the advice and recommendation of the Federal Reserve Bank of New York. It was well after two o'clock Saturday morning (about two thirty as I remember) when this decision was made. . . .[58]

Herein lay the snag that explains in part the inaction of President Hoover. Roosevelt was unwilling to accept any responsibility before he assumed office, and Hoover balked at the idea of doing anything of dubious legality which did not implicate the incoming President. Doubtless personal and political considerations weighed in the decisions of both of these men. Roosevelt probably did not object to the issue of a Presidential proclamation, but he simply refused to join with Hoover.

On no other occasion during the first twenty years of Federal Reserve history did purely political considerations play so prominent a role in the determination of monetary policy, nor did the

Board deserve more blame for its failure to assume the initiative. In all likelihood this particular banking crisis could have been averted.

Epilogue

The collapse of the banking system in March calamitously ended the first twenty years of Federal Reserve monetary policy. The bold experiment in central banking inaugurated in 1914 to relieve seasonal and emergency currency stringency came to grief over the unwillingness, not the incapacity, of the monetary authorities to preserve the solvency of a banking system already weakened by a prolonged business depression. That unwillingness was the direct result of the failure of an overwhelming majority of the governors of the Federal Reserve Banks and members of the Federal Reserve Board to understand how open market operations could be used to counteract recessions and depressions. More than any other single factor, it was confusion over the interpretation of excess reserves that accounts for the Federal Reserve's inaction during January and February, 1933. The behavior of the System in 1924 and 1927 did not provide the relevant guideposts for action in 1932 and 1933. Whatever relevance these two previous episodes may have had to the experience during the first six months of 1930, they were not directly relevant to events in 1932 and 1933. Liberal purchases of government securities in the last two weeks of February could have in all probability, barring some unforeseen international reaction, staved off the banking crisis that occurred in March.

The consistency with which Reserve Bank governors acted during the first twenty years is not remarkable, considering the fact that there had been so little turnover in the management of individual Federal Reserve Banks. Before 1935 the organizational structure of the System was characterized by a strong type of federalism with power diffused broadly rather than concentrated centrally. It imparted necessarily a sense of inertia and conservativism to monetary policy that leadership, even if it had been entirely effective in New York or Washington, could not possibly have overcome. One could conclude from the behavior and performance of the Reserve Bank governors that they learned slowly and adapted poorly to their expanding responsibilities.

But this point of view overlooks the problem of how knowledge was communicated from the academic ranks of monetary economists to the administrators of monetary policy. It is naive to assume that whatever economists "know" is the obligation of the monetary administrators to find out. Keeping the administrators of monetary policy apprised of what is going on in the academic world is a problem whose solution still remains far from satisfactory. There is no doubt that the role of the economist as policy maker and critic has evolved tremendously during the past thirty years. Until more is known about the channels through which this knowledge *should* have passed during those eventful years, only tentative judgments can be made about what System officials *ought* to have known. Yet whatever optimism we might feel about the performance of the Federal Reserve in the future must stem from the belief that continued expansion of the role of economists in public policy decisions will improve monetary behavior.

Notes

INTRODUCTION

1) Lester V. Chandler, *Benjamin Strong, Central Banker* (Washington, D.C.: Brookings Institution, 1958).
2) He used extensively the Board's mimeographed X-letters and the proceedings of the governors' conferences. Seymour E. Harris, *Twenty Years of Federal Reserve Policy,* 2 vols. (Cambridge, Mass.: Harvard University, 1933). The two other important studies of roughly the same period by Charles O. Hardy and Harold Reed depend entirely upon public statements and official reports of Federal Reserve officials. Charles O. Hardy, *Credit Policies of the Federal Reserve System* (Washington, D.C.: Brookings Institution, 1932), and Harold Reed, *Federal Reserve Policy, 1921–1930* (New York: McGraw-Hill, 1930). E. A. Goldenweiser's more recent study obviously was based in part on official records as well as his own personal memoranda but there are no direct references to these records in his book: *American Monetary Policy* (New York: McGraw-Hill, 1951).
3) Milton Friedman and Anna Jacobson Schwartz, *A Monetary History of the United States 1867–1960,* National Bureau of Economic Research (Princeton, N.J.: Princeton University, 1963).
4) *Leffingwell Papers* (Library of Congress), Letterbooks.
5) These records include Board minutes from 1914–33, minutes and related papers of the Open Market Investment Committee and the Open Market Policy Conference, and correspondence and memoranda contained in the Board's official files. No restrictions were placed on my access to the above mentioned materials.

CHAPTER 1 *The McAdoo Policy and World War I Finance*

1) E. S. Shaw, "Money Supply and Stable Economic Growth," in N. H. Jacoby, ed., *United States Monetary Policy* (Columbia University: The American Assembly, 1958), p. 53; and *Money, Income, and Monetary Policy* (Chicago: Irwin, 1950), pp. 426–27, 430. Milton Friedman and Anna Jacobson Schwartz, *A Monetary History of the United States 1867–1960,* National Bureau of Economic Research (Princeton, N.J.: Princeton University, 1963), p. 216. H. Parker Willis, *The Federal Reserve System* (New York: Ronald Press, 1923), p. 1210.

2) McAdoo married Eleanor Wilson, the President's daughter, in May, 1914. His first wife had died in 1912.
3) C. S. Hamlin, *Diaries* (Library of Congress), III, 53.
4) *Ibid.*, p. 56.
5) *Ibid.*
6) W. G. McAdoo, *Crowded Years* (Boston and New York: Houghton Mifflin, 1931), p. 288.
7) H. Willis, *op. cit.*, p. 675.
8) *Ibid.*, p. 674.
9) *McAdoo Papers* (Library of Congress), Letters, November 5, 1915.
10) McAdoo, *Crowded Years,* p. 382.
11) *Federal Reserve Board Records,* file labeled: "Preferential discount rates, Liberty Loans."
12) *Federal Reserve Board Records, minutes* (Washington, D.C.: Board of Governors), April 17, 1917.
13) *Ibid.*, April 26, 1917.
14) *Ibid.*, October 19, 1917.
15) *Annual Report of the Secretary of the Treasury, 1920* (Washington, D.C.: Government Printing Office, 1921), p. 110.
16) *Ibid.*, p. 122.
17) Willis, *op. cit.*, pp. 1154–55.
18) *Ibid.*, p. 1204.
19) *Ibid.*, p. 1205.
20) *Ibid.*, p. 1283.
21) Russell C. Leffingwell, "Discussion" of O. M. W. Sprague, "The Discount Policy of the Federal Reserve Banks," *The American Economic Review,* XI (March 1921), 30.
22) R. F. Harrod, *Policy Against Inflation* (London: Macmillan, 1958), p. 3.
23) *Leffingwell Papers* (Library of Congress), Letterbooks, XXXIII, 65–66 (author's italics).
24) *Ibid.*, XXXVIII, 113–29, letter dated December 12, 1919. Jacob Hollander, *War Borrowing* (New York: Macmillan, 1919).
25) Leffingwell, *op. cit.* XXXVIII, 118.
26) *Ibid.*
27) *Ibid.*, pp. 123–25.
28) *Federal Reserve Bulletin,* June, 1918, p. 486.
29) *Ibid.* (author's italics).
30) W. L. Crum, J. F. Fennelly, Lawrence Seltzer, *Fiscal Planning for Total War* (New York: National Bureau of Economic Research, 1942).
31) Adolph Miller, "War Finance and Inflation," *Annals of the American Academy,* LXXV (January 1918). J. M. Keynes, *How to Pay for the War* (London: Macmillan, 1940).
32) Miller, *op cit.*, p. 133.
33) *Ibid.*, p. 134.
34) The Federal Reserve Board was instrumental in establishing and administering the Capital Issues Committee to control the amount of security issues above a stated amount, the War Finance Corporation

to supply financial aid to firms, and the War Industries Board. See Willis, *op. cit.*, pp. 1262–72.

CHAPTER 2 *Postwar Financial Policy: The Inflation Phase, 1918–1920*

1) *Supra,* Chapter 1, p. 15.
2) C. S. Hamlin, *Diaries* (Library of Congress), IV, 194.
3) *Sixth Annual Report of the Federal Reserve Board* (Washington, D.C.: Government Printing Office, 1920), p. 2.
4) Hamlin, *op. cit.*, IV, 255. There was no single rate at which member banks could borrow from the Federal Reserve Banks but a complex of rates depending upon the kind of collateral offered and the maturity of the loan.
5) *Ibid.*, p. 256.
6) *Ibid.*, p. 263. Apparently Hamlin incorrectly dated these remarks. The minutes of the Board show that the decision not to raise rates was made on January 20.
7) John R. Commons, "Statement," *Stabilization Hearings,* Hearings before the Committee on Banking and Currency, House of Representatives, 69th Congress, 1st Session, Pt. 2, 1927, p. 1077; W. P. G. Harding, *The Formative Period of the Federal Reserve System* (New York: Houghton Mifflin, 1925), p. 123; Lester Chandler, *Benjamin Strong, Central Banker* (Washington, D. C.: Brookings Institution, 1958), p. 121.
8) *Federal Reserve Board Records,* proceedings of governors' conferences with Federal Reserve Board (Washington, D.C.: Board of Governors, March 20, 21, and 22, 1919), p. 354.
9) *Ibid.*, minutes, April 16, 1919.
10) *Ibid.*, files labeled: "Preferential Discount Rate for Paper Secured by Government Obligations."
11) *Ibid.*, auxiliary minutes, September 4, 1919.
12) Harding, *op. cit.*, p. 149. See also Adolph Miller, "Federal Reserve Policy," *The American Economic Review,* XI (June 1921), 181.
13) Hamlin, *op. cit.*, V, 26.
14) *Ibid.*, p. 17.
15) *Supra,* Chapter 1, p. 19.
16) *Leffingwell Papers* (Library of Congress), Letterbooks XXXIII, 65.
17) Russell C. Leffingwell, "Discussion" of O. M. W. Sprague, "The Discount Policy of the Federal Reserve Banks," *The American Economic Review,* XI (March 1921), 33.
18) *Agricultural Inquiry,* hearing before the Joint Commission of Agricultural Inquiry, 67th Congress, 1st Session, Vol. 2, 1922, pp. 503–4.
19) Hamlin, *op. cit.*, V, 57.
20) *Board Records,* auxiliary minutes, September 4, 1919.
21) *Ibid.*
22) *Ibid.*
23) *Ibid.*
24) Hamlin, *op. cit.*, V, 41–42.

25) *Ibid.*, p. 43.
26) R. G. Hawtrey, "The Federal Reserve System of the United States," *The Journal of the Royal Statistical Society*, LXXXV (March 1922), 247.
27) Hamlin, *op. cit.*, V, 49.
28) *Ibid.*
29) *Ibid.*, pp. 54–55.
30) *Ibid.*, p. 56.
31) *Board Records*, proceedings of governors' conference November 19, 20, and 21, 1919, p. 272.
32) *Ibid.*, p. 273. Governor Strong in a note of levity made the following remark: "I will warrant that the limit has been raised in every poker game in the United States in the last year." Strauss asked, "Do you expect to bring down the limit of the poker games by raising the discount rate?" To that Strong retorted, "Yes. That will be the effect in time." (p. 236).
33) Hamlin, *op. cit.*, V, 66–67. The Money Committee was an informal organization of New York Bankers with Governor Strong as chairman whose purpose it was to exercise selective control of loans to the stock exchange. See Chandler, *op. cit.*, pp. 122 ff.
34) For a different interpretation see Milton Friedman and Anna Jacobson Schwartz, *A Monetary History of the United States 1867–1960*, National Bureau of Economic Research (Princeton, N.J.: Princeton University, 1963), pp. 228–29. They assert that the Board's failure to raise rates sooner was solely the consequence of inept judgment and the loss of personal courage.
35) *Board Records*, discount rates, annual file, 1919.
36) *Leffingwell Papers*, XXXVII, 365.
37) *Ibid.*, p. 21.
38) *Ibid.*, pp. 70–71.
39) Hamlin, *op. cit.*, V, 110.
40) *Board Records*, Board's files labeled: "Preferential Discount Rate for Paper Secured by Government Obligations."
41) Friedman and Schwartz, *op. cit.*, p. 230.
42) Hamlin, *op. cit.*, V, 150.
43) Miller, *op. cit.*, p. 33.
44) One of the weaknesses of the Friedman and Schwartz narrative during this episode is their neglect of the Treasury position and the views of those responsible for formulating and administering Treasury policy. They approve of the conclusions of the Joint Congressional Commission of Agricultural Inquiry that the Federal Reserve Board and the Federal Reserve Banks were directly responsible for the failure to take action in 1919. Yet no Treasury official was called to testify. What the commission learned about Treasury policy they learned from Governor Harding and Governor Strong.

CHAPTER 3 *Postwar Financial Policy: The Deflation Phase, 1920–1921*

1) *Federal Reserve Bulletin* (Washington, D. C.: Federal Reserve Board, February, 1920), p. 118.
2) Stanley Lebergott, "Annual Estimates of Unemployment in the United States, 1900–1954," *The Measurement and Behavior of Unemployment,* National Bureau of Economic Research (Princeton, N.J.: Princeton University, 1957), p. 215.
3) Lester Chandler, *Benjamin Strong, Central Banker* (Washington, D.C.: Brookings Institution, 1958), pp. 183–85. Milton Friedman and Anna Jacobson Schwartz, *A Monetary History of the United States 1867–1960,* National Bureau of Economic Research (Princeton, N.J.: Princeton University, 1963), pp. 237–38, 249. Federal Reserve Banks were required to hold a gold reserve equal to at least 40% of their issue of Federal Reserve Notes and 35% of their total deposit liabilities, namely deposits of member banks. The average reserve ratio for the twelve Federal Reserve Banks had fallen to a low of 42.2% in May, 1920, and did not rise above that amount throughout the remainder of the year.
4) *Agricultural Inquiry,* hearing before the Joint Commission of Agricultural Inquiry, 67th Congress, 1st Session, Vol. 2, 1922, p. 714.
5) W. P. G. Harding, *The Formative Period of the Federal Reserve System* (New York: Houghton Mifflin, 1925), p. 200.
6) R. G. Hawtrey, "The Federal Reserve System of the United States," *The Journal of the Royal Statistical Society,* LXXXV, March, 1922, p. 249.
7) R. G. Hawtrey, *The Pound at Home and Abroad* (London: Longmans, 1961), p. 59.
8) David F. Houston, *Eight Years with Wilson's Cabinet,* Vol. 2 (New York: Doubleday, Page, 1926), p. 108.
9) Friedman and Schwartz, *op. cit.,* p. 237. E. S. Shaw, "Money Supply and Stable Economic Growth," *United States Monetary Policy* (The American Assembly: Columbia University, 1958), p. 57.
10) Chandler, *op. cit.,* pp. 169 ff.
11) *Federal Reserve Bulletin,* March, 1916, p. 102. An address delivered on January 25 before the New York Credit Men's Association.
12) Milton Friedman has given a different interpretation: "the Federal Reserve System . . . established a separate official body charged with explicit responsibility for monetary conditions and supposedly clothed with adequate power to achieve monetary stability or, at least, to prevent pronounced instability." Milton Friedman, *A Program for Monetary Stability* (New York: Fordham University, 1959), p. 14.
13) *Federal Reserve Bulletin,* November, 1918, p. 1048–49.
14) *Ibid.,* p. 1049.
15) *Ibid.,* p. 1050.
16) There is a strong resemblance between the above analysis and what Keynes and Robertson have both labeled the "finance motive"; that

is, the temporary demand for money by business firms while goods are in process of distribution from producer to consumer. This, of course, is not exactly what Keynes meant by "demand for finance," but he admitted in a brush with Robertson that his use was only a special case of finance required by any productive process. Keynes argued that bank credit in the sense of "finance" was a *revolving fund* which did not "absorb or exhaust any resources." J. M. Keynes, "Alternative Theories of the Rate of Interest," *The Economic Journal,* XLVII (June 1937), 247. Robertson was quick to point out that it could only be so regarded if the banking system kept the aggregate of working capital intact. D. H. Robertson, "Mr. Keynes and 'Finance'," *The Economic Journal,* XLVIII (June 1938), 316.

17) *Board Records,* X-letter 3022a, January 13, 1921, p. 3.
18) C. S. Hamlin, *Diaries* (Library of Congress), VI, 32, 33. Williams resigned shortly thereafter.
19) *Ibid.,* p. 66.
20) *Ibid.,* pp. 76–77.
21) *Board Records,* proceedings of governors' conference April 12–15, 1921, pp. 28–29.

CHAPTER 4 *The Managed Money Interlude: 1921–1923*

1) S. E. Harris, *Twenty Years of Federal Reserve Policy,* 2 vols. (Cambridge, Mass.: Harvard University, 1933). Laughlin Currie, *The Supply and Control of Money in the U.S.* (Cambridge, Mass.: Harvard University, 1934).
2) Adolph Miller, "Federal Reserve Policy," *The American Economic Review,* XI (June 1921), 192.
3) Oliver M. W. Sprague, "The Discount Policy of the Federal Reserve Banks," *The American Economic Review,* XI (March 1921), 28.
4) Miller, *op. cit.,* p. 193.
5) *Ibid.*
6) *Tenth Annual Report of the Federal Reserve Board* (1923), p. 30.
7) *Twelfth Annual Report of the Federal Reserve Board* (1925), p. 2.
8) *Stabilization Hearings,* hearings before the Committee on Banking and Currency, House of Representatives, 70th Congress, 1st Session, 1928, p. 13.
9) *Ibid.,* pp. 19–21.
10) J. M. Keynes, *Monetary Reform* (New York: Harcourt, 1924), p. 199. R. F. Harrod, *Policy Against Inflation* (London: Macmillan, 1958), p. 34.
11) *Stabilization Hearings, op. cit.,* pp. 20–21.
12) *Ibid.,* p. 21.
13) Lester Chandler, *Benjamin Strong, Central Banker* (Washington, D.C.: Brookings Institution, 1958), p. 199.
14) *Tenth Annual Report, op. cit.,* p. 33.
15) *Ibid.* (author's italics).
16) Lloyd Mints, *A History of Banking Theory* (Chicago: University of Chicago, 1945), pp. 266–67.

17) *Tenth Annual Report, op. cit.*, p. 34.
18) *Ibid.*, pp. 33–34 (italics in the original).

CHAPTER 5 *The Application of the Quantitative Test: 1922–1923*

1) *Federal Reserve Board Records,* file labeled: "Discount Rates," memorandum, dated March 14, 1922.
2) *Ibid.*, memorandum dated April 3, 1922. Gilbert's view is consistent with the money supply model presented in Chapter 3.
3) C. S. Hamlin, *Diaries* (Library of Congress), VI, 171.
4) *Board Records,* discount rates, 1922.
5) *Board Records,* Miller Papers. Box number 3. These papers are uncatalogued and do not form part of the official files of the Board of Governors.
6) *Ibid.*, p. 3.
7) *Stabilization Hearings,* hearings before the House Committee on Banking and Currency, 70th Congress, 1st Session, 1928, p. 295.
8) *Federal Reserve Bulletin,* November, 1922, p. 1267 (author's italics).
9) Lester Chandler, *Benjamin Strong, Central Banker* (Washington, D.C.: Brookings Institution, 1958), p. 218.
10) *Ibid.*, p. 221.
11) *Federal Reserve Bulletin,* March, 1923, p. 283.
12) *Ibid.*, May, 1923, p. 539.
13) *Ibid.*, p. 541.
14) *Board Records,* X-Letter 3696, April 7, 1923. See also: Chandler, *op. cit.*, pp. 209 ff.
15) Hamlin, *op. cit.*, VII, 86–87.
16) *Board Records,* Open Market Investment Committee, May 23, 1923. Letter of Governor Crissinger to J. H. Case, Deputy Governor of the Federal Reserve Bank of New York, dated May 31, 1923.
17) *Tenth Annual Report of the Federal Reserve Board,* p. 15.
18) *Federal Reserve Bulletin,* May, 1923, p. 539.

CHAPTER 6 *The Strong Policy: The 1923–1924 Recession*

1) Lester Chandler, *Benjamin Strong, Central Banker* (Washington, D.C.: Brookings Institution, 1958), p. 241.
2) Charles O. Hardy, *Credit Policies of the Federal Reserve System* (Washington, D.C.: Brookings Institution, 1932), p. 108. Milton Friedman and Anna Jacobson Schwartz, *A Monetary History of the United States, 1867–1960,* National Bureau of Economic Research (Princeton, N.J.: Princeton University, 1963), p. 269.
3) Arthur I. Bloomfield, *Monetary Policy under the International Gold Standard, 1880–1914* (New York: Federal Reserve Bank of New York, 1959), p. 24.
4) *Federal Reserve Bulletin,* February, 1924, p. 78.
5) *Board Records,* Open Market Investment Committee, December 3, 1923, minutes.

6) *Board Records,* Open Market Investment Committee, November 12, 1942, Report of the Open Market Investment Committee to the Joint Conference November 1924.
7) *Board Records,* Open Market Investment Committee, December 3, 1923; memorandum from W. R. Burgess to J. H. Case dated November 30, 1923.
8) *Ibid.*
9) *Ibid.*, January 14, 1924; memorandum from W. R. Burgess to J. H. Case.
10) *Ibid.*, February 8, 1924; memorandum from W. R. Burgess and J. H. Case to Benjamin Strong.
11) *Ibid.*, April 22, 1924; Memorandum on the Credit Situation.
12) C. S. Hamlin, *Diaries* (Library of Congress), VIII, 124–25. Edmund Platt was a member of the Board 1920–1930.
13) *Board Records,* proceedings of governors' conference, May 6, 1924, p. 9.
14) *Ibid.*, pp. 63–64.
15) Hamlin, *op. cit.*, VIII, 133.
16) *Ibid.*, p. 131.
17) *Ibid.*, pp. 147–48.
18) *Ibid.*, pp. 154–55.
19) *Board Records,* Open Market Investment Committee, May 29, 1924; memorandum from Burgess to Strong, May 27, 1924.
20) *Ibid.*, Report of the Open Market Investment Committee to the Joint Conference, November, 1924.
21) *Federal Reserve Bulletin,* July 1924, p. 533.
22) *Stabilization Hearings,* hearings before the Committee on Banking and Currency, House of Representatives, 69th Congress, 1st Session, Part 1, 1927, p. 317.
23) Hamlin, *op. cit.*, VIII, 170.
24) Chandler, *op. cit.*, p. 243.
25) Sir Henry Clay, *Lord Norman* (London: St. Martin's Press, 1957), p. 143.
26) Chandler, *op. cit.*, p. 283.
27) Randolph Burgess, "What the Federal Reserve System Is Doing To Promote Business Stability," *Proceedings of the American Academy of Political Science, 1926–1928,* XII, 146.
28) *Stabilization Hearings,* 1926, p. 336.
29) *Tenth Annual Report of the Federal Reserve Board,* p. 10 (author's italics).
30) *Stabilization Hearings,* 1928, p. 116.
31) Harold Reed, *Federal Reserve Policy, 1921–1930* (New York: McGraw-Hill, 1930), p. 60.
32) Hardy, *op. cit.*, pp. 79–81.

CHAPTER 7 *The Quiet Years: The Application of the Qualitative Test, 1925–1926*

1) E. A. Goldenweiser, *American Monetary Policy* (New York: McGraw-Hill, 1951), p. 143.
2) Stanley Lebergott, "Annual Estimates of Unemployment in the United States, 1900–1954," *The Measurement and Behavior of Unemployment,* National Bureau of Economic Research (Princeton, N.J.: Princeton University, 1957), 215.
3) Goldenweiser, *op. cit.,* p. 144. Goldenweiser was director of the Division of Research and Statistics from 1927 to 1945.
4) Charles O. Hardy, *Credit Policies of the Federal Reserve System* (Washington, D.C.: Brookings Institution, 1932), p. 122.
5) *Stabilization Hearings,* 1927, p. 784.
6) *Eleventh Annual Report of the Federal Reserve Board,* p. 283.
7) C. S. Hamlin, *Diaries* (Library of Congress), IX, 170.
8) Harold Reed, *Federal Reserve Policy, 1921–1930* (New York: McGraw-Hill, 1930), p. 91.
9) *Ibid.,* p. 92.
10) Hamlin, *op. cit.,* XI, 25.
11) *Ibid.,* p. 23.
12) *Ibid.,* p. 32.
13) *Ibid.,* pp. 42–43.
14) *Ibid.,* pp. 49–50.
15) *Ibid.,* p. 125.
16) *Ibid.,* p. 133.
17) Hardy, *op. cit.,* p. 123.
18) Hamlin, *op. cit.,* XII, 99.
19) *Ibid.,* pp. 107–08.

CHAPTER 8 *The 1927 Recession: An International Test of Credit Policy*

1) C. S. Hamlin, *Diaries* (Library of Congress), XIII, 59.
2) *Federal Reserve Board Records,* Open Market Investment Committee, May 9, 1927; "Preliminary Memorandum Relative to Open Market Policy," dated May 11, 1927.
3) *Ibid.,* minutes, May 12, 1927.
4) Hamlin, *op. cit.,* XIII, 165.
5) *Ibid.*
6) *Fourteenth Annual Report of the Federal Reserve Board* (1927), p. 9.
7) *Ibid.,* p. 15.
8) Lester Chandler, *Benjamin Strong, Central Banker* (Washington, D.C.: Brookings Institution, 1958), pp. 375 ff.
9) Hamlin, *op. cit.,* XIV, 12–13.
10) *Harrison Papers* (Butler Library, Columbia University), Cable Books, Bank of England, April–August, 1927.

11) *Goldenweiser Papers* (Library of Congress), Correspondence, XIX, 40–52.
12) Chandler, *op. cit.*, p. 440.
13) *Supra,* Chapter 4, pp. 62–63.
14) Hamlin, *op. cit.*, XIV, 27.
15) *Ibid.*, p. 28.
16) *Ibid.*, p. 17.
17) *Board Records,* Open Market Investment Committee, July 27, 1927, minutes.
18) Hamlin, *op. cit.*, XIV, 19.
19) *Ibid.*, p. 29.
20) *Ibid.*, p. 27.
21) *Harrison Papers,* Cable Books, Bank of England. Also Hamlin, *op. cit.*, XIV, 39.
22) *Board Records,* Open Market Investment Committee, November 1, 1927; preliminary memorandum dated October 18, 1927.
23) *Ibid.*, report to governors' conference.
24) John K. Galbraith, *The Great Crash, 1929* (Boston and New York: Houghton Mifflin, 1955), p. 14.

CHAPTER 9 *The Stock Market Mania: 1928*

1) C. S. Hamlin, *Diaries* (Library of Congress), XIV, 105.
2) *Ibid.*, pp. 106–07.
3) *Federal Reserve Board Records,* Open Market Investment Committee, January 12, 1928, "Memorandum on Condition of Business," p. 6.
4) *Ibid.*, p. 7.
5) Hamlin, *op. cit.*, XIV, 113–14.
6) *Ibid.*, pp. 116–7.
7) *Goldenweiser Papers* (Library of Congress), memorandum dated January 28, 1928, on meeting of the Federal Reserve Board January 24.
8) *Board Records,* Open Market Investment Committee, March 26, 1928.
9) Hamlin, *op. cit.*, XIV, 153. Miller's remark was probably made in the heat of an argument, and he exaggerated his position.
10) The demand deposit base for computing reserves was reduced. Net demand deposits were defined as gross demand deposits (except U.S. government deposits) minus due to other banks and the net excess (if any) of demand deposits due to other banks over demand balances due from other domestic banks and cash items in the process of collection. When corporate demand or time balances were drawn upon for lending in the stock market, one of the effects might be a reduction in interbank deposits.
11) *Banking and Monetary Statistics* (Washington, D.C.: Board of Governors of the Federal Reserve System, 1943), pp. 72–3.
12) Goldenweiser, *op. cit.*, memorandum dated September 24, 1928.
13) Sir Dennis Robertson, *Economic Commentaries* (London: Staples, 1956), p. 69.
14) Lester Chandler, *The Economics of Money and Banking,* 4th edition (New York: Harper and Row, 1964), p. 495.

15) *Fifteenth Annual Report of the Federal Reserve Board* (1928), p. 10.
16) *Board Records,* Open Market Investment Committee, July 18, 1928; "Report on the Credit Situation."
17) *Ibid.*
18) *Ibid.,* August 13, 1928, letter from Governor Young to George Harrison dated August 16, 1928; quoted by Hamlin, *op. cit.,* XV, 7–8.
19) Hamlin, *ibid.,* XV, 8. Governor Young, Platt, and the Comptroller voted yes; Miller and James voted no.
20) *Ibid.,* p. 27.
21) *Ibid.,* p. 119.
22) *Fifteenth Annual Report* (1928), pp. 6–7.
23) *Board Records,* Open Market Investment Committee. November 15, 1928; "Preliminary Memorandum dated November 14, 1928."
24) Seymour Harris, *Twenty Years of Federal Reserve Policy,* Vol. 2 (Cambridge, Mass., Harvard University, 1933), p. 437.
25) *Ibid.,* p. 539.
26) Hamlin, *op. cit.,* XV, 124–25.
27) *Ibid.,* XVI, p. 123.

CHAPTER 10 *The Miller-Hamlin Policy of Direct Pressure: 1929*

1) C. S. Hamlin, *Diaries* (Library of Congress), XV, 200.
2) *Ibid.,* January 4, 1929.
3) *Harrison Papers,* Conversations, Vol. 1, 1926–31; memorandum dated January 25, 1929, pp. 2–4.
4) *Goldenweiser Papers* (Library of Congress), talks with Governor Young on March 6, 1929.
5) *Federal Reserve Board Records,* Open Market Investment Committee, preliminary memorandum dated January 7, 1929.
6) At a Federal Reserve Board meeting on January 24, 1929, Adolph Miller requested that the governor call a meeting so that he might submit a draft of a letter on the proper use of Federal Reserve credit facilities proposed by him in accordance with a resolution adopted on December 31, 1928.
7) *Board Records,* minutes.
8) Goldenweiser, *op. cit.,* meeting of Federal Reserve Board on March 22, 1929; memorandum dated March 23, 1929, p. 2.
9) Harrison, *op. cit.,* Conversations, Vol. 1, 1926–31; memorandum to files dated February 11, 1929, pp. 2–7.
10) Hamlin, *op. cit.,* p. 160.
11) Goldenweiser, *op. cit.,* talk with Governor Young on March 6, 1929, p. 4.
12) *Federal Reserve Bulletin,* April 1929, pp. 243–44.
13) Adolph Miller, "Federal Reserve Policies: 1927–1929," *The American Economic Review,* XXV (September 1935), 456–457.
14) Hamlin, *op. cit.,* XV, 198–99.
15) *Ibid.,* p. 200.
16) *Ibid.,* XVI, p. 27.

17) John K. Galbraith, *The Great Crash, 1929* (Boston and New York: Houghton Mifflin, 1955), p. 16.
18) *Ibid.*, p. 38.
19) Harrison, *op. cit.*, Conversations, Vol. 1, 1926–31; memorandum to files dated February 11, 1929, p. 5.
20) Hamlin, *op. cit.*, 169–70.
21) Harrison, *op. cit.*, Conversations, Vol. 1, 1926–31; memorandum dated April 25, 1929; telephone conversation with Undersecretary Mills on April 25.
22) *Board Records*, Board minutes, May 22, 1929.
23) Hamlin, *op, cit.*, XVI, 77.
24) Harrison, *op. cit.*, miscellaneous letters and reports, Vol. 1, 1920–1931; letter of Gates McGarrah to Governor Young, May 31, 1929.
25) Hamlin, *op. cit.*, XVI, 94–95.
26) That is not to say that they did not fully understand the mechanism of bank credit expansion on the basis of net addition to reserves. But on some unexplained empirical grounds they thought reserves injected through the bill market found their way much more slowly to the stock market.
27) Hamlin, *op. cit.*, pp. 96–97.
28) Harrison, *op. cit.*, miscellaneous letters and reports, Vol. 1, 1920–1931, letter to McGarrah from Board, June 12, 1929.
29) Goldenweiser, *op. cit.*, memorandum of meeting of Governor Harrison with members of the Board August 7, 1929, dated August 8, 1929.
30) *Ibid.*, p. 3.
31) Hamlin, *op, cit.*, XVI, 155.

CHAPTER 11 *The Aftermath of the Stock Market Collapse: 1929–1932*

1) *Stabilization of Commodity Prices,* U.S. House Banking and Currency Committee, Subcommittee, Hearings: (72:1) (1932), p. 475. So much has been written on the collapse of the stock market and the events leading up to that fatal week that I have seen no reason for reviewing the same material again. For an informative as well as a readable account see J. K. Galbraith, *The Great Crash, 1929* (Boston: Houghton Mifflin, 1955).
2) *Harrison Papers,* miscellaneous letters and reports, Vols. 1 and 2; letter sent to all governors of the Federal Reserve Banks dated November 27, 1929.
3) C. S. Hamlin, *Diaries* (Library of Congress), XVI, 189, 191.
4) Hamlin, *op. cit.*, XVII, 40.
5) *Banking and Monetary Statistics* (Washington, D.C.: Board of Governors of the Federal Reserve System, 1943), p. 384 (Wednesday Figures).
6) Hamlin, *op. cit.*, XVI, 191.
7) *Federal Reserve Board Records,* Open Market Policy Conference, January 28 and 29, 1930; explanatory statement of Governor Norris.

8) Hamlin, *op. cit.*, XVII, 87.
9) *Supra*, Chapter 6, pp. 83–84; 91–92.
10) *Stabilization Hearings*, before the House Committee on Banking and Currency, 70th Congress, 1st Session, p. 283.
11) *Ibid.*, p. 116.
12) Hamlin, *op. cit.*, XVII, 89.
13) *Ibid.*, p. 95.
14) *Ibid.*, p. 113.
15) *Goldenweiser Papers* (Library of Congress), memorandum dated April 24, 1930.
16) Hamlin, *op. cit.*, XVII, 140.
17) *Ibid.*, p. 145.
18) Hamlin, *op. cit.*, XVIII, June 23, 1930.
19) *Ibid.*, p. 85.
20) Harrison, *op. cit.*, Discussion Notes, Vol. 1, memorandum of meetings of Board of Directors, April 24 and May 1, 1930.
21) *Ibid.*, July 17, 1930.
22) *Ibid.*, Executive Committee of Board of Directors meeting May 19, 1930.
23) Harrison, *op. cit.*, miscellaneous letters and reports, Vol. 1, letter dated July 3, 1930.
24) *Ibid.*, letter from Governor Seay dated July 9, 1930.
25) *Ibid.*, letter from Governor Calkins dated July 10, 1930.
26) *Ibid.*, letter from Governor Talley dated July 15, 1930.
27) *Ibid.*, letter from Governor Geery dated July 7, 1930.
28) *Ibid.*, letter to all governors except Talley and Fancher dated July 18, 1930.
29) Harrison, *op. cit.*, Discussion Notes, Vol. 1, meeting of officers' council, September 17, 1930.
30) Hamlin, *op. cit.*, XVIII, 63.
31) Raimund W. Goldschmidt, *The Changing Structure of American Banking* (London: George Routledge and Sons, 1933), p. 225.
32) Hamlin, *op. cit.*, XVIII, 194.
33) *Ibid.*, p. 201.
34) Goldenweiser, *op. cit.*, "Notes on trip to New York, March 12–13," March 16, 1931.
35) *Ibid.*, "Dinner at University Club in New York, Monday, April 13," April 15, 1931.
36) Hamlin, *op. cit.*, XIX, 51.
37) Goldenweiser, *op. cit.*, "Talk with Governor Meyer on June 18," June 19, 1931.
38) Hamlin, *op. cit.*, XIX, 122–24.
39) Goldenweiser, *op. cit.*, "Confidential Memoranda 1922–33," notes on Open Market Investment Committee meeting, August 11, 1931.
40) Hamlin, *op. cit.*, XIX, 148.
41) *Board Records*, Open Market Policy Conference, November 30, 1931; preliminary memorandum dated November 27, 1931.

42) Harrison, *op. cit.*, Discussion Notes, memorandum of meeting of New York Bank Board of Directors, October 8, 1931.
43) *Ibid.*, Discussion Notes, Vol. 1, memorandum of meeting of Board of Directors, October 15, 1931.
44) William Adams Brown, Jr., *The International Gold Standard Reinterpreted, 1914–1934,* National Bureau of Economic Research, Vol. 2 (New York: 1940), pp. 1180–81.
45) Harrison, *op. cit.*, Discussion Notes, Vol. 1, memorandum, Executive Committee, October 26, 1931.
46) *Board Records,* New York–Bank of France negotiations; letter of Governor Harrison to Governor Meyer dated December 18, 1931.
47) "Restoring and Maintaining the Average Purchasing Power of the Dollar," Hearings, Committee on Banking and Currency, U.S. Senate, 72nd Congress, 1st Session: 1932, p. 195.
48) Hamlin, *op. cit.*, XIX, 178.
49) Hamlin, *op. cit.*, XX; inserted after p. 40.
50) Herbert Hoover, *The Memoirs of Herbert Hoover, The Great Depression 1929–1941* (New York: Macmillan, 1952), p. 116.
51) *Ibid.*, pp. 116–17.
52) Henry H. Villard, "The Federal Reserve System's Monetary Policy in 1931 and 1932," *The Journal of Political Economy,* XL (December 1937).
53) Seymour Harris, *Twenty Years of Federal Reserve Policy,* Vol. 2 (Cambridge, Mass.: Harvard University, 1933), pp. 629–30.
54) *Ibid.*, p. 623.

CHAPTER 12 *From Easy Money to the Collapse of the Banking Mechanism: 1932–1933*

1) *Harrison Papers,* memorandum on meetings of Executive Committee, January 4, 1932. Board of Directors meeting, January 28, 1932, February 18, 1932, and February 25, 1932.
2) Milton Friedman and Anna Jacobson Schwartz, *A Monetary History of the United States 1867–1960,* National Bureau of Economic Research (Princeton, N.J.: Princeton University, 1963), p. 406.
3) Harrison, *op. cit.*, discussion notes, Vol. 2, memorandum, Board of Directors meeting, January 21, 1932.
4) *Goldenweiser Papers* (Library of Congress), notes on credit policy in 1932, "Confidential Memoranda, 1922–33," file dated January 7, 1932.
5) *Federal Reserve Board Records,* Open Market Policy Conference, February 24–25, 1932; preliminary report.
6) Stabilization of Commodity Prices, Hearings before Subcommittee of Committee on Banking and Currency, House of Representatives, 72nd Congress, 1st Session, 1932; part II, p. 467.
7) *Ibid.*, p. 495.
8) *Board Records,* Open Market Policy Conference Executive Committee, June 16, 1932.

9) Harrison, *op. cit.*, Discussion Notes, Vol. 2, Board of Directors meeting, April 28, 1932.
10) *Ibid.*, Board of Directors meeting, May 12, 1932.
11) *Board Records,* Open Market Policy Conference, April 12, 1932.
12) Harrison, *op. cit.*, Discussion Notes, Vol. 2, meeting of Executive Committee of Board of Directors, April 4, 1932.
13) *Board Records,* Open Market Policy Conference, April 12, 1932.
14) C. S. Hamlin, *Diaries* (Library of Congress), XX, 160.
15) *Ibid.*, p. 162.
16) *Board Records,* Open Market Policy Conference, May 17, 1932.
17) *Nineteenth Annual Report of the Federal Reserve Board* (1932), pp. 10–11.
18) *Ibid.*, p. 16.
19) Stabilization of Commodity Prices, Hearings before Subcommittee of the Committee on Banking and Currency, House of Representatives, 72nd Congress, 1st Session, 1932, Pt. 2, p. 460.
20) *Ibid.*, p. 461.
21) *Ibid.*, p. 462.
22) *Ibid.*
23) *Ibid.*, p. 495.
24) *Nineteenth Annual Report* (1932), p. 13.
25) Hamlin, *op. cit.*, XXII, 40.
26) *Ibid.*
27) Lester Chandler, *Benjamin Strong, Central Banker* (Washington, D.C.: Brookings Institution, 1958), pp. 239–40.
28) *Ibid.*, p. 240.
29) Seymour Harris, *Twenty Years of Federal Reserve Policy,* Vol. 2 (Cambridge, Mass.: Harvard University, 1933), p. 679.
30) Harrison, *op cit.*, Discussion Notes, Vol. 2, meeting of Board of Directors, July 7, 1932.
31) *Board Records,* Open Market Policy Conference, January 4, 1933.
32) Hamlin, *op. cit.*, XXII, January 4, 1933 (typewritten, following page 40).
33) *Board Records,* Open Market Policy Conference, January 4, 1933.
34) Hamlin, *op. cit.*, pp. 40–43.
35) Harrison, *op. cit.*, Discussion Notes, Vol. 3, Executive Committee meeting January 16, 1933.
36) *Ibid.*, Conversations, Vol. 2, summary of conversations on evening of January 18, 1933; memorandum to Governor Harrison from Burgess.
37) Hamlin, *op. cit.*, XXII, 61.
38) Harrison, *op. cit.*, Discussion Notes, Vol. 3, Board of Directors meeting, February 16, 1933.
39) Harris, *op. cit.*, Vol. 2, p. 840.
40) Harrison, *op. cit.*, Discussion Notes, Vol. 3, Executive Committee meeting, February 20, 1933. Similar statement repeated at Board of Directors meeting on February 23, 1933: "The present open market machinery would not permit of prompt action with respect to pur-

chases of Government securities and we decided to open the bill window."

41) *Ibid.*, Board of Directors meeting, February 23, 1933.
42) *Ibid.*, Board of Directors meeting, February 27, 1933.
43) *Ibid.*, Board of Directors meeting, February 27, 1933.
44) *Board Records,* minutes, February 16, 1933.
45) Herbert Hoover, *The Memoirs of Herbert Hoover,* Vol. 3 (New York: Macmillan, 1952), p. 210.
46) *Board Records,* minutes, February 25, 1933.
47) Harrison, *op. cit.,* Vol. 3, Board of Directors meeting, December 22, 1932, p. 50.
48) Hamlin, *op. cit.*, XXII, 99.
49) *Board Records,* minutes, February 27, 1933.
50) *Ibid.*
51) Hoover, *op. cit.*, p. 211.
52) Hamlin, *op. cit.*, XXII, 109.
53) *Ibid.*
54) *Board Records,* Banking Holiday file. Also quoted by Herbert Hoover, *The Memoirs of Herbert Hoover, op. cit.*, pp. 211–12.
55) *Board Records,* minutes, March 3, 1933.
56) *Ibid.*
57) *Ibid.*
58) *Board Records,* Banking Holiday file, letter of George Harrison to C. S. Hamlin, August 15, 1933.

Select Bibliography

GENERAL

Annual Report of the Board of Governors of the Federal Reserve System, Washington, D.C.

Annual Report of the Secretary of the Treasury, Washington, D.C.

Federal Reserve Bulletin, Board of Governors of the Federal Reserve System, Washington, D.C.

Goldenweiser, E. A., *Papers,* Library of Congress, Washington, D.C.

Hamlin, Charles S., *Diaries,* Library of Congress, Washington, D.C.

Harrison, George L., *Papers,* Butler Library, Columbia University.

Leffingwell, Russell C., *Letterbooks,* Library of Congress, Washington, D.C.

McAdoo, William G., *Papers,* Library of Congress, Washington, D.C.

BOOKS

Anderson, Clay, *A Half-Century of Federal Reserve Policymaking 1914–1964.* Philadelphia: Federal Reserve Bank of Philadelphia, 1965.

Barger, Harold, *The Management of Money.* Chicago: Rand McNally, 1964.

Beckhart, Benjamin, *The Discount Policy of the Federal Reserve System.* New York: Holt, 1924.

Bloomfield, Arthur, *Monetary Policy Under the International Gold Standard, 1880–1914.* New York: Federal Reserve Bank of New York, 1959.

Board of Governors of the Federal Reserve System, *Banking and Monetary Statistics.* Washington, D.C.: Board of Governors, 1943.

Bogart, Ernest, *War Costs and Their Financing.* New York: Appleton, 1921.

Brown, William Adams, Jr., *The International Gold Standard Reinterpreted, 1914–1934.* 2 vols., New York: National Bureau of Economic Research, 1940.

Brunner, Karl and Allan H. Meltzer, *The Federal Reserve's Attachment to the Free Reserve Concept.* Washington, D.C.: Subcommittee on Domestic Finance, Committee on Banking and Currency, House of Representatives, 88th Congress, 2nd Session, 1964.

Chandler, Lester, *Benjamin Strong, Central Banker.* Washington, D.C.: Brookings Institution, 1958.

———, *The Economics of Money and Banking.* 4th Edition, New York: Harper, 1964.

Clay, Sir Henry, *Lord Norman.* London: St. Martin's, 1957.

Crum, William, John F. Fennelly, and Lawrence H. Seltzer, *Fiscal Planning for Total War*. New York: National Bureau of Economic Research, 1942.

Currie, Laughlin, *The Supply and Control of Money in the United States*. Cambridge, Mass.: Harvard University, 1934.

Friedman, Milton, *A Program for Monetary Stability*. New York: Fordham University, 1959.

———, and Anna Jacobson Schwartz, *A Monetary History of the United States 1867–1960*. National Bureau of Economic Research. Princeton: Princeton University, 1963.

Galbraith, John K., *The Great Crash 1929*. Boston: Houghton Mifflin, 1955.

Goldenweiser, Emanuel A., *American Monetary Policy*. New York: McGraw-Hill, 1951.

Goldschmidt, Raimund W., *The Changing Structure of American Banking*. London: George Routledge and Sons, 1933.

Harding, William P. G., *The Formative Period of the Federal Reserve System*. Boston and New York: Houghton Mifflin, 1925.

Hardy, Charles, *Credit Policies of the Federal Reserve System*. Washington, D.C.: Brookings Institution, 1932.

Harris, Seymour, *Twenty Years of Federal Reserve Policy*. 2 vols., Cambridge, Mass.: Harvard University, 1933.

Harrod, Roy, *Policy Against Inflation*. London: Macmillan, 1958.

Hawtrey, Ralph G., *The Pound at Home and Abroad*. London: Longmans, 1961.

Hollander, Jacob, *War Borrowing*. New York: Macmillan, 1919.

Hoover, Herbert, *The Memoirs of Herbert Hoover, The Great Depression 1929–1941*. Vol. 3, New York: Macmillan, 1952.

Houston, David, *Eight Years with Wilson's Cabinet*. 2 vols., New York: Doubleday, Page, 1926.

Keynes, John M., *How To Pay for the War*. London: Macmillan, 1940.

———, *Monetary Reform*. New York: Harcourt, 1924.

———, *A Treatise on Money*. 2 vols., London: Macmillan, 1950.

McAdoo, William, *Crowded Years*. Boston and New York: Houghton Mifflin, 1931.

Mints, Lloyd, *A History of Banking Theory*. Chicago: University of Chicago, 1945.

Moreau, Emile, *Souvenirs d'un Gouveneur de la Banque de France*. Editions M.-Th. Genin, Librarie de Medicis, Paris.

Noyes, Alexander D., *The War Period of American Finance, 1908–1925*. New York and London: G. P. Putnam's Sons, 1926.

Reed, Harold, *Federal Reserve Policy, 1921–1930*. New York: McGraw-Hill, 1930.

Robertson, Sir Dennis, *Economic Commentaries*. London: Staples, 1956.

Samuelson, Paul, and Everett Hagen, *After the War 1918–1920*, Washington, D.C.: National Resources Planning Board, June 1943.

Shaw, Edward, *Money, Income and Monetary Policy*. Chicago: Irwin, 1950.

Van Sant, E. R., *The Floating Debt of the Federal Government 1919–1936*. Baltimore: Johns Hopkins, 1937.

Warburg, Paul M., *The Federal Reserve System, Its Origin and Growth*. 2 vols., New York: Macmillan, 1930.

Whittlesey, Charles R., *The Banking System and War Finance*. New York: National Bureau of Economic Research, February 1943.

Willis, Henry P., *The Federal Reserve System.* New York: Ronald Press, 1923.

ARTICLES

Burgess, Randolph, "What the Federal Reserve System Is Doing to Promote Business Stability," *Proceedings of the American Academy of Political Science,* XII, 785–93.

Hawtrey, Ralph G., "The Federal Reserve System of the United States," *Journal of the Royal Statistical Society,* LXXXV (March 1922), 224–55.

Keynes, John M., "Alternative Theories of the Rate of Interest," *The Economic Journal,* XLVII (June 1937), 241–52.

Leffingwell, Russell, "Discussion," *The American Economic Review,* XI (March 1921), 30–36.

Miller, Adolph, "Federal Reserve Policy," *The American Economic Review,* XI (June 1921), 177–206.

———, "Responsibility for Federal Reserve Policies: 1927–1929," *The American Economic Review,* XXV (September 1935), 442–58.

———, "War Finance and Inflation," *Annals of the American Academy of Political and Social Science,* LXXV (January 1918), 113–34.

Mitchell, Wesley C., "The Crisis of 1920 and the Problem of Controlling the Business Cycle," *The American Economic Review, Papers and Proceedings,* XII (March 1922), 20–32.

Robertson, Dennis, "Mr. Keynes and 'Finance,'" *The Economic Journal,* XLVIII (June 1938), 314–18.

Shaw, Edward, "Money Supply and Stable Economic Growth," *United States Monetary Policy.* Columbia University: The American Assembly, 1958, 49–71.

Slichter, Sumner, "The Period 1919–1936 in the United States: Its Significance for Business Cycle Theory," *The Review of Economics and Statistics,* XIX (February 1937), 1–19.

Sprague, Oliver M. W., "The Discount Policy of the Federal Reserve Bank," *The American Economic Review,* XI (March 1921), 16–29.

Villard, Henry H., "The Federal Reserve System's Monetary Policy in 1931 and 1932," *The Journal of Political Economy,* XLV (December 1937), 721–39.

CONGRESSIONAL DOCUMENTS

Agricultural Inquiry: Hearing Before the Joint Commission of Agricultural Inquiry, 67th Congress, 1st Session, 1922.

Operation of the National and Federal Reserve Banking System: Hearings Before a Subcommittee of the Committee on Banking and Currency. U.S. Senate, 71st Congress, 3rd Session, 1931.

Purchases of Liberty Bonds and Victory Notes for the Five Per Cent Bond Purchase Fund: House of Representatives, Document No. 905, 66th Congress, 3rd Session, 1920.

Restoring and Maintaining the Average Purchasing Power of the Dollar, Hearings, Committee on Banking and Currency, U. S. Senate, 72nd Congress, 1st Session, 1932.

Stabilization: Hearings Before the Committee on Banking and Currency, House of Representatives, 69th Congress, 1st Session, 1927.

Stabilization: Hearings Before the House Committee on Banking and Currency, 70th Congress, 1st Session, 1928.

Stabilization of Commodity Prices: Hearings Before Subcommittee of Committee on Banking and Currency, House of Representatives, 72nd Congress, 1st Session, 1932.

Index